DISTRIBUTED EMBEDDED SYSTEMS: DESIGN, MIDDLEWARE AND RESOURCES

IFIP – The International Federation for Information Processing

IFIP was founded in 1960 under the auspices of UNESCO, following the First World Computer Congress held in Paris the previous year. An umbrella organization for societies working in information processing, IFIP's aim is two-fold: to support information processing within its member countries and to encourage technology transfer to developing nations. As its mission statement clearly states,

> *IFIP's mission is to be the leading, truly international, apolitical organization which encourages and assists in the development, exploitation and application of information technology for the benefit of all people.*

IFIP is a non-profitmaking organization, run almost solely by 2500 volunteers. It operates through a number of technical committees, which organize events and publications. IFIP's events range from an international congress to local seminars, but the most important are:

- The IFIP World Computer Congress, held every second year;
- Open conferences;
- Working conferences.

The flagship event is the IFIP World Computer Congress, at which both invited and contributed papers are presented. Contributed papers are rigorously refereed and the rejection rate is high.

As with the Congress, participation in the open conferences is open to all and papers may be invited or submitted. Again, submitted papers are stringently refereed.

The working conferences are structured differently. They are usually run by a working group and attendance is small and by invitation only. Their purpose is to create an atmosphere conducive to innovation and development. Refereeing is less rigorous and papers are subjected to extensive group discussion.

Publications arising from IFIP events vary. The papers presented at the IFIP World Computer Congress and at open conferences are published as conference proceedings, while the results of the working conferences are often published as collections of selected and edited papers.

Any national society whose primary activity is in information may apply to become a full member of IFIP, although full membership is restricted to one society per country. Full members are entitled to vote at the annual General Assembly, National societies preferring a less committed involvement may apply for associate or corresponding membership. Associate members enjoy the same benefits as full members, but without voting rights. Corresponding members are not represented in IFIP bodies. Affiliated membership is open to non-national societies, and individual and honorary membership schemes are also offered.

DISTRIBUTED EMBEDDED SYSTEMS: DESIGN, MIDDLEWARE AND RESOURCES

IFIP 20th World Computer Congress, TC10 Working Conference on Distributed and Parallel Embedded Systems (DIPES 2008), September 7-10, 2008, Milano, Italy

Edited by

Bernd Kleinjohann
University of Paderborn / C-LAB
Germany

Lisa Kleinjohann
University of Paderborn / C-LAB
Germany

Wayne Wolf
Georgia Institute of Technology
USA

Springer

Editors
Bernd Kleinjohann
University of Paderborn
Germany

Lisa Kleinjohann
University of Paderborn
Germany

Wayne Wolf
Georgia Institute of Technology
Savannah, GA
USA

p. cm. (IFIP International Federation for Information Processing, a Springer Series in Computer Science)

ISSN: 1571-5736 / 1861-2288 (Internet)
ISBN: 978-1-4419-3505-2 eISBN: 978-0-387-09661-2

Softcover reprint of the hardcover 1st edition 2008

Printed on acid-free paper

springer.com

IFIP 2008 World Computer Congress (WCC'08)

Message from the Chairs

Every two years, the International Federation for Information Processing hosts a major event which showcases the scientific endeavours of its over one hundred Technical Committees and Working Groups. 2008 sees the 20th World Computer Congress (WCC 2008) take place for the first time in Italy, in Milan from 7-10 September 2008, at the MIC - Milano Convention Centre. The Congress is hosted by the Italian Computer Society, AICA, under the chairmanship of Giulio Occhini.

The Congress runs as a federation of co-located conferences offered by the different IFIP bodies, under the chairmanship of the scientific chair, Judith Bishop. For this Congress, we have a larger than usual number of thirteen conferences, ranging from Theoretical Computer Science, to Open Source Systems, to Entertainment Computing. Some of these are established conferences that run each year and some represent new, breaking areas of computing. Each conference had a call for papers, an International Programme Committee of experts and a thorough peer reviewed process. The Congress received 661 papers for the thirteen conferences, and selected 375 from those representing an acceptance rate of 56% (averaged over all conferences).

An innovative feature of WCC 2008 is the setting aside of two hours each day for cross-sessions relating to the integration of business and research, featuring the use of IT in Italian industry, sport, fashion and so on. This part is organized by Ivo De Lotto. The Congress will be opened by representatives from government bodies and Societies associated with IT in Italy.

This volume is one of fourteen volumes associated with the scientific conferences and the industry sessions. Each covers a specific topic and separately or together they form a valuable record of the state of computing research in the world in 2008. Each volume was prepared for publication in the Springer IFIP Series by the conference's volume editors. The overall Chair for all the volumes published for the Congress is John Impagliazzo.

For full details on the Congress, refer to the webpage http://www.wcc2008.org.

Judith Bishop, South Africa, Co-Chair, International Program Committee
Ivo De Lotto, Italy, Co-Chair, International Program Committee
Giulio Occhini, Italy, Chair, Organizing Committee
John Impagliazzo, United States, Publications Chair

WCC 2008 Scientific Conferences

TC12	**AI**	Artificial Intelligence 2008
TC10	**BICC**	Biologically Inspired Cooperative Computing
WG 5.4	**CAI**	Computer-Aided Innovation (Topical Session)
WG 10.2	**DIPES**	Distributed and Parallel Embedded Systems
TC14	**ECS**	Entertainment Computing Symposium
TC3	**ED_L2L**	Learning to Live in the Knowledge Society
WG 9.7 **TC3**	**HCE3**	History of Computing and Education 3
TC13	**HCI**	Human Computer Interaction
TC8	**ISREP**	Information Systems Research, Education and Practice
WG 12.6	**KMIA**	Knowledge Management in Action
TC2 **WG 2.13**	**OSS**	Open Source Systems
TC11	**IFIP SEC**	Information Security Conference
TC1	**TCS**	Theoretical Computer Science

IFIP

- is the leading multinational, apolitical organization in Information and Communications Technologies and Sciences
- is recognized by United Nations and other world bodies
- represents IT Societies from 56 countries or regions, covering all 5 continents with a total membership of over half a million
- links more than 3500 scientists from Academia and Industry, organized in more than 101 Working Groups reporting to 13 Technical Committees
- sponsors 100 conferences yearly providing unparalleled coverage from theoretical informatics to the relationship between informatics and society including hardware and software technologies, and networked information systems

Details of the IFIP Technical Committees and Working Groups can be found on the website at http://www.ifip.org.

Contents

6 Distributed Operating Systems and Timing

7 Task and Data Partitioning

Preface

This year, the IFIP Working Conference on Distributed and Parallel Embedded Systems (DIPES 2008) is held as part of the IFIP World Computer Congress, held in Milan on September 7-10, 2008. The embedded systems world has a great deal of experience with parallel and distributed computing. Many embedded computing systems require the high performance that can be delivered by parallel computing. Parallel and distributed computing are often the only ways to deliver adequate real-time performance at low power levels.

This year's conference attracted 30 submissions, of which 21 were accepted. Prof. Jörg Henkel of the University of Karlsruhe graciously contributed a keynote address on embedded computing and reliability. We would like to thank all of the program committee members for their diligence.

Wayne Wolf, Bernd Kleinjohann, and Lisa Kleinjohann

Acknowledgements

We would like to thank all people involved in the organization of the IFIP World Computer Congress 2008, especially the IPC Co-Chairs Judith Bishop and Ivo De Lotto, the Organization Chair Giulio Occhini, as well as the Publications Chair John Impagliazzo. Further thanks go to the authors for their valuable contributions to DIPES 2008. Last but not least we would like to acknowledge the considerable amount of work and enthusiasm spent by our colleague Claudius Stern in preparing the proceedings of DIPES 2008. He made it possible to produce them in their current professional and homogeneous style.

IFIP TC 10 Working Conference on Distributed and Parallel Embedded Systems (DIPES 2008) IFIP World Computer Congress, September 7-10, 2008, Milan, Italy

General Chair

Wayne Wolf	Georgia Institute of Technology, USA

PC-Chair

Bernd Kleinjohann	University of Paderborn, C-LAB, Germany

Program Committee

Jean Arlat	LAAS CNRS, France
Christophe Bobda	University of Potsdam, Germany
Arndt Bode	Technical University München, Germany
João M. P. Cardoso	Technical University of Lisbon, Portugal
Luigi Carro	UFRGS, Brazil
Matjaž Colnarič	University of Maribor, Slovenia
Tom Conte	North Carolina State University, USA
Alfons Crespo Lorente	Technical University of Valencia, Spain
Nikil Dutt	University of California, Irvine, USA
Petru Eles	Linköping University, Sweden
Rolf Ernst	Technical University Braunschweig, Germany
Bernhard Eschermann	ABB Switzerland Ltd., Switzerland
João M. Fernandes	University of Minho, Portugal
Uwe Glässer	Simon Fraser University, Canada
Luís Gomes	New University of Lisbon, Portugal
Rajesh Gupta	University of California, San Diego, USA
Wolfgang Halang	Fernuniversität Hagen, Germany
Uwe Honekamp	Vector Informatik GmbH, Germany
Pao-Ann Hsiung	National Chung Chen University, Taiwan
Ahmed Jerraya	CEA-LETI, MINATEC, France
Kane Kim	University of California, Irvine, USA
Raimund Kirner	Technical University Vienna, Austria
Bernd Kleinjohann	University of Paderborn, C-LAB, Germany

Lisa Kleinjohann	University of Paderborn, C-LAB, Germany
Hermann Kopetz	Technical University Vienna, Austria
Johan Lilius	Turku Centre for Computer Science, Finland
Ricardo J. Machado	University of Minho, Portugal
Erik Maehle	University of Lübeck, Germany
Vincent Mooney	Georgia Institute of Technology, USA
Frank Mueller	North Carolina State University, USA
Carlos E. Pereira	UFRGS, Brazil
Luís Pinho	Polytechnical Institute of Porto, Portugal
Peter Puschner	Technical University Vienna, Austria
Franz J. Rammig	University of Paderborn, Germany
Achim Rettberg	University of Oldenburg, Germany
Bernhard Rinner	Klagenfurt University, Austria
Luis-Miguel Santana Ormeno	ST Microelectronics, France
Hènrique Santos	University of Minho, Portugal
Klaus Schneider	University of Kaiserslautern, Germany
Edwin Sha	University of Texas, Dallas, USA
Zili Shao	Hong Kong Polytechnic University, Hong Kong
Joachim Stroop	dSPACE, Germany
P. S. Thiagarajan	National University of Singapore, Singapore
François Terrier	CEA LIST, France
Lothar Thiele	ETH Zürich, Switzerland
Flavio R. Wagner	UFRGS, Brazil
Wayne Wolf	Georgia Institute of Technology, USA
Dieter Wuttke	Technical University Ilmenau, Germany
Alex Yakovlev	University of Newcastle, UK
Laurence T. Yang	St. Francis Xavier University, Canada

Organizing Committee

Lisa Kleinjohann	University of Paderborn, C-LAB, Germany
Claudius Stern	University of Paderborn, C-LAB, Germany

Co-Organizing Institutions

IFIP TC 10, WG 10.2, and WG 10.5

Hierarchically Distributing Embedded Systems for Improved Autonomy

Claudius Stern, Philipp Adelt, Willi Richert, and Bernd Kleinjohann

Abstract Distribution of functionality among nodes is a contemporary research issue for embedded systems, e.g. in the field of autonomous mobile robot groups. In such groups, the concept of distribution is mainly used to achieve flexibility and robustness that could not be reached by a single robot. Here it will be used as a design-paradigm for a robot's *internal* architecture. In this paper, a hierarchically distributed robot architecture will be introduced which leads to an improved autonomy of the overall system.

Key words: distributed embedded systems, autonomous systems, robot control

1 Introduction

Distribution is a contemporary research issue for embedded systems. Currently, in the field of distributing a task to a group of nodes much research work is done (e.g. [2, 15]). By distributing a task, the probability for a system-wide failure or for continuously incorrect execution decreases because of the diversity and independency of the distributed system parts.

In robotic soccer, which is a challenging research and application field for the combination of real time embedded systems design with intelligent autonomous behavior, distribution is applied at two levels. At the multi-robot level the paradigm of distribution is mainly used to build homogeneous cooperating teams of robots. At the level of single robots this paradigm can considerably support robustness and flexibility. That will be shown in this paper describing the Paderkicker robots.

The Paderkicker team [9] consists of five robots that already participated successfully in several international competitions including the RoboCup 2006 World

Claudius Stern · Philipp Adelt · Willi Richert · Bernd Kleinjohann
Universität Paderborn, C-LAB
e-mail: claudis, padelt, richert, bernd@c-lab.de

Please use the following format when citing this chapter:

Stern, C., et al., 2008, in IFIP International Federation for Information Processing, Volume 271; *Distributed Embedded Systems: Design, Middleware and Resources*; Bernd Kleinjohann, Lisa Kleinjohann, Wayne Wolf; (Boston: Springer), pp. 1–9.

Championship. Our platform asks for the whole range of research areas needed for a successful deployment in the real world. This includes embedded real-time architectures [3, 5, 10], realtime vision [11, 12, 13], learning and adaptation from limited sensor data, skill learning [7] and methods to propagate learned skills and behaviours in the robot team [8].

In this paper we focus on the hierarchically distributed architecture of the Paderkicker robots. In Section 2 we describe the current system with its components. Section 3 then focuses on the modular system design of the Paderkicker robot, covering the functional design as well as the architecture of hardware. Section 5 gives an overview of the vision module which includes three individual real-time image processing modules whose outputs then are merged. The behavior module is described in Section 4. Section 8 concludes the paper and a short survey of future development directions and research fields is given regarding the architecture described in this paper.

2 Robot outline

The current generation of the Paderkicker robots is equipped with an omnidirectional drive which enables the robot to do translational and rotational movements simultaneously. This is a great advantage over the prior generation described in [9] that featured a differential drive with two driven wheels. Here a four wheel omnidirectional drive is used instead of a three wheel one. The construction of the wheel suspension ensures that all four wheels are pressed onto the ground which leads to enhanced stability.

Besides the driving system, the ball handling system has been redesigned from scratch. The ball handling system consists of two main components: the ball kicking system and the dribbling system. The previously used mechanical kicking system has been replaced by an electromagnetic solenoid which provides more control over the kicking power and reduces the actuation latency. The ball dribbling system has been redesigned to be more robust concerning collisions. All servo motors have been mechanically decoupled with rubber blocks so that even hard collisions will not harm the servos with excessive mechanical shocks.

The same mechanical decoupling has been applied to the servos of the active vision system to tolerate collisions with high kicked balls. In contrast to omnivision systems that are currently used by many other teams, three individual pan-tilt cameras are used in the vision system. Each camera may independently focus and track a different object of interest like ball, goal or other robots.

3 System design

In this section the structure of the Paderkicker robot will be shown. First, the functional architecture will be described. Then we will show how this logical structure maps onto a hardware structure. After the description of the underlying structures, the behavior system as well as the vision system will be introduced.

3.1 Functional architecture

During the system design process, four main functional units were identified (vision, driving, ball handling and behavior) and designed in a modular way. A robot of the Paderkicker team consists of a behavior module, the vision module, the driving module, and the ball handling module. The function of the last three is self-explaining by their respective names. The behavior module is the topmost module in a robot's hierarchy. It controls the robot's overall behavior.

The different modules are realized in a distributed way as described below. All components communicate with a message format which is used in the entire system independent of the respective medium for communication.

The functional units were further divided into sub-modules as depicted in Figure 1. This structure allows the independent development of the different functional units. Furthermore, the functional units were designed to work autonomously on their own presenting an already abstracted interface to the rest of the system. A dedicated interface sub-module manages the communication and merges data. This hierarchical structure enables the functional unit "Behavior module" to act on a very high level of abstraction.

As an example, the driving module is designed to work autonomously and part of the robot's low-level behavior has been mapped to it. Distributing the drive-control task to a group of sub-modules instead of using only one monolithic module leads to more flexibility and robustness. The sub-modules within are realized on individual microcontroller boards working as a distributed system. Each microcontroller board realizes an individual motor controller and odometry data logger with a short measurement-control latency and therefore can react very fast. Each board also incorporates an emergency handling unit which leads to a more robust behavior of the whole driving module.

Other teams hardly describe their overall software architecture. Often they describe in detail the behavior system and its mechanisms but not the underlying overall structure. Nevertheless, a common approach is a layered structure, e.g. used by the 5dpo–2000 team [6] or the AIS–BIT Robots team [4]. The AIS–BIT Robots team uses two layers at different abstraction levels. The first layer deals with low-level processing of sensor data and image data. The second layer then deals with abstract behaviors. Both layers contain different modules but the modules within one layer are not further hierarchically arranged.

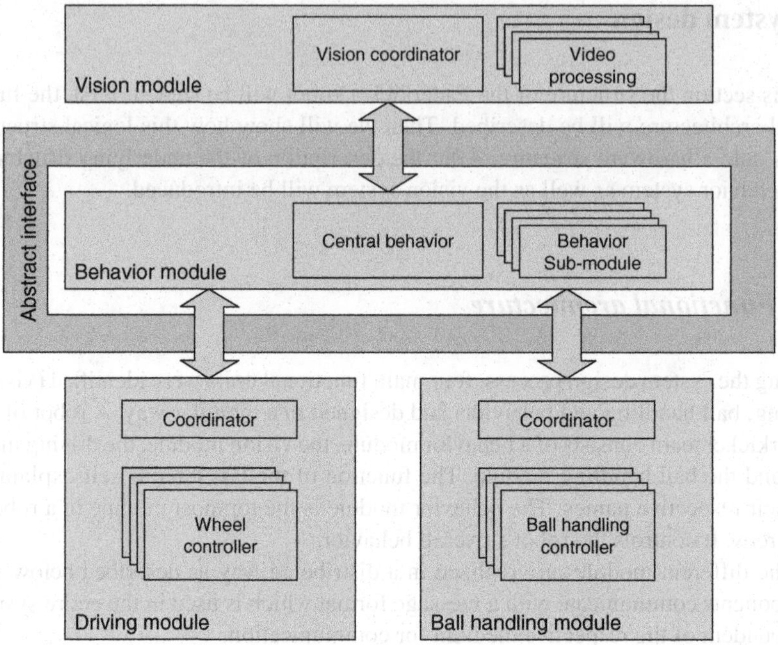

Fig. 1 Paderkicker hierarchical module structure

3.2 *Hardware architecture*

The functional structure described above is mapped onto a hardware architecture as depicted in Figure 2. The central processing unit is a Pentium M ULV PC board running Linux. The vision algorithms and the behavior system are realized here. The Mini-ITX board is equipped with a Mini PCI wireless LAN card and handles team communication.

As described above, the modules for ball handling and driving are divided into sub-modules. These sub-modules are realized on microcontroller boards equipped with an Atmel microcontroller which comes with an on-chip CAN bus interface. Groups of microcontroller boards communicate over CAN with the members of the according group. One dedicated microcontroller board in each group manages the communication with the central Mini-ITX board over a USB connection.

4 Behavior based system

The actual version of the behavior system is realized as a parallel distributed software system (Figure 3), where parallel running processes are responsible for the dedicated functional hardware units vision, driving, and ball handling. In addition,

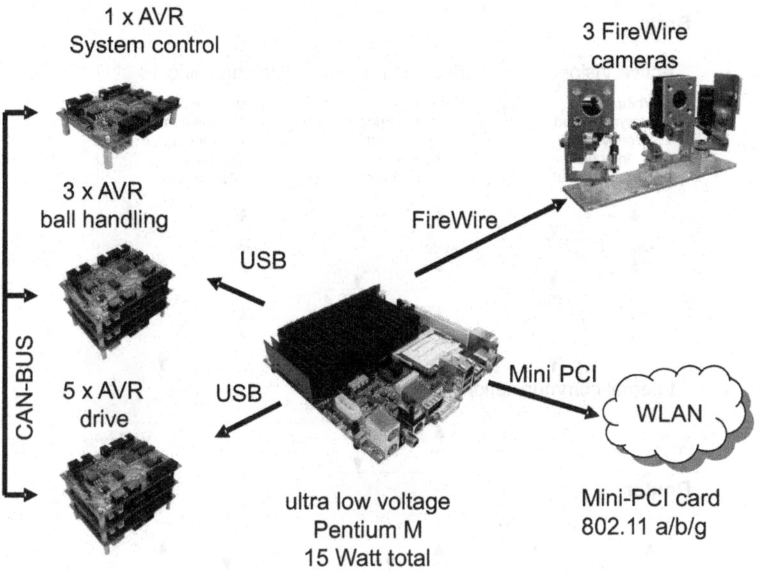

Fig. 2 Paderkicker hardware architecture

a new timing concept now allows the different subsystems like the above mentioned to run at different cycle duration. Using a double buffered shared memory approach it is no problem if e.g. the cycle time of the vision system increases because the analyzed image contains more detectable objects than usual or if the ball handling component has to run at a higher frequency than the driving component.

The architecture's design is driven by the need of the sub-modules *Active Vision*, *Driving*, and *Ball Handling* to run at different sample rates. In the former architecture all the functionality was done in the same module at the same speed. The problem was that functionality that needs to run at a high speed got at some point corrupted data from modules running at slower speed, which lead to unpredictable behavior in some cases. To avoid this, at first the different functionality was identified and regrouped in separate sub-modules. Then we introduced a double-buffered communication mechanism that separates the actual data on which the individual modules are working on from the communication process.

Each sub-module has its own *Sense-Plan-Act* cycle. The *Act* part is of course no real action but rather new data for the other modules or part of the final action which first has to be sent to the hardware via the *Router*. All sub-modules are running concurrently. While they are implemented at the moment as Java Threads it is no difficulty to let them reside on even different processors.

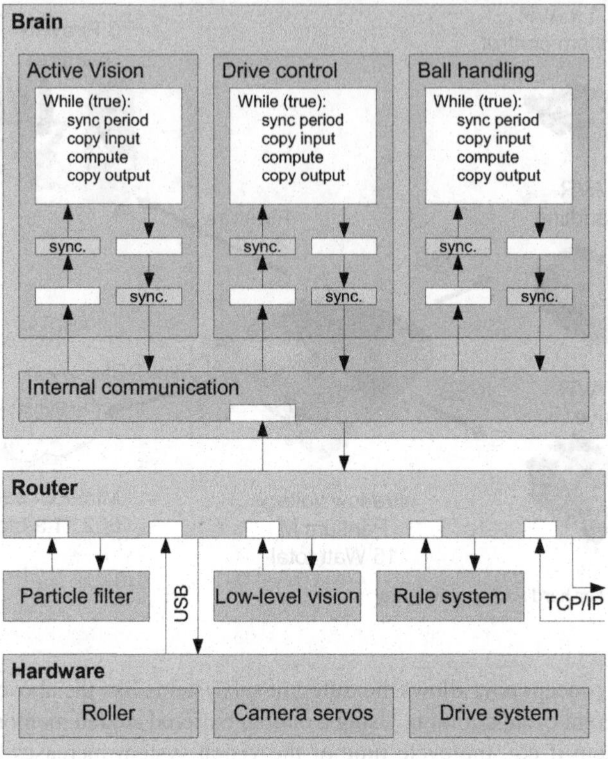

Fig. 3 Asynchronous architecture for the behavior module

5 Vision system

The vision system also has been designed using the paradigm of hierarchical distribution. The vision systems span four levels of abstraction, beginning with the low-level vision based on an optimized algorithm for low latency real-time color segmentation [12]. The original algorithm has been adapted to run on a PC under an ordinary Linux system. Three digital FireWire cameras are mounted on pan-tilt units to cover the whole 360° view. Each camera is handled by an independent task doing the low-level image processing. On the next level of hierarchy the outputs of these tasks are merged into a robot-centric view of the surrounding objects and landmarks. Figure 4 shows a visualization of the particle filter. Each triangle indicates a hypothesis of the robot's position with the hollow triangle being the resulting position estimation of the robot in the world coordinate system. An abstract interface is presented to the next level of hierarchy enabling the user of the interface to specify e.g. scan modes of the cameras.

The next level of abstraction includes two particle filters [1] and a specialized control module. One particle filter estimates the robot's position relative to known landmarks. The second particle filter estimates the position of the ball relative to the

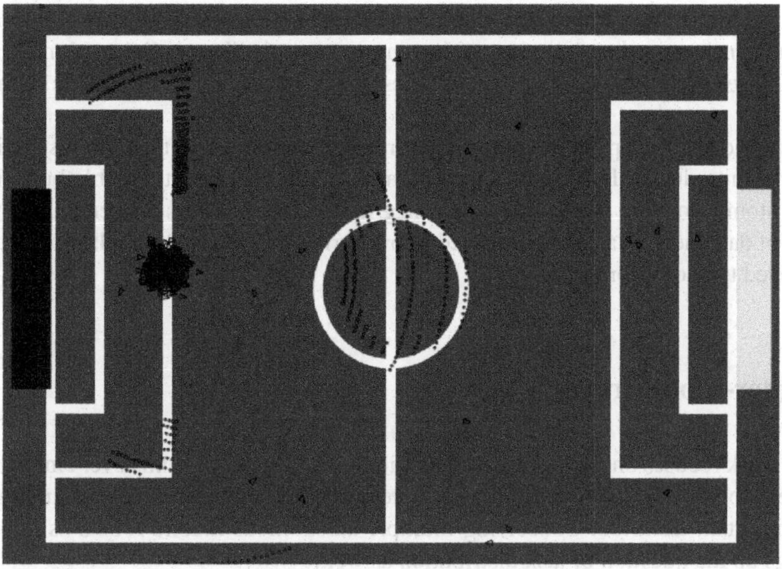

Fig. 4 Visualization of the particle filter and the robot's perceived artefacts (dots).

robot. The control module again presents an abstract interface to the next level of abstraction. Using this interface two views are accessible. One "global view" with global world coordinates including all absolute coordinates of objects and landmarks. However, the second view is robot-centric using relative coordinates.

The behavior based system descibed in Section 4 is located on the highest level of abstraction. A dedicated module within this system takes care about the behavior of the underlying vision system, e.g. which part of the field is to be examined or whether the ball has to be tracked.

Compared to systems using an omnivision camera [14], on our system the resolution is higher for a given viewing direction. Furthermore the system allows the over-sampling of a specified region of interest. Due to the constant usage of abstraction throughout the system this is done autonomously, e.g. for the position of the ball. This enables the system to recognize even distant objects that would be indistinguishable in a typical omnivision setup with only one fixed camera.

6 Coordination of functional units

The architecture does not impose limits upon the way data is exchanged between functional units. Most units will work asynchronously regarding each other and can work in a time-triggered or event-triggered manner. An example for an asynchronous time-triggered operation are the cameras attached to the vision system that will deliver data in periodic intervals that cannot practically be synchronized with the rest of the system. The high-level behavior system is running at a different rate unsynchronized to the cameras. In contrast, sensors like a ball detection sensor can trigger event processing and event messages that are non-deterministic in their timing.

To bridge the gap between such different execution semantics, an abstraction layer is introduced. It decouples the communication of the unit. Double buffering with atomic copying is used to ensure integrity for data transfers. Depending on the type of data, new data either is queued or overwrites an old value for a last-recently-received type of information.

7 Inter-robot strategy

This work focuses on the hierarchical distribution of functional units over embedded systems onboard a robot. Nevertheless, integrating the robot with its surrounding is an important task, too. Conceiving multiple autonomous mobile robots as a team brings up the question of task distribution as well.

Different from onboard the robot, task distribution is dynamic and depends on external non-deterministic parameters like the amount of robots available. Merging multiple robots of different types into a heterogeneous team allows for specialized task fulfillment but further complicates task allocation.

In general a strategy is needed to conquer a given objective with the available resources. In the existing homogeneous Paderkicker robot team the external architecture comprises a central dedicated server that oversees availability and state of the robots. It holds the strategy to be executed and dynamically decides which robot executes what task. This design has several drawbacks. The central component is a single point of failure that can render a complete team inoperable when it fails. Since communication reliability is of major concern in almost all situations, the team was designed to complete a task autonomously once the role is assigned.

To enhance this situation further, in the future the task decision process will also be distributed among the robots. This allows for decentralized strategic components that can be locally implemented on a robot. Integrating new and yet unknown robots with unique features does not imply having to change a central server rule-set anymore. Instead the robot specific parts of task assignment strategies can be implemented locally and therefore be distributed among the set of robots.

8 Outlook and conclusion

The future direction clearly indicates an even further distributed approach internal as well as external of a single robot. A distributed communication framework will act as a framework towards autonomous decision making in teams. By using a modular design and distributing functional units of the system onboard a robot among embedded systems, the stability of the whole system increases. Distributing the driving low-level behavior over multiple microcontrollers leads to faster reactions, e.g. regarding the compensation of transmission slip.

References

1. M.S. Arulampalam, S. Maskell, N. Gordon, and T. Clapp. A tutorial on particle filters for online nonlinear/non-gaussian bayesian tracking. *Signal Processing, IEEE Transactions on [see also Acoustics, Speech, and Signal Processing, IEEE Transactions on]*, 50(2):174–188, Feb 2002.
2. Krishnakumar Balasubramanian, Jaiganesh Balasubramanian, Jeff Parsons, Aniruddha Gokhale, and Douglas C. Schmidt. A platform-independent component modeling language for distributed real-time and embedded systems. *J. Comput. Syst. Sci.*, 73(2):171–185, 2007.
3. D. Beier, R. Billert, B. Brüderlin, Bernd Kleinjohann, and Dirk Stichling. Marker-less vision based tracking for mobile augmented reality. In *Proceedings of the Second International Symposium on Mixed and Augmented Reality (ISMAR 2003)*, Tokyo, Japan, October 2003.
4. Stefan Christen, Ronny Hartanto, Benjamin Maus, Walter Nowak, Sven Olufs, Paul G. Ploger, Michael Reckhaus, Christian Rempis, Azamat Shakhimardanov, and Lars Weber. AIS–BIT Robots Team Description 2006. Technical report, FH Bonn-Rhein-Sieg and Fraunhofer AIS, 2006.
5. Natascha Esau, Bernd Kleinjohann, Lisa Kleinjohann, and Dirk Stichling. Visitrack – video based incremental tracking in real-time. In *Proceedings of the 6th IEEE International Symposium on Object-oriented Real-time Computing (ISORC '03)*, Hakodate, Japan, May 2003.
6. Antnio Paulo Moreira, Paulo Costa, Andr Scolari, Armando Sousa, and Paulo Marques. 5dpo–2000 Team Description for RoboCup 2006. Technical report, FEUP - Faculdade de Engenharia da Universidade do Porto, 2006.
7. Willi Richert and Bernd Kleinjohann. Towards robust layered learning. In *IEEE International Conference on Autonomic and Autonomous Systems (ICAS'07)*, June 2007.
8. Willi Richert, Bernd Kleinjohann, and Lisa Kleinjohann. Evolving agent societies through imitation controlled by artificial emotions. In *International Conference on Intelligent Computing, ICIC 2005*, number 3644 in LNCS, pages 1004–1013. Springer-Verlag Berlin, June 2005.
9. Willi Richert, Bernd Kleinjohann, Markus Koch, and Philipp Adelt. The paderkicker team: Autonomy in realtime environments. In *Proceedings of the Working Conference on Distributed and Parallel Embedded Systems (DIPES 2006)*, October 2006.
10. Dirk Stichling. *VisiTrack - Inkrementelles Kameratracking fr mobile Echtzeitsysteme*. PhD thesis, Universitt Paderborn, Fakultt fr Elektrotechnik, Informatik und Mathematik, 2004.
11. Dirk Stichling and Bernd Kleinjohann. CV-SDF – a model for real-time computer vision applications. In *IEEE Workshop on Application of Computer Vision*, Orlando, Florida, December 2002. IEEE.
12. Dirk Stichling and Bernd Kleinjohann. Low latency color segmentation on embedded real-time systems. In *Design and Analysis of Distributed Embedded Systems*. Kluwer Academic Publishers, November 2002.
13. Dirk Stichling and Bernd Kleinjohann. Edge vectorization for embedded real-time systems using the CV-SDF model. In *Proceedings of the 16th International Conference on Vision Interfaces (VI 2003)*, Halifax, Canada, June 2003.
14. Felix v. Hundelshausen, Sven Behnke, and Raúl Rojas. An omnidirectional vision system that finds and tracks color edges and blobs. *Lecture Notes In Computer Science*, 2377:374–379, 2002.
15. Jules White and Douglas C. Schmidt. Automated configuration of component-based distributed real-time and embedded systems from feature models. *Proceedings of the 17th Annual Conference of the International Federation of Automatic Control*, 2008.

Sorting Units for FPGA-Based Embedded Systems

Rui Marcelino, Horácio Neto, and João M. P. Cardoso

Abstract Sorting is an important operation for a number of embedded applications. As sorting large datasets may impose undesired performance degradation, acceleration units coupled to the embedded processor can be an interesting solution for speeding-up the computations. This paper presents and evaluates three hardware sorting units, bearing in mind embedded computing systems implemented with FPGAs. The proposed architectures take advantage of specific FPGA hardware resources to increase efficiency. Experimental results show the differences in resources and performances among the three proposed sorting units and also between the sorting units and pure software implementations for sorting. We show that a hybrid between an insertion sorting unit and a merge FIFO sorting unit provides a speed-up between 1.6 and 25 compared to a quicksort software implementation.

Key words: sorting, FPGAs, embedded systems, special-purpose architecture

1 Introduction

Search and sorting are becoming important operations for embedded computing. Even modest devices are being furnished with amounts of storage that were unthinkable only a couple of years ago. Handheld portable devices, such as PDAs and cell phones, have now the capacity to store large datasets and finding the contents the user wants is becoming critical. For example, an MP3 player with 160 GB can store about 40,000 songs!

Rui Marcelino
UALG/EST – Campus da Penha – Faro, Portugal
e-mail: rmarcel@ualg.pt

Horácio Neto · João M. P. Cardoso
UTL/IST/INESC-ID – Rua Alves Redol – Lisboa, Portugal
e-mail: hcn@inesc.pt, jmpc@acm.org

Please use the following format when citing this chapter:

Marcelino, R., Neto, H. and Cardoso, J.M.P., 2008, in IFIP International Federation for Information Processing, Volume 271; *Distributed Embedded Systems: Design, Middleware and Resources*; Bernd Kleinjohann, Lisa Kleinjohann, Wayne Wolf; (Boston: Springer), pp. 11–22.

Also, new emerging applications, like sensor data logs, internet traffic, transactions logs, where the information occurs in the form of data streams [1], show how important are database and data stream management systems. The performance of queries in these systems is often dominated by the cost of the sorting algorithm [2]. Hence, sorting units able to improve performance may play an important role.

Our goal is to research efficient sorting units to couple to a general purpose processor (GPP) for FPGA-based embedded systems (see Figure 1). In this paper we present three sorting units and compare the execution time of those units to pure software solutions (e.g., quicksort). The three sorting units proposed explore parallel processing, streaming, and FPGA resources. To combine key properties of those sorting units we also present and evaluate a hybrid sorting unit.

This paper is organized as follows. In section 2 we review related work on sorting machines. Section 3 describes our proposed architectures. Section 4 shows experimental results. Finally, section 5 draws some conclusions.

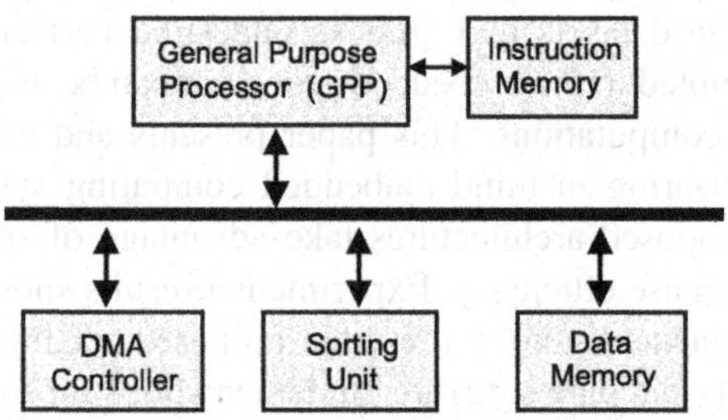

Fig. 1 Block diagram of the target system. The *sorting units* are instantiated as an OPB custom core and the data to be sorted are stored in BRAMs connected to the OPB bus.

2 Background and Related Work

Sorting has been exhaustively studied in the area of computer science and many sorting algorithms exist [3]. On GPPs, quicksort is the fastest of the common sorting algorithms for general case sorting [3]. Albeit the performance of quicksort, sorting remains a time spending operation.

A number of approaches have been studied to accelerate sorting operations on GPPs, namely the use of hyper-threaded technology to accelerate quicksort in the Intel compiler [4], and the use of graphics processors [2].

Concerning application-specific architectures, two different approaches have been considered for accelerating sorting operations, one focusing on variations on the sorting networks [5], and the other exploring systolic linear arrays [9]. Although those approaches may achieve high-performance sorting, both rely on a large number of simultaneous load/stores to feed the sorting unit. This hampers their practical use with current technology.

Sorting networks are based on levels with arrays of 2-input swap-comparators. Martinez et al. [6] propose, for the Burrows Wheeler Transform operation, a hardware sorting network with two levels of pipelining, where the data is sorted in an iterative scheme. The sorting unit deals with 128 characters and results show a large FPGA area occupation and a maximum clock frequency of about 50 MHz.

Zhang and Zheng [7] present a parallel sorting algorithm using a fixed size sorting network. Their architecture is composed by three components: input queues, pipelined sorting network, and a termination detection circuit. Results for different queues size and numbers are shown.

Lin and Liu [8] propose a cascade of compare-swap cells to build the sorting circuit. The data to be sorted propagate through the sorting unit. They argue their approach is scalable and is suitable for VLSI implementations. However, they present an ASIC implementation in a 0.32 m CMOS technology, dealing only with 32 elements of 16 bits and achieving a 66 MHz maximum clock frequency.

Parahami and Kwai [9] propose a cell for systolic linear arrays where the control signals are pipelined with the data to be sorted. In their work, two parallel comparisons are performed in each cell. Bednara et al. [10] present a hybrid hardware/software implementation of a sorting algorithm that uses merge-sort for its sequential part and a Parhami and Kwai [9] type systolic array for the parallel part. In their approach, the sorting unit is implemented in FPGAs and is coupled to a microprocessor.

Recently, Ratnayke and Amer [11] propose an FPGA implementation variation of the counting sort algorithm. This algorithm is a histogram based sorter and explores the BRAM structures of the FPGAs for the modified counting sort algorithm. The sorting unit was implemented in a Virtex II-Pro FPGA and the results show that a significant number of FPGA resources is required to sort a large number of elements.

In this work, we exploit three different sorting units to couple to a host softcore processor, bearing in mind the trade-off between hardware resources and performance. The target system is tested using FPGA devices. Next sections describe those sorting units.

3 Sorting Units

The three approaches for hardware sorting units proposed herein are:

- Odd-Even Sorting Network Machine, based on sorting networks where we reduce the traditional area used for sorting network implementations by using an iterative scheme.
- Insertion Sorting Machine, based on a scalable and linear array.
- FIFO-based Merge Sorting Machine, based on the available and efficient FPGAs FIFO support using BRAMs.

Next, we describe in detail each one of the sorting units mentioned above.

3.1 Odd-Even Sorting Network Machines

Hardware solutions using sorting networks, such as the one proposed in [7], require a large number of hardware resources to implement the complete network. To save hardware resources we propose a solution based on Batchers odd-even [5] sorting network with reuse of resources. We use an iterative sorting unit, where the sorting network is reduced to a single row. In this approach, the maximum computational time complexity is O(*n*), being *n* the number of elements to sort.

The basic element of sorting networks is the comparator-swap block, shown in Figure 2(a), which performs the elementary sort between two elements. The block receives the two data elements to be sorted A, B and outputs the two sorted elements L and H, where L means "less than" or "equal", and H means "greater than". In addition a /CHANGE signal flags if a swap between the two input data elements has been done or not.

As the hardware implementation of the sorting network may require too many resources, especially when dealing with a large number of inputs, a split of the network in iterative sequential stages is performed. On this implementation, referred herein as "*sequential network*", the hardware is reused to implement all the required computing stages of the sorting network with a smaller number of physical stages. Note that this sorting network requires a simple control unit and is used for its simplicity, regularity and scalability.

Two schemes have been implemented using the odd-even transposition sorting algorithm. The first one, named sorting network with one pipeline level (SN-I), refers to a machine employing hardware reuse in every clock cycle. For this, a basic comparator-swap is used as shown in Figure 2(a), but without output registers. Registers are placed at the end of the stage to store the results every clock cycle (see Figure 2(b)). A switch network, implemented by an array of multiplexers, is included between the comparators and the output registers. The switch network is responsible for the data alignment, as show in Figure 3, then the output is fed to the input of the unit and this loop is continuously repeated until the data input items are sorted. Until all the elements become sorted, pairs of elements are switched every clock cycle. The sorting is finished when no swap is performed in two consecutives clock cycles of the machine, considering all comparator-swap blocks, or when it reaches the final number of iterations (*n*). This is detected by the control logic that reads the output global flag, /CHANGE, which is an AND of all the individual /CHANGE flags.

The second approach implemented is a sorting network with two pipeline levels (SN-II). The sorting scheme used is the same, the odd-even transposition sorting network, but the data alignment is performed by the use of two comparator levels (see Figure 4). Now the comparator-swap blocks have the outputs registered, creating a 2-stage pipelined machine. These two-stages are reused every two clock cycles. As before, the sorting finishes when the control logic detects that no swap was performed on all comparator-swap blocks in two consecutives clock cycles or when it reaches the final number of iteration (*n*).

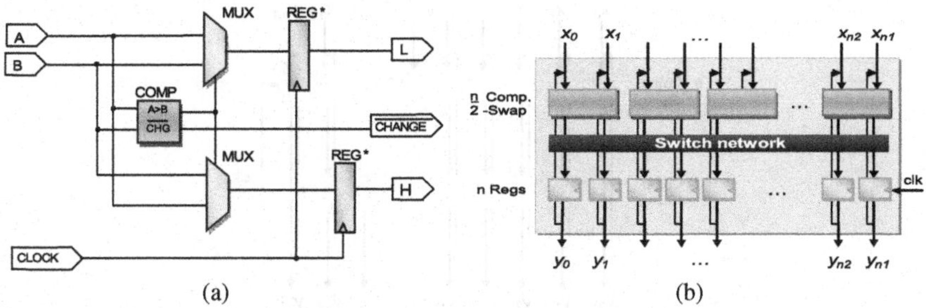

Fig. 2 (a) Comparator-Swap block, the output registers are not used in the SN-I machine implementation (b) SN-I, one pipeline level sorting unit

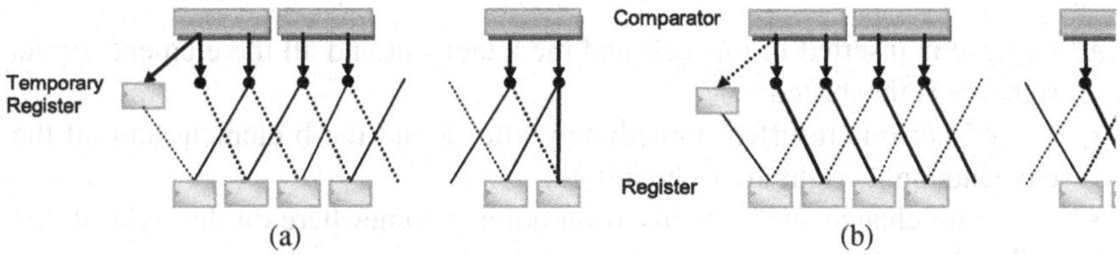

Fig. 3 Switch network for data alignment on SN-I, an extra temporary register have been used: (a) Odd; (b) Even

3.2 Insertion Sorting Machine

The insertion sorting machine is represented by the dependence graph shown in Figure 5(a), where each node represents a comparison/insert cell. The number of cells equals the number of elements to be sorted. A new element to be sorted/inserted is broadcasted to all nodes and comparisons are performed in order to find the right node for inserting this new element. Depending on the sort direction, ascending or descending, the most right node reflects the minimum or the maximum element. The data are read from the machine through the right cell in a sequential way (one by one), or in a parallel way. In this machine, the sorting operation is overlapped with the input data operations.

Considering the ascending sorting mode, where the element with the lowest value will be at the right element of the sorting array, as represented in Figure 5(a). In one cell we have an element a from the previous cell, and an element b in the current cell register. For ascending mode of sort the comparator performs the following condition: $b \leq a$. The new element to be inserted c is compared with the data held in all the cell registers. In the general case, where the element a has not the largest possible value, we have one of three possibilities for each cell of the array:

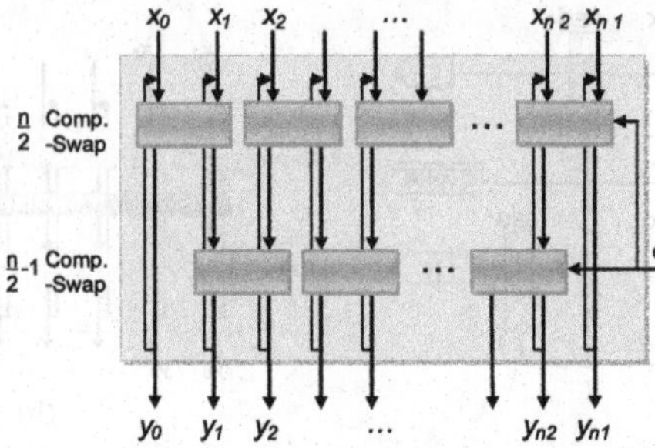

Fig. 4 SN-II, two pipeline levels sorting unit. In this machine the comparator-swap has the output registers.

- $c \geq a$: c is inserted in this cell and the a element and all the elements on its right are right shifted.
- $a > c \geq b$: c is inserted immediately after a and the b element and all the elements on its right are right shifted.
- $c < b$: no change since the insertion point is somewhere on the right of this cell.

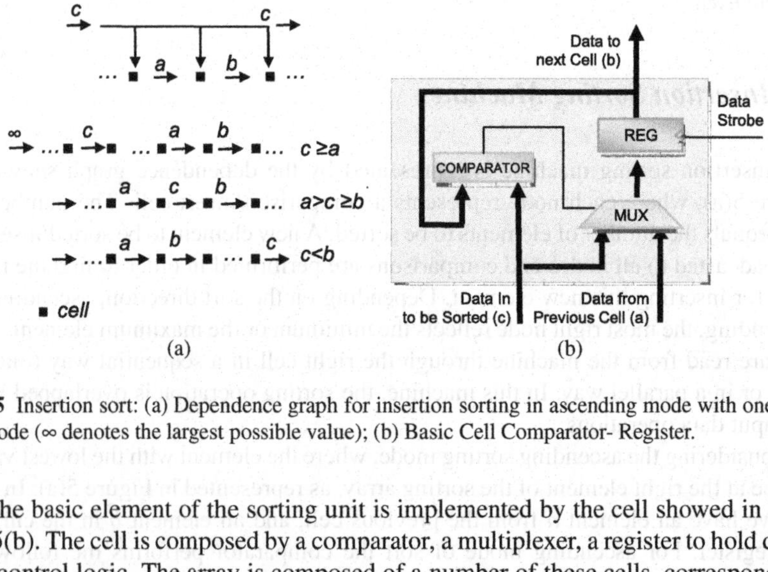

Fig. 5 Insertion sort: (a) Dependence graph for insertion sorting in ascending mode with one cell per node (∞ denotes the largest possible value); (b) Basic Cell Comparator- Register.

The basic element of the sorting unit is implemented by the cell showed in Figure 5(b). The cell is composed by a comparator, a multiplexer, a register to hold data, and control logic. The array is composed of a number of these cells, corresponding to the number of elements to be sorted (see Figure 6). Two tags work in a pipeline fashion interconnecting the cells. One tag represents the active cells and works like a carry flag (CY) that is propagated through the cells, as the elements are inserted in the sorting unit. The other tag (LE) reflects the comparison result between the new element to sort and the element presented in the register of each cell. If the new element is greater than the element presented in the register this tag is reset, other way is set. The two tags drive the control logic located in the cell, in order to define the exact cell where this new element is inserted.

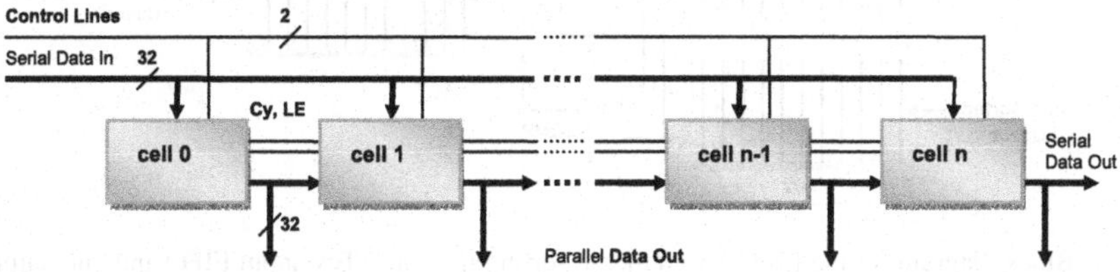

Fig. 6 Insert Sorting circuit block diagram for n-elements.

3.3 FIFO-based Merge Sorting Machine

Our FIFO-based merge sorting unit uses the merge scheme shown in Figure 7. The sorting structure consists of three FIFO queues: two input FIFOs and one output FIFO. The input FIFOs have depth $n/2$ and the output FIFO has depth n. This unit assumes that the data in the two input FIFOs have been sorted before.

A truly FIFO-based implementation needs to start by sorting two data elements, each one in a different input FIFO and then repeatedly performs sorting of two sets of $k/2$ elements to achieve k sorted elements until it reaches the last iteration where n elements are sorted based on the two sets of $n/2$ elements previously sorted. This approach might be, however, inefficient and thus a different strategy can be used to feed the FIFO-based merge sorting unit with the two sorted sets of $n/2$ elements each. For example, we can use a Sorting Network Unit or an Insertion Sorting Unit to sort those two sets of $n/2$ elements.

The merging process is performed by presenting the data of the two previous sorted input FIFOs to the inputs of a comparator and a multiplexer. The comparator output defines which element is "greater than" and signals the multiplexer control line in order to select the appropriate element to be written to the output FIFO. A new data element is sorted every clock cycle and the process repeats until all the data are processed. The computational time complexity of this approach is O(n), being n the number of elements to sort.

Although not exploited in this work, it is possible to build sorting units of this kind using more than 2-input FIFOs and more than two levels of FIFOs. Topologies based on trees of FIFOs can be used and might be suitable when it is possible to sort concurrently the data elements in the input FIFOs.

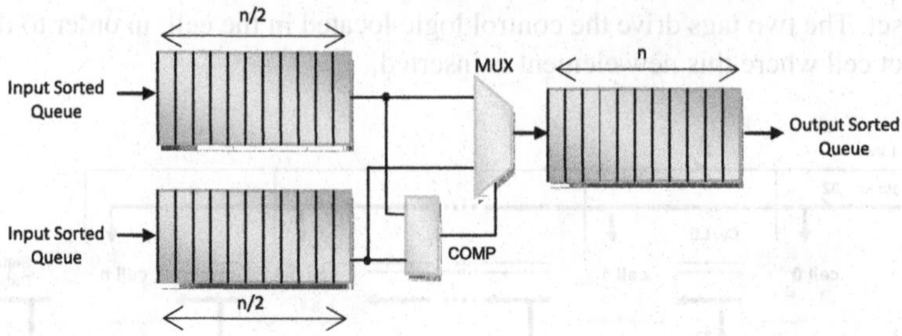

Fig. 7 Block diagram for the FIFO-based merge sorting machine. Two input FIFO and one output FIFO are used.

4 Experimental Results

The sorting units and their control units have been specified in parameterized behavioral RTL-VHDL code. A Xilinx Spartan 3 FPGA (xc3s400-5fg456) has been used to characterize the FPGA implementation of those units. For this particular study we use sorting units working with 32-bit data elements.

The Embedded Development Kit (EDK) and WebISE, release 8.2i, from Xilinx were used for system development and configuration, logic synthesis and placement and routing. For prototyping and test, we use a system with a Xilinx 32-bit MicroBlaze *softcore* processor. For the particular cases presented herein, the sorting units are instantiated as an OPB custom core and the data to be sorted are stored in BRAMs connected to the OPB bus. For data transfer between the BRAMs and the sorting units a DMA controller is included. The MicroBlaze was configured with default parameters, i.e., without the optional datapath units, and without caches. The stack memory was adjusted for the quicksort algorithm requirements. The software implementations were compiled using the C compiler included in the EDK (mb-gcc), with the -O2 option selected.

Our analysis is performed in two steps, one regarding the FPGA resources and the other the execution time of the sorting units being evaluated. All the results obtained by the proposed sorting units are compared with the software algorithm quicksort. In these experiments both the sorting units and the *softcore* processor were running at the same clock frequency (50 MHz for the validations done using the FPGA board). Note, however, that higher speed-ups could be obtained if we consider maximum frequencies for each unit as the maximum clock frequency of MicroBlaze in the FPGA used is around 100 MHz.

Table 1 summarizes the FPGA resources used for the sorting units and the maximum clock frequencies achieved. For the comparisons, we use units with size $n = 128$. The results indicate that the Sorting Network with two levels (SN-II) needs 20% more FPGA resources than the Sorting Network with one level (SN-I). The amount of FPGA resources required for the Insertion Sorting unit is similar to SNI. As can be seen, the FIFO-based merge sorting unit uses mainly BRAMs and much less FPGA resources than the other sorting units.

For execution time analysis, we use sets with 16K 32-bit unsigned integers (N). Those sets were randomly generated (uniform distribution). The data communication between the memory and the sorting unit is performed by a DMA controller.

The FIFO-based Merge Sorting Unit requires that two blocks of data with $n/2$ elements be previously sorted and stored in the input FIFOs. In this case, the sorting unit will then give the n elements sorted. To sort those $n/2$ elements we tested the use of a Sorting Network and an Insertion Sorting Unit. The sorting units are able to directly sort a certain pre-defined number of elements (n). Sorting data N size over n needs a merge-sort scheme. For that, we use a software implementation of a merge-sort (identified as software-merge), where each block of data to be sorted (with size n) is sorted by the hardware sorting unit.

Table 1 Maximum clock frequencies and FPGAs resources obtained after Place and Route for the sorting units.

Sorting Unit	LUTs	FFs	Slices	BRAM	Frequency (MHz)
SN I ($N = 128$)	14,629	3,976	7,438	0	80
SN II ($N = 128$)	18,764	8,345	8,906	0	160
Insertion Sorting Machine ($N = 128$)	12,954	4,296	6,486	0	198
FIFO-based Merge Sorting ($N = 128$)[1]	516	444	384	3	104

[1] This machine uses the same resources and achieves the same maximum clock frequency for sizes below or equal $n = 512$.

Figure 8 shows the speed-ups of the hybrid proposed solution (Insertion + FIFObased merge sorting unit) over software quicksort. The hybrid units used here are of size 32, 64, and 128. As can be seen, the speed-up is high and increases with the size of the sorting units. For machines with size 256 with 128 pre-sorted queue, which is the maximum size of sorting units we have experimented with the FPGA used, a speed-up of about 25 has been achieved.

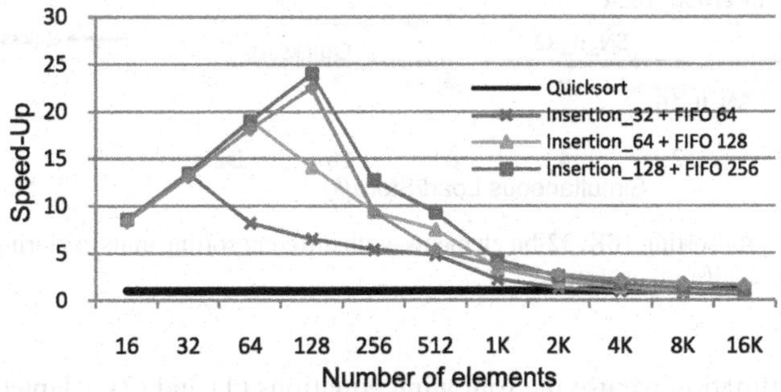

Fig. 8 Speed-ups for different FIFO-based merge sorting units over software quicksort.

As previously referred, when the number of data elements to be sorted surpasses the number of elements sorted by each execution of the sorting unit, a software-merge algorithm is used. In this later case, a degradation in the speed-ups is present (the inflexion points in the chart shown in Figure 8). Note that the software- merge adds a computational time complexity $O(n \cdot \log n)$, being n the number of elements to sort.

Figure 9 gives estimations for sorting a set of 16K elements with three sorting units. We exploit the case of having support for simultaneous load/store operations to communicate data to the sorting units. For the estimations, we use two completely parallel Sorting Networks (SN-II), able to directly sort 16 and 32 elements. The second machine is a 1024-element Insertion Sorting Unit. The third machine is a FIFO-based Merge Sorting Unit able to output 512 sorted elements using two sets of 256 elements sorted by an Insertion Sorting Unit. The results take into account typical DMA load/store latencies, acquired from experimental measurements. For calculating the execution time when sorting 16K elements, the overhead of a *software-merge* has been included.

These results indicate that the Sorting Network SN-II with size 16 (*SN_II_16*) achieves worse results than software quicksort, even with 16 simultaneous load/store operations. The SN-II with size 32 (*SN_II_32*) surpasses quicksort when considering more than 2 simultaneous load/store operations. The Insertion Sort Unit with size 1024 (*Insertion_1024*) achieves for all the cases better performance than quicksort, but since the data is fed to the sorting unit sequentially no gain is obtained by performing simultaneous load/store operations. The highest speed-ups are obtained by the Insertion 256 + FIFO-based merge sorting unit with size 512 (*Insertion_256 + FIFO_512*). In this case, the speed-up increases between 1 to 2 simultaneous load/store operations, as is explained by the fact that this particular unit uses 2 input FIFOs.

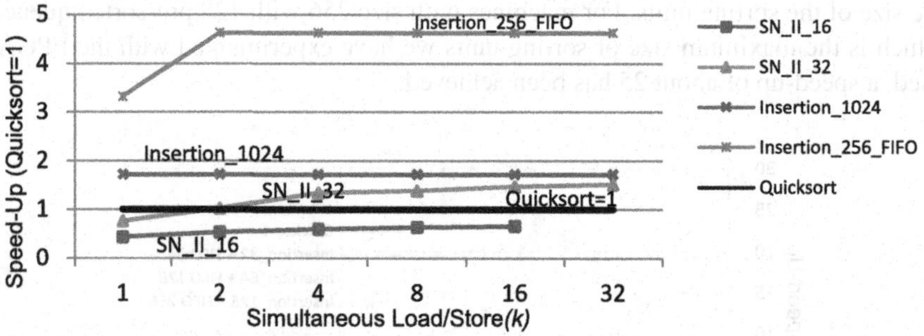

Fig. 9 Speedups for sorting 16K, 32-bit elements, with different sorting units exploring the number of simultaneous load/store operations

For the estimation we use the following equations (1) and (2), adapted from [5]:

$$T_{(n)} = \frac{n}{k}(t_{load} + t_{store}) + t_{sort\ unit(n)} \quad (1)$$

where $T_{(n)}$ is the total time to sort n elements, considering that n is the maximum number of elements to sort directly on the sorting unit, k represents the simultaneous load/store operations, t_{load} the time to load data from the memory, t_{store} the time to store data in the memory, and $t_{sort\ unit(n)}$ the time required by the sorting unit to sort n elements, considering the data are been loaded

$$T_{software\ merge(N)} = \left[\left(p^2 - p + 4\right) 2^p - 1\right] T_{(n)} \tag{2}$$

where $T_{software\ merge(N)}$ is the total time to sort N, elements using software merge, and $p = log(N)$. For larges sorts typically the number N is much greater than n.

5 Conclusions

We describe in this paper three different approaches for hardware sorting units. The sorting units proposed have been coupled to a microprocessor in an FPGAbased embedded system. The sorting units explore different architectures: sorting networks with one or two levels, an insertion sorting array, and a particular sorting unit based on FIFOs. We evaluated these units by coupling them to the peripheral on-chip bus in a system based on a softcore microprocessor (Xilinx MicroBlaze) and implemented in an FPGA. The results show the execution times achieved and the resources needed by each sorting unit. From our preliminary study, the best unit, when a small number of load/store operations can be simultaneously performed (1 or 2), is a hybrid between an insertion sorting and an FIFO-based merge sorting. This sorting unit provides speed-ups between 1.6 and 15 compared to a quicksort pure software solution running in the microprocessor of the system. Even when the number of simultaneously load/store operations is higher (3 or more), the FIFO-based merge sorting unit is from the three units tested in this paper the fastest.

Acknowledgments

This work has been partially supported by the project COBAYA, funded by the Portuguese Foundation for Science and Technology (FCT).

References

1. Golab L., Özsu M.T.: Issues in data stream management, ACM SIGMOD Record, v.32 n.2, p.5–14, June, San Diego, California (2003)
2. Govindaraju, N., Raghuvanshi, N., Henson, M., Tuft, D., Manocha, D.: GPUTera- Sort: high performance graphics co-processor sorting for large database management, in Proceedings of the 2006 ACM SIGMOD international conference on Management of data, June 26-29, Chicago, IL, USA (2006)

3. Knuth, D.E.:The Art of Computer Programming, Vol. 3 - Sorting and Searching. Addison-Wesley (1973)
4. Rajiv, R.D.P.:Accelerating Quicksort on the Intel® Pentium® 4 Processor with Hyper-Threading Technology, http://softwarecommunity.intel.com/articles/eng/2422.htm, October (2007)
5. Batcher, K.:Sorting Networks and Their Applications. Proc. AFIPS Spring Joint Computer Conf. Vol. 32, pp. 307–314, Atlantic City, NJ, USA, 30 April - 2 May (1968)
6. Martínez J., Cumplido, R.R., Feregrino, C.:An FPGA-based parallel sorting architecture for the Burrows Wheeler transform, Proceedings International Conference on Reconfigurable Computing and FPGAs, 28-30 Sept., Puebla City, Mexico (2005)
7. Zhang, Y., Zheng, S.Q.: An Efficient Parallel VLSI Sorting Architecture, VLSI Design, vol. 11, no. 2, pp. 137–147, (2000)
8. Lin, C.S., Liu, B.D.:Design of a Pipelined and Expandable sorting Architecture with Simple Control Scheme. IEEE International Symposium on Circuits and Systems, Volume: 4, pp. 217–220, 26-29 May. Scottsdale, Arizona, USA (2002)
9. Parhami, B., Kwai, D.M.: Data-driven control scheme for linear arrays. Application to a stable insertion sorter, IEEE Trans. On Parallel and Distributed Systems, January 1999, Vol. 10, No. 1, pp. 23–28, (1999)
10. Bednara, M., Beyer, O., Teich, J., Wanka, R.: Tradeoff Analysis And Architecture Design Of Hybrid Hardware/Software Sorter, Application-Specific Systems, Architectures, and Processors. Proceedings of the IEEE International Conference on Application-Specific Systems, Architectures, and Processors, Proceedings, pp. 299, 10-12 July, Boston, MA, USA (2000)
11. Ratnayake, K., Amer, A.: An FPGA Architecture of Stable-Sorting on a Large Data Volume : Application to Video Signals, 41st Annual Conference on Information Sciences and Systems, pp. 431–436, 14-16 March, Baltimore, USA (2007)

Error-Exploiting Video Encoder to Extend Energy/QoS Tradeoffs for Mobile Embedded Systems

Kyoungwoo Lee, Minyoung Kim, Nikil Dutt, and Nalini Venkatasubramanian

Abstract Energy/QoS provisioning is a challenging task for video applications in power-constrained mobile embedded systems. Many error-resilient video encodings allow us to exploit errors and generate a range of acceptable tradeoff spaces by controlling the amount of errors in the system. This expanded tradeoff space allows system designers to comparatively evaluate different operating points with varying QoS and energy consumption by aggressively exploiting error-resilience attributes, and can potentially result in significant energy savings. Specifically, we propose an error-aware video encoding technique that intentionally injects errors (drops frames) while ensuring QoS in accordance with error-resilience. The novelty of our approach is in *active exploitation of errors* to vary the operating conditions for further optimization of system aspects. Our experiments show that our error-exploiting video encoding can reduce the energy consumption for an encoding device by 37% in video conferencing over a wireless network, without video quality degradation, compared to a standard video encoding technique for a test video stream. Furthermore, we present the adaptivity of our approach by incorporating the feedback from the decoding side to achieve the QoS requirement under dynamic network status.

1 Introduction

Due to the rapid deployment of wireless communications, video applications on mobile embedded systems such as video telephony and video streaming have grown dramatically. A major challenge in mobile video applications is how to efficiently allocate the limited energy resource in order to deliver the best video quality. A significant amount of power in mobile embedded systems is consumed by video pro-

---

Kyoungwoo Lee · Minyoung Kim · Nikil Dutt · Nalini Venkatasubramanian
Department of Computer Science, School of Information and Computer Sciences, University of California, Irvine, CA 92697, USA
e-mail: {kyoungwl, minyounk, dutt, nalini}@ics.uci.edu

Please use the following format when citing this chapter:

Lee, K., et al., 2008, in IFIP International Federation for Information Processing, Volume 271; *Distributed Embedded Systems: Design, Middleware and Resources*; Bernd Kleinjohann, Lisa Kleinjohann, Wayne Wolf; (Boston: Springer), pp. 23–34.

cessing and transmission. Also, error resilient video encodings demand extra energy consumption in general to combat the transmission errors in wireless video communications. Thus, it is challenging and essential for system designers to explore the possible tradeoff space and to increase the energy saving while ensuring the quality satisfaction even under dynamic network status. In this paper, we introduce the notion of *active error exploitation* to effectively extend the tradeoff space between energy consumption and video quality, and present an adaptive error-exploiting video encoding to maximize the energy saving with minimal quality degradation.

Tradeoffs between energy consumption and QoS (Quality of Service) for mobile video communication have been investigated earlier [3, 5, 12, 14, 17]. It is interesting to observe that the delivered video data is *inherently error-tolerant*: spatial and temporal correlations between consecutive video frames are used to increase the compression efficiency, and results in errors at the reconstructed video data. These naturally induced errors from the encoding algorithms degrade the video quality, but they may not be perceived by the human eye. This inherent error-tolerance of video data can be exploited to increase the energy reduction for mobile embedded systems. For instance, relaxing the acceptable quality of the video reduces the overhead for the exhaustive searching algorithm by exploring a partial area instead of the entire region. Further, we exploit errors actively for the purpose of energy reduction. In our study, one way of active error exploitation is to intentionally drop frames before the encoding process. By dropping frames, we eliminate the entire video encoding process for these frames and thereby reduce energy consumption while sacrificing some loss in the video quality. Note that the effects of dropping frames on video quality are partially canceled with the nature of error-tolerance in video data.

To cope with transmission errors such as packet losses, error-resilient video encoding techniques [2, 9, 15, 16, 18] have been investigated to reduce the effects of transmission errors on QoS. Most existing error resilient techniques judiciously adapt their resilience levels considering the network status. Interestingly, our approach, combining these error-resilient techniques with intentional dropping frames, presents several pros and cons. First, we can improve the video quality to the level that error-resilient techniques achieve by considering these frame drops as packet losses occurring in the network. Second, we can increase the error margins that video encoders potentially exploit for maximal energy reduction, i.e., we can drop more frames. On the other hand, the error-resilience increases the compressed video data in general, and so raises the energy consumption for data transmission. Thus, this active error-exploitation approach with error resilient techniques significantly enlarges the tradeoff space among energy consumption for compression, energy consumption for transmission, and QoS in mobile video applications. Furthermore, our error exploiting video encoding scheme extends the applicability of error resilient schemes, even when the network is error-free.

In this paper, we propose a new knob, *error injection rate* (*EIR*) that controls the amount of data to be dropped. This EIR knob can be used to explore the tradeoff space between the energy consumption and video quality, unlike in previous approaches. Specifically, we present an error-exploiting video encoding with EIR based on an existing error-resilient video encoding, PBPAIR (Probability-Based

Power-Aware Intra-Refresh) [9]. Our new approach, called Error-Exploiting PBPAIR or *EE-PBPAIR*, is composed of two units: *error-injection unit* and *error-canceling unit*. The error-injection unit drops frames intentionally according to EIR. And the error-canceling unit applies PBPAIR to encode video data resilient against intentional frame drops. Active error exploitation can reduce the overheads for transmission and even the decoding, and results in the energy savings of all components in an encoding-decoding path in distributed mobile embedded systems. However, very aggressive error injection in EE-PBPAIR can degrade the video quality significantly, and there is a need to monitor the delivered video quality in distributed systems and to adjust the EIR to ensure satisfactory quality. Thus, we also present *adaptive EE-PBPAIR*, which adapts the EIR based on the quality feedback from the decoding side while minimizing the energy consumption.

The contributions and results of our work are:

- We propose the notion of active error exploitation, that extends the energy/QoS tradeoff space for video encoding on power-constrained embedded systems.
- We present an error-exploiting video encoding, *EE-PBPAIR*, by dropping frames intentionally in accordance with an error resilient scheme, PBPAIR [9].
- We present a feedback-based quality adjustment technique by adapting the EIR to meet the quality constraint – *adaptive EE-PBPAIR*.
- We demonstrate the efficacy of our approach: as compared to a standard video encoding based on H.263 [7], EE-PBPAIR reduces the energy consumption of an encoding device by up to 37% over a video stream without quality degradation, and by up to 49% at the cost of 10% quality degradation.

2 Background

Energy and QoS aware adaptations have been studied for video applications on mobile embedded systems in a cross-layer manner [12, 17]. In particular, Mohapatra et al. [12] explored the effects of video encoding parameters such as quantization scale, IP-ratio, and motion estimation algorithms on energy consumption and QoS, and proposed an integrated power management technique with middleware adaptations aware of system configurations. On the other hand, Eisenberg et al. [3] exploited the knowledge of the concealment method at the decoder to reduce the transmission power. However, although energy/QoS aware schemes have studied the tradeoff between energy consumption and QoS, they did not take into account error resilience against unreliable transmission and active error exploitation.

One of the most effective methods to achieve error-resilient video is to introduce the intra-coded frame (I-frame) periodically: since I-frames are decoded independently, they protect the propagation of the transmission errors and even encoding errors in previous frames. However, the transmission of I-frames causes delay and jitter (due to relatively large size) compared to predictively-coded frames (P-frames), and the loss of I-frames is more sensitive on QoS than that of P-frames [2, 9]. To mitigate both the propagation of the transmission errors and the overheads of large I-frames, recently intra-MB (Macroblock) refresh approaches have been proposed

[2, 9, 16]. Intra refresh techniques distribute intra-MBs among frames, which not only removes the overheads of I-frames but also improves the error-resilience. While most intra-MB refresh techniques have been focused on alleviating the effects of the transmission errors on the video quality, Kim et al. [9] proposed an energy-efficient and error-resilient video encoding named PBPAIR, and presented tradeoffs among error resilience, encoding efficiency, and energy consumption for video encoding. However, existing error resilient techniques have focused on how to manage the errors from network in a passive manner (*passive error exploitation*). On the contrary, our *active error exploitation* maximizes the feature of applications by intentional error injection – an approach has not been applied to video encoding earlier.

Our approach actively exploits the error tolerance of video data by injecting errors intentionally at the application level, and an error resilient video encoder along with *adaptive error injection* minimizes the effect of injected errors on the QoS. Therefore, our error-exploiting video encoding approach aggressively exploits error resilience to achieve the maximal energy gain while ensuring the QoS, and further opens opportunities to expand the tradeoff spaces between QoS and energy consumption in mobile embedded systems.

3 Our Approach

3.1 Fundamentals of Active Error Exploitation

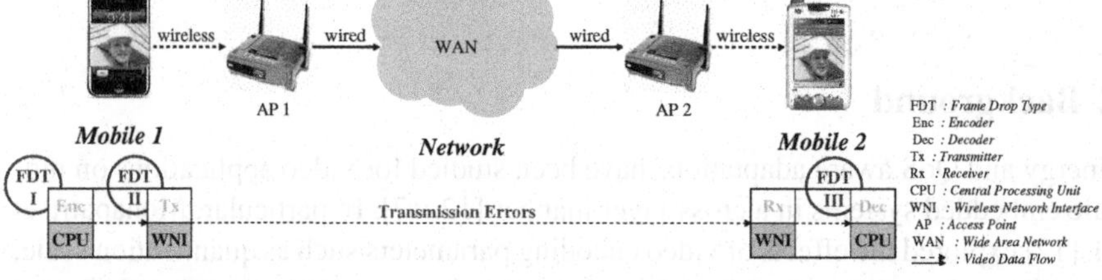

Fig. 1 System Model and Frame Drop Types I/II/III for Active Error Exploitation

Fig. 1 shows our system model for mobile video conferencing. This mobile video conferencing system consists of two mobile devices and the network environment. Each mobile device is modeled as a mobile embedded system composed of a CPU and a WNI, where video data is encoded (or decoded) and transmitted (or received). The network consists of WAN and two wireless access points, each of which provides the wireless communication channel for each mobile device. For simplicity, we consider one path from an encoder to a decoder for mobile video conferencing.

We *exploit errors actively*. In our study, active exploitation of errors means intentional frame dropping in mobile embedded systems. For the purpose of energy reduction, video frames can be dropped by any component in Fig. 1. For instance, the Decoder can drop the delivered video data to reduce the decoding energy (*Frame Drop Type III* as in Fig. 1). Another possibility is that the Transmitter drops video data to save the communication energy, and error resilient techniques take care of the dropped data in advance (*Frame Drop Type II*). Further, the Encoder can drop frames intentionally before the encoding process, and encode the rest of frames robust against the dropped frames, which are considered as lost packets in network (*Frame Drop Type I*). Note that dropping frames at the Encoder is the most effective in terms of energy reduction since it affects the energy consumption across all the following components in an encoding-decoding path as drawn in Fig. 1, and the energy consumption for encoding (Enc EC) is relatively high compared to those for the other components in our system model. Therefore, in this particular work, we only consider *Frame Drop Type I* (i.e., intentional frame drop at the Encoder) for active error-exploitation approach. *Type II* and *III* remain as our future work.

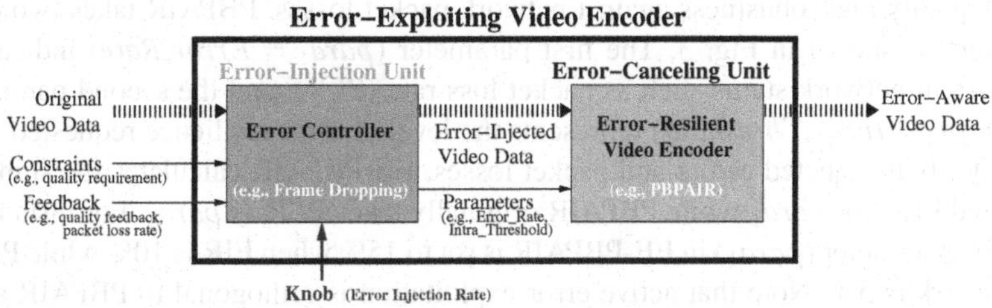

Fig. 2 Error-Exploiting Video Encoder: Error-Injection Unit and Error-Canceling Unit

Our error-exploiting video encoder is composed of two units, *error-injection unit* and *error-canceling unit*, as shown in Fig. 2. The *error-injection unit* controls the amount of errors for the purpose of energy reduction, and the *error-canceling unit* reduces the effects of the injected errors on the video quality using an error-resilient video encoder. The *Error Controller* acts as an *error-injection unit*, taking into account the constraint (e.g., required video quality) and the feedbacks from the decoding side (e.g., reconstructed video quality) and from the network (e.g., packet loss rate); furthermore, it intentionally injects the amount of errors according to a new knob – error injection rate (EIR), and generates the error-injected video data as illustrated in Fig. 2. Finally, the *Error-Resilient Video Encoder* acts as an *error-canceling unit*, and generates the error-aware video data by encoding the error-injected video data with parameters in preparation for downstream network packet losses as well as intentionally injected errors.

3.2 EE-PBPAIR: An Error-Exploiting Video Encoder

We now present *EE-PBPAIR* (Error-Exploiting PBPAIR), an approach that injects errors intentionally by "Dropping Frames" as an *error-injection unit*, and encodes video resiliently with "PBPAIR" as an *error-canceling unit* as shown in Fig. 2.

Dropping frames is one way of injecting errors intentionally. In this study, we consider a simple frame dropping approach, PFD (Periodic Frame Dropping). PFD periodically drops frames according to EIR. For instance, PFD with 10% of EIR drops every 10th frame. PFD evenly distributes the effects of frame dropping on QoS over a video stream. Note that the quality will be deliberately maintained by the fea-

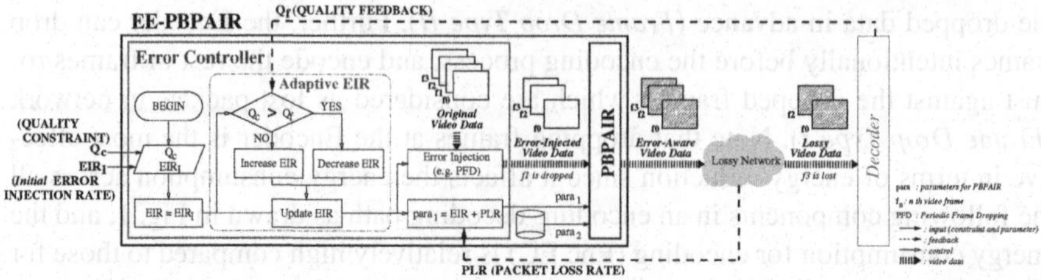

Fig. 3 Flow of Error Controller and Adaptive EIR in EE-PBPAIR for Mobile Video Applications

ture of error-resilient PBPAIR. We use PBPAIR as an error-resilient video encoder since the authors in [9] have demonstrated its energy efficiency while maintaining video quality and robustness against network packet losses. PBPAIR takes two parameters as shown in Fig. 3. The first parameter ($para_1 = Error\_Rate$) indicates the current network status such as packet loss rate (PLR), and the second parameter ($para_2 = Intra\_Threshold$) represents the level of error resilience requested. To consider both injected errors and packet losses, EE-PBPAIR calculates the sum of EIR and PLR for $para_1$ while PBPAIR originally takes PLR as $para_1$. For instance, the first parameter ($para_1$) in EE-PBPAIR is set to 15% when EIR is 10% while PLR in network is 5%. Note that active error exploitation is orthogonal to PBPAIR and can be applied to any error-resilient and energy-efficient video encoding technique which adapts algorithmic parameters according to the network status.

Our error-exploiting video encoder saves the energy consumption in several ways: i) intentional frame dropping saves energy consumption since EE-PBPAIR skips frame encodings according to EIR. ii) the energy consumption for video encoding is reduced since EE-PBPAIR adaptively introduces the more intra-MBs instead of inter-MBs for error resilience due to the intentional frame drops. iii) intentional frame dropping can reduce the encoded video file size, which propagates the energy saving downstream to the Transmitter, the Receiver, and even the Decoder.

A high EIR increases the energy reduction for encoding but decreases the QoS, if it is beyond a manageable point for error-resilient encoding. To keep the QoS degradation minimal, our approach is able to constrain the EIR based on the feedback from the decoding side. Fig. 3 describes this adaptive EIR feature in *Error Controller*. *Error Controller* takes the quality constraint Q_c and sets the initial error injection rate EIR_I. Then it receives the feedback such as Q_f and *PLR* as shown in the feedback loop of Fig. 3. If Q_f is less than Q_c, the current EIR is bad in terms of QoS, and so the EIR is decreased. Otherwise, it is increased (the flow of "Adaptive EIR" in Fig. 3). Based on EIR, the error injection module periodically drops frames. Thus, *Error Controller* forwards the error-injected video data to the *PBPAIR* as shown in Fig. 3. Also $para_1$ is delivered to the *PBPAIR*, which encodes the error-injected video data robust against the amount of errors indicated as $para_1$, with $para_2$ selected by PBPAIR methodology. Consequently, the encoded video data is now error-aware, i.e., it is cognizant of injected errors and packet losses as illustrated in Fig. 3. This adaptive video encoder adjusts EIR to meet the quality constraint with minimal energy consumption. So we believe that our adaptive approach can be effectively used to adjust our video encoder under a dynamic network environment for maximal energy reduction while ensuring the QoS. Note that the frequencies of feedbacks such as Q_f and *PLR* are beyond this work, and we assume that feedback channels are reliable.

4 Experiments

4.1 Experimental Setup

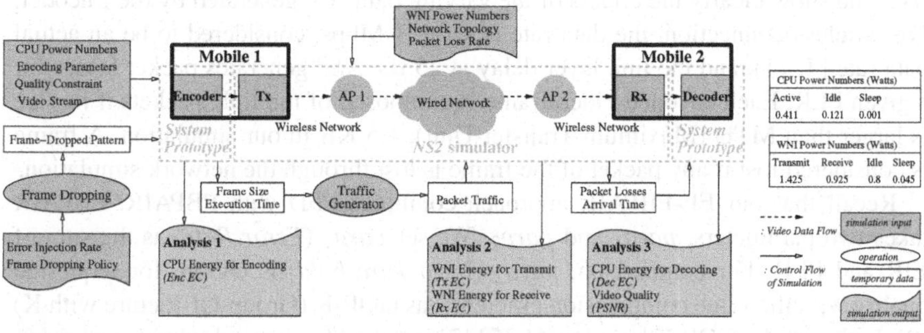

Fig. 4 Experimental Framework for Mobile Video Conferencing System - *System Prototype* + *NS2*

For interactive multimedia applications such as mobile video conferencing in distributed embedded systems, an end-to-end experimental system framework is a necessity since all components in a distributed system work interactively and affect other components in terms of energy consumption and performance. Thus, we evaluated EE-PBPAIR on top of an end-to-end framework as shown in Fig. 4 consisting of a *System Prototype* [10] and *NS2* simulator [13]. The *System Prototype* emulates a mobile embedded system and is detailed in our technical report [10].

The left side of Fig. 4 shows the preprocessing step, where a pattern of dropped frames is generated according to an EIR. CPU power numbers, video encoder parameters, network status (PLR), and quality constraint are inputs to *System Prototype*, where a video encoder compresses a video stream. *System Prototype* analyzes the first set of results – Analysis 1 – such as the energy consumption for encoding (*Enc EC*), and calculates the encoded size and the encoding completion time of each video frame, which are used for generating the network traffic for the following network simulation. Analysis 1 succinctly shows the CPU energy for encoding at the sender. Next, *NS2* simulates the generated network traffic with a set of configurations including the network topology and WNI power values, and estimates the energy consumption (*Tx* and *Rx EC*) for WNIs – Analysis 2. Thus Analysis 2 captures the end-to-end networking effects, including those of the transmitter and the receiver. Finally at the receiver, the *System Prototype* decodes the transmitted video data based on generated packet losses and frame arrival times from *NS2*, and evaluates the energy consumption for decoding (*Dec EC*) and the video quality measured in PSNR (Peak Signal to Noise Ratio) in Analysis 3. Thus Analysis 3 captures the CPU energy for decoding at the receiver (Power consumption numbers for CPU [6] and WNI [8] are configured as shown in the tables on the right side of Fig. 4). By combining Analysis 1, Analysis 2 and Analysis 3, we are able to measure the entire end-to-end energy savings for our proposed scheme.

Using *NS2*, we simulate the network consisting of two IEEE 802.11 WLANs (Wireless Local Area Network) and a wired network connecting them as shown in Fig. 4. Each WLAN is composed of one access point (AP 1 or AP 2), and one mobile device (Mobile 1 or Mobile 2). We exclude the effects of traffic from other mobile stations since they affect the energy consumption of WNI in our mobile devices. Instead, we limit the data rate of WNI, which constrains the encoded bit rate, and show clearly the effects of the varying data size generated by the Encoder. For wireless connection, the data rate is set at 1 Mbps, considered to be an actual data rate [4, 11], and the link layer delay at 25 μs. *NS2* generates packet losses for a given PLR. Each encoded video frame is composed of multiple packets if its size is larger than MTU (Maximum Transfer Unit), 1.5 KB in our simulation. A frame is considered lost if any packet of the frame is lost through the network simulation.

Recall that our EE-PBPAIR approach combines PFD with PBPAIR. PBPAIR takes two parameters, $para_1$ and $para_2$. We set $para_1$ (*Error_Rate*) as the sum of EIR and PLR. For comparison, $para_2$ (*Intra_Threshold*) is chosen for requested quality with the same compression efficiency as GOP-K (Group-Of-Picture with K) [9]. In this study, GOP-K based on H.263 [7] is defined as a standard video encoder, where K indicates the number of P-frames between I-frames. In GOP-K, we change K for resilience against the transmission errors in network as in [1, 9]. As a test video sequence, *FOREMAN* in QCIF format (176×144 pixels) is used. To constrain the bandwidth, we consider that the bitrate is 64 kbps (kilobits per second) and frame rate is 5 fps (frames per second).

4.2 Experimental Results

We present three sets of results. First we show the energy reduction due to active error exploitation (Section 4.2.1). Second, we demonstrate the expanded design space allowing better exploration of tradeoff alternatives (Section 4.2.2). Finally, Section 4.2.3 demonstrates the efficacy of adaptive EE-PBPAIR that maintains quality under dynamic network conditions by incorporating the quality feedback.

4.2.1 Energy Reduction from Active Error-Exploitation

To show the effectiveness of our proposed technique, we evaluates EE-PBPAIR with 10% EIR in comparison to GOP-3 considering 10% of PLR in network.

Fig. 5(a) shows the effectiveness of an error-exploiting approach on the energy reduction. The plots present the normalized energy consumption and the video quality of EE-PBPAIR to those of GOP-3, and clearly show that EE-PBPAIR is very effective compared to GOP-3 in terms of each category of energy consumption with slight quality degradation. Specifically, EE-PBPAIR consumes 34% less energy than GOP-3 for encoding (Enc EC) since it drops 10% of video frames and compresses more macro-blocks with less expensive intra encodings than predictive encodings. In terms of energy consumption for transmitting video data (Tx EC), EE-PBPAIR

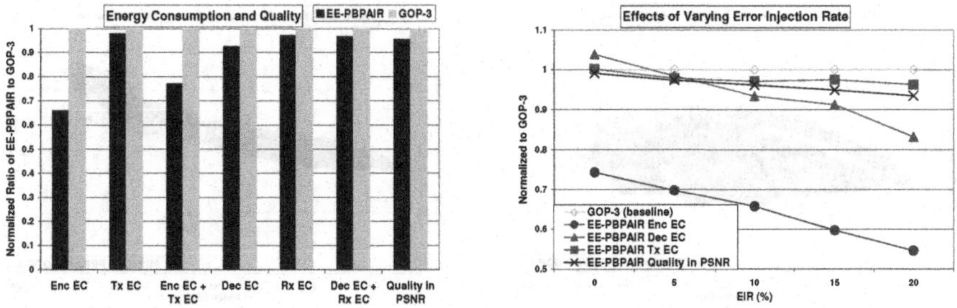

(a) EIR = 10% (b) EIR = 0% to 20%

Fig. 5 Effects of Error Injection Rate on Energy Consumption and Video Quality in EE-PBPAIR compared to GOP-3 (PLR = 10%, FOREMAN 300 frames)

sends a similar amount of data within less time than GOP-3, which results in the slight energy reduction. Thus, the energy consumption for the source (Enc EC and Tx EC) is reduced by 23% with EE-PBPAIR, at the cost of 4% quality degradation. Note that 1% quality degradation indicates about 0.31 dB reduction from the PSNR value for GOP-3. At the destination, EE-PBPAIR reduces the energy consumption by 8% for the decoding (Dec EC), which mainly results from dropping 10% frames at the source. Note also that more intra-encoded MB results in more energy consumption for the decoding but 10% frame dropping compensates for this effect. EE-PBPAIR saves the energy consumption for the receiver (Rx EC) by 3% mainly due to the smaller duration for receiving. The energy consumption at the destination (Dec EC + Rx EC) is reduced by 5%. These results are very effective in energy reduction with respect to all energy categories at the cost of slight quality degradation, which is an acceptable tradeoff for power-hungry mobile embedded systems.

We now illustrate how EIR is effective as a knob to tradeoff the quality for energy reduction. To observe the effects of varying EIR on quality and energy consumption, we compare EE-PBPAIR with GOP-3 by varying EIR from 0% to 20%. Fig. 5(b) shows the normalized video quality and each energy consumption of EE-PBPAIR to those of GOP-3. Since we adapt $para_2$ of PBPAIR to minimize the transmission overhead, the energy consumption for the data transmission (Tx EC) of EE-PBPAIR with varying EIR is close to that of GOP-3. With an increase of EIR, quality is still managed within an insignificant degradation of quality, and this quality management is mainly because of the error-resilient feature of EE-PBPAIR. With 20% EIR, the loss of quality is 7% in PSNR. Fig. 5(b) clearly shows that increasing the EIR significantly saves energy consumption for encoding (Enc EC). Since the portion of intra-MBs for each frame is increasing for error resilience, the energy consumption for the decoding is higher than GOP-3 with low EIR between 0% and 5%. However, with an increase of EIR, the number of frames to be decoded is decreasing and thus the energy consumption decreases. With 20% EIR, we obtain 45% energy reduction for encoding, and 17% reduction for decoding at the cost of 7% quality degradation.

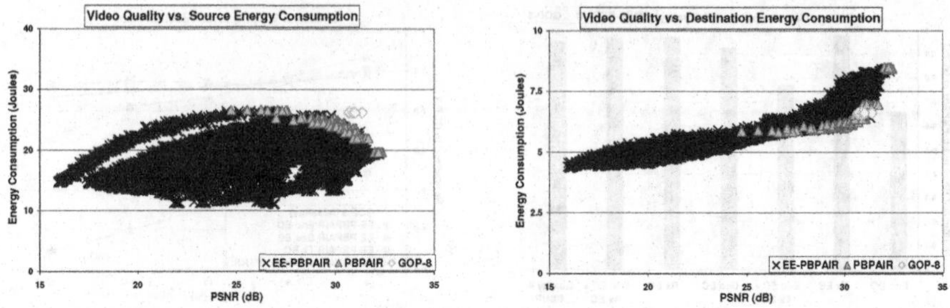

(a) Video Quality in PSNR vs. Source Energy Consumption (Enc EC + Tx EC)

(b) Video Quality in PSNR vs. Destination Energy Consumption (Dec EC + Rx EC)

Fig. 6 Extended Tradeoff Space between Video Quality and Energy Consumption by EE-PBPAIR in comparison to GOP-8 and PBPAIR (EIR = 0% to 50%, PLR = 5%, FOREMAN 300 frames)

4.2.2 Extended Energy/QoS tradeoff

Fig. 6(a) plots the energy consumption at the source vs. quality of EE-PBPAIR compared to PBPAIR and GOP-8, and clearly shows that design space of EE-PBPAIR is much larger and more effective than those of PBPAIR and GOP-8. As compared to PBPAIR, the tradeoff space of EE-PBPAIR subsumes all spaces for PBPAIR since indeed EE-PBPAIR with 0% of EIR is PBPAIR. As compared to GOP-8, EE-PBPAIR generates a better design space in terms of the energy reduction (by up to 37%) without losing video quality, and presents even better video quality with less energy consumption. Further, relaxing the quality requirement (such as 10% QoS degradation) compared to GOP-8 increases the energy reduction at the source by up to 49%. Thus, EE-PBPAIR very effectively expands the design space between the source energy consumption and video quality by exploiting the intentional errors. Fig. 6(b) depicts the tradeoff space between the energy consumption at the destination and the video quality, and clearly shows that EE-PBPAIR greatly extends the spaces explored by PBPAIR and GOP-8. However, the energy saving at the destination using EE-PBPAIR is less effective than that at the source since the resilience approach encodes more intra-MBs, which decreases the energy saving resulting from the intentional error injection. Even then, EE-PBPAIR can save the energy consumption by 3% without losing QoS compared to GOP-8.

4.2.3 Adaptive EE-PBPAIR: Ensuring Quality under Dynamic Network

To show the effectiveness of our adaptive EE-PBPAIR by updating EIR, we model a dynamic network and compare adaptive EE-PBPAIR to static EE-PBPAIR (i.e., EE-PBPAIR with a fixed EIR). For this experiment, PLR begins with 20% and decreases by 5% every 20 runs and after 5% PLR it increases by 5% until it reaches 15%. Each run captures 300 frames of video encoding. The horizontal axis in Fig. 7 represents this scenario with varying PLR. The quality constraint is set to 29.6 dB in PSNR, which is about 10% quality degradation from GOP-3 without any losses. Static EE-PBPAIR encodes the video data with a fixed EIR = 30% (since 30% EIR degrades the video quality significantly in some dynamic network situations as shown in Fig. 7(a)) while adaptive EE-PBPAIR starting with 30% EIR and updates it

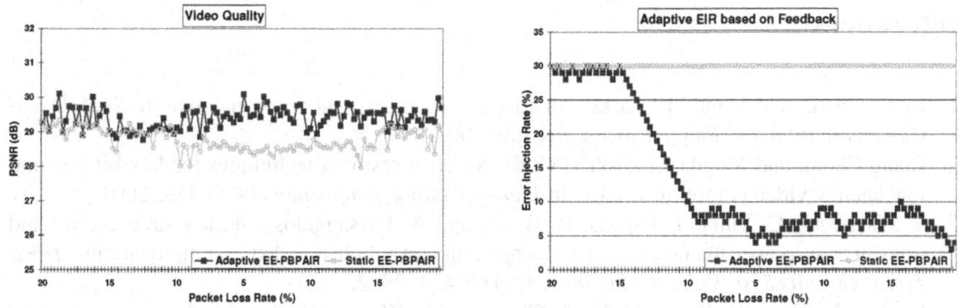

(a) Adaptive EE-PBPAIR delivers better video quality than static EE-PBPAIR

(b) Adaptive error injection rate according to quality feedback

Fig. 7 Adaptive EE-PBPAIR Robust to Varying PLR under Dynamic Network Status

according to the quality feedback. Fig. 7(a) draws the PSNR values for adaptive EE-PBPAIR in comparison to static EE-PBPAIR, and shows that the delivered quality of adaptive EE-PBPAIR is consistently better than that of static EE-PBPAIR. EE-PBPAIR adapts the EIR according to the feedback with respect to the video quality as shown in Fig. 7(b). In conclusion, this EIR adaptivity with EE-PBPAIR adjusts the quality of service based on the feedback for mobile video applications in distributed embedded systems while minimizing the energy consumption.

5 Summary and Future Work

Mobile video applications pose significant challenges for battery-constrained embedded systems due to high processing power for compression algorithms and transmission of a large volume of video data. Fortunately, video applications tolerate errors inherently, and we exploit this error tolerance of video data for the purpose of the energy savings. Active error exploitation – – intentional frame dropping together with error-resilient video encoding – – can achieve significant energy gains while ensuring the video quality. We present a new approach that injects errors intentionally to balance the dual goals of energy efficiency and satisfactory QoS.

In this paper, we demonstrated our approach in two phases for video conferencing applications running on resource-limited mobile systems. First we presented EE-PBPAIR that combines an error-resilient video encoder (PBPAIR) with intentional frame dropping to significantly reduce the energy consumption for the entire encoding-decoding path of the video conferencing application. Our experiments also demonstrated that the active error exploitation of EE-PBPAIR allows system designers to consider larger tradeoff spaces than previous approaches: GOP-K and PBPAIR. Further, we proposed an adaptive EE-PBPAIR by controlling a new knob, error-injection rate (EIR), in order to satisfy the delivered quality based on the feedback under the dynamic network status.

Our future work includes intelligent frame dropping techniques for further energy reduction with minimal quality degradation. We also plan to extend active error exploitation to the system level combined with error-aware architectures and network protocols to maximize the energy reduction for distributed embedded systems.

References

1. Liang Cheng and Magda El Zarki. An adaptive error resilient video encoder. In *SPIE Visual Communication and Image Processing*, July 2003.
2. Liang Cheng and Magda El Zarki. PGOP: An error resilient techniques for low bit rate and low latency video communications. In *Picture Coding Symposium (PCS)*, Dec 2004.
3. Y. Eisenberg, C. Luna, T. Pappas, R. Berry, and A. Katsaggelos. Joint source coding and transmission power management for energy efficient wireless video communications. *IEEE Trans. Circuits Syst. Video Technology*, 12:411–424, 2002.
4. L. Guo, X. Ding, H. Wang, Q. Li, S. Chen, and X. Zhang. Exploiting idle communication power to improve wireless network performance and energy efficiency. In *IEEE International Conference on Computer and Communications (INFOCOM)*, pages 1–12, April 2006.
5. Al Harris, Cigdem Sengul, Robin Kravets, and Prashant Ratanchandani. Energy-efficient multimedia communications in lossy multi-hop wireless networks. *IFIP Mobile and Wireless Communication Networks*, 162:461–472, 2005.
6. Intel Corporation, http://www.intel.com/. *Intel PXA255(R) Processor: Developer's Manual.*
7. ITU-T. *H.263 Draft: Video Coding for Low Bitrate Communication*, May 1996.
8. Yu Jiao and Ali R. Hurson. Adaptive power management for mobile agent-based information retrieval. In *IEEE Advanced Information Networking and Applications (AINA)*, pages 675–680, March 2005.
9. M. Kim, H. Oh, N. Dutt, A. Nicolau, and N. Venkatasubramanian. PBPAIR: An energy-efficient error-resilient encoding using probability based power aware intra refresh. *ACM SIGMOBILE Mobile Computing and Communications Review*, 10:58–69, July 2006.
10. Kyoungwoo Lee, Minyoung Kim, Nikil Dutt, and Nalini Venkatasubramanian, Tech Rep. (http://www.ics.uci.edu/∼kyoungwl/eepbpair/). *Adaptive EE-PBPAIR: A Novel Error-Exploiting Video Encoder Incorporating End-to-End QoS Feedback*, Dec 2007.
11. Jens Meggers, Gregor Bautz, and Anthony Sang-Bum Park. Providing video conferencing for the mobile user. In *IEEE Conference on Local Computer Networks*, page 526, March 1996.
12. S. Mohapatra, R. Cornea, H. Oh, K. Lee, M. Kim, N. Dutt, R. Gupta, A. Nicolau, S. Shukla, and N. Venkatasubramanian. A cross-layer approach for power-performance optimization in distributed mobile systems. In *Next Generation Software Program in conjunction with IPDPS*, page 218.1, April 2005.
13. NS2. Network Simulation version 2, http://www.isi.edu/nsnam/ns/.
14. Clark N. Taylor, Sujit Dey, and Debashis Panigrahi. Energy/latency/image quality tradeoffs in enabling mobile multimedia communication. In *Proc. of Software Radio: Technologies and Services*, pages 55–66. Springer Verlag, Jan 2001.
15. Y. Wang, S. Wenger, J. Wen, and A. K. Katsaggelos. Review of error resilient coding techniques for real-time video communications. *IEEE Signal Processing Magazine*, 17:61–82, July 2000.
16. S. Worrall, A. Sadka, P. Sweeney, and A. Kondoz. Motion adaptive error resilient encoding for mpeg-4. In *IEEE International Conference on Acoustics, Speech, and Signal Processing (ICASSP)*, volume 3, May 2001.
17. Wanghong Yuan, Klara Nahrstedt, Sarita V. Adve, Douglas L. Jones, and Robin H. Kravets. Design and evaluation of a cross-layer adaptation framework for mobile multimedia systems. In *Proceedings of SPIE/ACM Multimedia Computing and Networking Conference (MMCN)*, January 2003.
18. Rui Zhang, Shankar L. Regunathan, and Kenneth Rose. Video coding with optimal inter/intra-model switching for packet loss resilience. *IEEE Journal on Selected Areas in Communications*, 18(6):966–976, June 2000.

Specification-based Verification of Embedded Systems by Automated Test Case Generation

Christoph M. Kirchsteiger, Christoph Trummer, Christian Steger, Reinhold Weiss, and Markus Pistauer

Abstract It is time and resource intensive to derive test cases manually from the requirements specification to fully verify that the embedded system design fulfills its specification. However, automatic parsing to generate test cases is often not possible due to the informal, non-machine readable structure of the specification document. Formal specification languages would ease the parsing process, however they are difficult to use and rarely accepted. A promising trade-off are semi-formal specification languages, which are both easy-to-parse and easy-to-use.
This paper presents a novel approach developed in the SIMBA[1] project to tightly integrate a semi-formal requirements specification document into the design flow of embedded system designs. It considers the specification as a series of semi-formal textual use cases and automatically generates specification-based SystemC test cases. During a simulation with the System-under-Verification (SuV) the test cases are executed to determine whether the SuV fulfills the specification. A demonstration is given by a case study of an RFID controller. It shows that errors in the specification and discrepancies between the design and its specification are detected.

Christoph M. Kirchsteiger · Christoph Trummer · Christian Steger · Reinhold Weiss
Institute for Technical Informatics, Graz University of Technology, Inffeldgasse 16/1, 8010 Graz, Austria
e-mail: (c.kirchsteiger, trummer, steger, rweiss)@tugraz.at

Markus Pistauer
CISC Semiconductor Design & Consulting GmbH, Lakeside B07, 9020 Klagenfurt, Austria
e-mail: m.pistauer@cisc.at

[1] This project has been funded by the Austrian Federal Ministry for Transport, Innovation, and Technology under the FFG contract FFG 812424

Please use the following format when citing this chapter:

Kirchsteiger, C.M., et al., 2008, in IFIP International Federation for Information Processing, Volume 271; *Distributed Embedded Systems: Design, Middleware and Resources*; Bernd Kleinjohann, Lisa Kleinjohann, Wayne Wolf; (Boston: Springer), pp. 35–44.

1 Introduction

In today's design of embedded systems, 70% of the entire design effort is spent on functional verification. Functional verification is mainly driven by finding adequate test cases to verify that the modeled system behaves according to its specification [21]. Clearly, deriving test cases manually by reading the large system specification document is very time and resource intensive and error-prone. On the other hand, it is infeasible to perform this task automatically due to the informal non-machine readable structure of the specification.

The approach presented here focuses on semi-formal description formats to specify requirements. A very promising and well-known semi-formal specification style are textual use cases [4]. Although they are similar to graphical UML use cases enhanced by UML sequence diagrams, they can be extended much more easily to cover additional domain-specific information (e.g. by inserting additional fields for non-functional requirements). Textual use cases are both widely accepted to communicate with a customer and suitable for automatic post-processing. They define the interaction and the behavior of a system under certain conditions (pre-/postconditions, trigger) as a sequence of interaction steps with the environment (=actors). Their structure is formal, table-based and composed of several fields for the name, the pre-/postconditions and the interaction scenarios. However, within each field the description is entirely informal. Thus, textual use cases are similar to natural language but used in a structured way, which makes them easy-to-learn for stakeholders from various domains.

A common textual use case description contains the following fields:

- Actor (communicates with the specified system)
- Pre-/postcondition and trigger
- Main success scenario (i.e. main interaction sequence)
- Extensions (i.e. alternative flows to the main scenario)

In this paper, we propose a novel design methodology (see Fig. 1) for the specification-based functional verification of embedded system models by simulation. We use simulation for verification without being concerned with the state-space explosion problem as in static verification techniques. The main steps of our approach as shown in Fig. 1 are highly automated and encompass both the error-correction of the original specification document and the functional verification of the system model. The generated test cases are based upon the SystemC Verification Library (SCV) [20] and can be used to verify both transaction-level models and RTL hardware designs [18].

The remainder of this paper is organized as follows: We start with an overview of related work in section 2. In section 3 we present our methodology and describe its implementation in section 4. Section 5 provides a case study of an Radio Frequency Identification controller (=RFID tag) to present the applicability of our methodology and its results. Finally we give a conclusion and list further work in section 6.

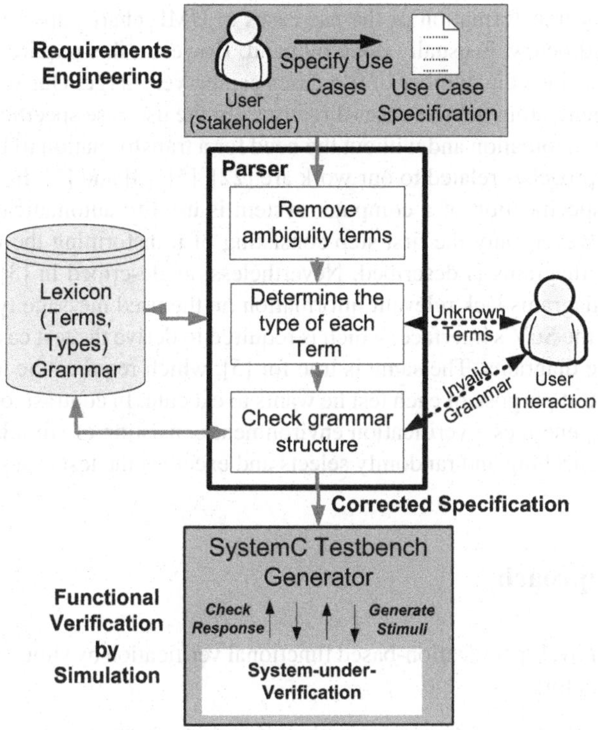

Fig. 1 Novel highly automated approach from textual use cases to a SystemC testbench for functional verification.

2 Related Work

Test case generation from the specification has been widely studied in the research community. Most of them, like [24], [13] and [1] favor formal specification languages as UML or SDL. However, in the hardware domain, which constitutes an important portion of embedded systems, most of the designs are specified in a document-based way. UML and other formal specification languages are hardly used and are considered as a large burden, which confronts time-to-market. Although these specification formats are unambiguous, precise and consistent, it is very difficult for stakeholders from various domains, who specify requirements, to get familiar with these formats. In contrast, our approach is based on semi-formal textual use case-based descriptions as defined in [4]. They are both widely accepted and easy-to-use by stakeholders and suitable for automatic post-processing.
There are a number of approaches, which are dealing with textual use case-based descriptions for test case generation. Most of them, like [9] and [10] focus on the formal transformation of use cases to UML state, message sequence or activity charts, which are then used to generate the test cases. Whereas, the automatic test case generation from UML charts is widely studied in the research community [16], [15],

[11] the formal transformation of the use cases to UML charts, apart from the approaches stated below, is usually done by hand. However, this requires a lot of interaction effort since the number of use cases can be very large. Our work resolves this issue by generating the test cases directly from the use case specification with a high degree of automation and without the need for a transformation to UML charts. Significant approaches related to our work are [22], [5], [3] and [7]. In [22] and [7] the use case specification of a computer system is used to automatically generate test cases. However, only the first step consisting of transforming the use cases to UML activity diagrams is described. Nevertheless, as described in [3], the generated activity diagrams lack relevant information on the used message types and the connection to the SuV's interface, which is required to derive the test cases automatically from the diagrams. The same is true for [5], which requires the test designer to specify the test purpose of each test he wants to execute. In contrast, our approach automatically generates a verification environment consisting of stimuli generation and response checking and randomly selects and executes the test cases.

3 Novel Approach

We propose a novel specification-based functional verification by simulation methodology that aims for:

- Check the specification to remove ambiguities and incorrect grammar.
- Automate the functional test case generation from textual use case specifications.
- Provide a functional verification by executing the test cases to determine the discrepancies between the embedded system model and its specification.

As shown in Fig. 1 our approach starts with a semi-formal use case specification of the System-under-Verification (SuV). The common textual use case descriptions [4] are extended by additional fields to cover constants, like message types or time delay constants. During the parsing of the use case specification we deal with typical natural language issues [8]. Therefore, we define a grammar and a lexical subset of the natural language to be used for specifying the use cases. This is done in collaboration with our industry partner, who has strong experience with common grammar structures and terms used for the specification. A list of guidelines is provided to keep the stakeholder to the given grammar structure and focus on terms from the lexical subset. It is not mandatory for the stakeholder to stick to these guidelines, although it decreases the required user interaction significantly. The interactions are also decreasing with the number of processed requirements as in the case of a missing term, which requires the user to specify the type of this unknown term. This decision is remembered the next time this term is analyzed without the need for an interaction by the user. After the parsing, the specification document is corrected and it is used as the input for the SystemC testbench generator, which generates the specification-based test cases. During a SystemC simulation these test cases are applied to the SuV to check if it corresponds to the specification. Output messages

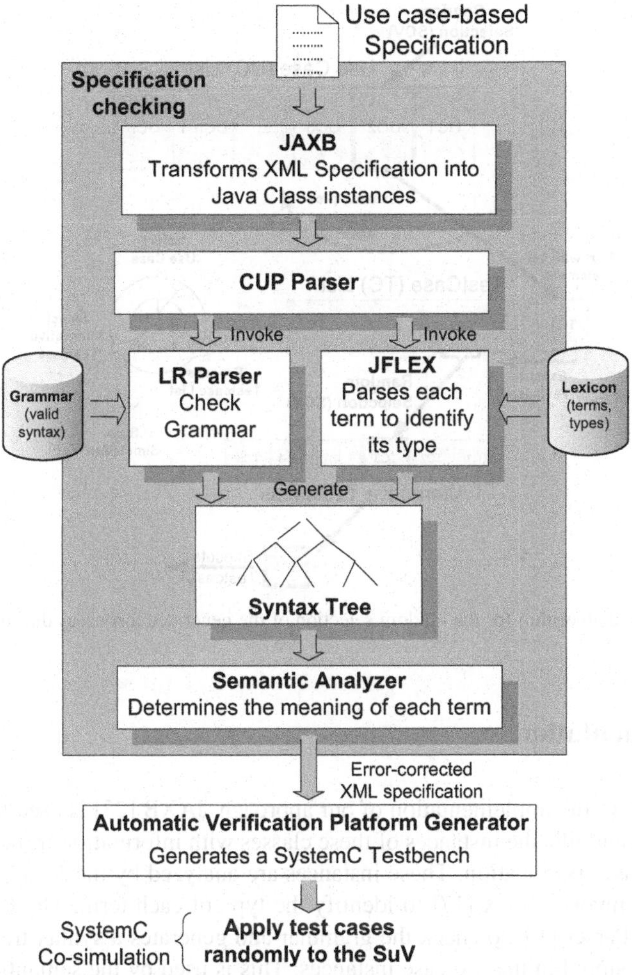

Fig. 2 Our implementation uses JAXB to extract data from the specification. The CUP Parser invokes the LR Parser and JFLEX to generate a syntax tree [2]. The semantic analyzer uses the syntax tree to provide the input for the test case generator.

convey information on the test progress, the test coverage as well as the test results to inform the verification engineer on-line about the current status of the simulation-based verification.

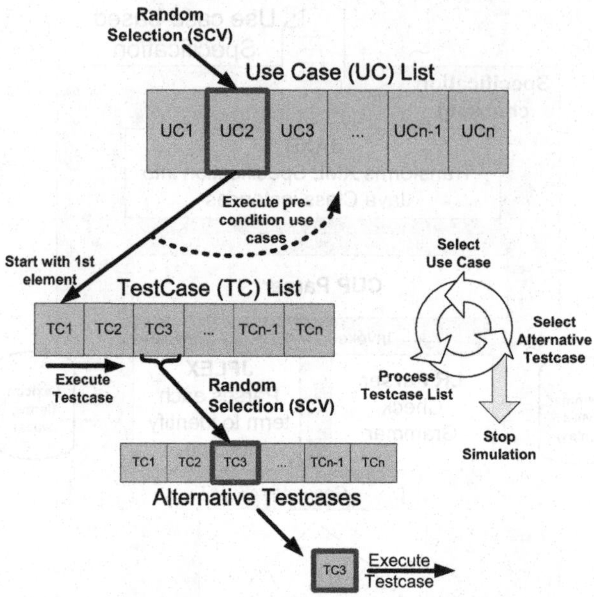

Fig. 3 Proposed algorithm for the random selection of the generated test cases during a SystemC simulation.

4 Implementation

Figure 2 shows the implementation of our approach. JAXB [23] is used to generate Java classes and fills the instances of these classes with information from the XML-based use case specification. These instances are analyzed by the Java CUP parser [12], which invokes JFlex [17] to identify the type of each term. The CUP parser uses an LR-Parser [19] to check the grammar and generates a syntax tree [2] from each phrase stored in the use case instances. This is used by the semantic analyzer to determine the meaning of each term and to generate the error-corrected XML specification. Finally, the Automatic Verification Platform Generator uses this XML specification to generate the SystemC testbench.

The SystemC testbench selects and executes SystemC test cases during a simulation and consists of the two threads: random test case selection and test execution. The algorithm of the random test case selection thread is shown in Fig. 3. The entire process in Fig. 3 is reiterated until each use case has been selected by a user-specified number of times or the simulation is stopped by the verification engineer. In each iteration our algorithm uses SCV constructs to randomly select a use case from the list of use cases. This list is generated each time the Automatic Verification Platform Generator reads the error-corrected XML specification input file and generates the SystemC testbench module. Each use case may contain a list of predecessor use cases. These are defined in the use case's precondition statement and are executed before the current use case is processed. Each use case contains a list of test cases, which correspond to the steps in its scenarios. Each test case may also contain a list of alternative test cases specified in the extension scenarios. When a use case is processed our algorithm goes through its test cases sequentially starting at the first element in the list. For each test case it determines if the test case has a list of alternative test cases. If so, it uses the SCV constructs to randomly select a test case from the list for execution. Otherwise, the current test case is selected and executed by the test execution thread, which generates the stimuli, estimates and stores the SuV's internal state, checks the SuV response and prints the test case's name and status for verification reporting. The test execution thread is a verification state machine generated from the input XML use case specification as shown in Fig. 4. For each step in the use case scenario, which corresponds to a test case, the verification state machine contains a case block to execute this step. The case block *SET_UP_TAG_1_RECEIVES_ACTION* in Fig. 4 corresponds to the specified use case step

Tag receives Query Message with matching SL Flag

from Fig. 5 and generates the corresponding stimuli to apply this step to the SuV. The case block *SET_UP_TAG_10_TRANSMITS_ACTION* checks the system response at step

Tag transmits 16bit Random Number

from Fig. 5. The functions marked as grey-tone are the corresponding transactor functions. A transactor component is also automatically generated by our methodology and is inserted between the SystemC testbench module and the SuV to map the test cases to the SuV. Since the interface of the SuV can change the transactor is adapted by the verification engineer to connect it to the interface of the SuV. The mapping of the transaction-level test cases to the SuV's interface would go beyond the topic of this paper and is not explained here any further.

5 A Case Study of an Radio-Frequency Identification Controller

To demonstrate our methodology we have implemented it in the HW/SW co-design tool *SyAD*® (System Architect Designer) [14]. *SyAD*® enables the development of system-level HW/SW co-designs and supports a multi-language and multi-level co-simulation framework of SystemC, VHDL, VHDL-AMS and MATLAB Simulink. As a case study we have considered a use case-based specification of an Radio-Frequency Identification controller (= RFID tag) state machine provided by our industrial cooperation partner. The specification document is derived from the controller state diagram specified in the EPCGlobal Class-1 Generation-2 UHF RFID protocol for communications [6]. The use case-based specification document covers the entire tag state diagram (see Fig. 6.19. in [6]) and encompasses 53 use case scenarios. Fig. 5 shows a small excerpt from the use case-based specification document. We applied our methodology implemented in *SyAD*® to the entire use case

```
int testbench::test_execution(){
  switch(state){
  case SET_UP_TAG_1_RECEIVES_ACTION :
    transmit_Message->set_value(QUERY_MESSAGE, SL_FLAG);
    send_to_DUT(transmit_Message);
    break;

  case ...

  case SET_UP_TAG_10_TRANSMITS_ACTION :
    message *received_message;
    receive_from_DUT(received_message, PC_EPC_CRC_MSG);
    if(check_message(received_message))
      return TB_PASSED;
    else
      return TB_FAILED;
    break;
  }
}
```

Fig. 4 Automatically generated source code of the test execution thread.

Name: *Set up Tag*
Description: *Use case accessed when tag enters the Reader field.*
Scope: *UHF RFID Tag (=Tag).*
Primary actor: *Interrogator (=Reader)*
Precondition/Trigger: *Tag (re)-enters the Reader Field*
Main Success Scenario:
1. Tag receives Query command with matching SL Flag from Reader
...
10. Tag transmits 16bit Random number
11. Tag exits use case and goes to "Reply Tag" Use Case
Alternate Flows:
1a. Tag receives Select command from Reader
...
LocNonfunctional Requirements:
Timing Constraints: *Step 1 until step 11 shall be done within t1.*

Fig. 5 Use case derived from the protocol specification of an RFID controller state machine.

specification and discovered 6 syntax errors (due to invalid grammar and missing verbs and articles) and added 8 unknown terms to the lexicon during the parsing steps. In a next step our Automatic Verification Platform Generator generated the SystemC testbench module consisting of 131 test cases derived from the use case specification document. Fig. 6 demonstrates the results of the simulation of the SystemC testbench with the SuV for 5, 10, 15 and 20 iterations of the SystemC test case selection algorithm from Fig. 3. Use case 1 (UC 1) is executed most of all, since it is in the precondition list of all other use cases. In contrast, UC 5 is less often executed since it does not occur in the precondition list of any other use case. The ratio of executed use case scenarios to the total number of use case scenarios specifies the covered amount of the specification by the simulated test cases. The left diagram in Fig. 3 shows a comparison of the number of identified errors and the verified portion of the specification for 5, 10, 15 and 20 iterations. A 80% functional coverage de-

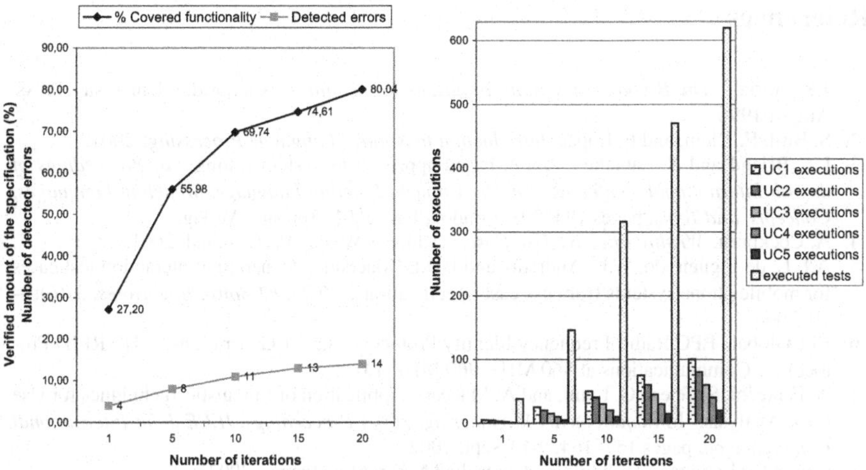

Fig. 6 Simulation results for 5, 10, 15 and 20 iterations of the proposed test case selection algorithm applied to the RFID controller model.

tects 14 errors and requires 20 iterations of the test case selection algorithm, which results in more than 600 executed tests as illustrated in Fig. 3

6 Conclusion and Further Work

In this paper we presented a novel functional verification methodology for embedded system designs. The methodology supports both the correction of errors in the specification document and the automated test case generation from the specification. The test cases are used to verify whether the system model fulfills its specification (=functional verification) and close the gap between the specification and the design.

Our approach focuses on textual case-based specifications, which are suitable for black-box test case generation. We used a case study based on the semi-formal specification of a higher class RFID controller to demonstrate and prove our methodology. We showed that our methodology can be used to correct the specification document and to automatically generate SystemC test cases, which are executed randomly during simulation to determine the discrepancies between the design and its specification. As a further step we plan to improve the verification reporting by introducing functional coverage monitors into our design flow. This provides on-line information on how much functionality has been verified.

References

1. J.R. Abrial. *The B-book : assigning programs to meanings*. Cambridge University Press, August 1996.
2. S. Bird, E. Klein, and E. Loper. *Introduction to Natural Language Processing*. 2001.
3. L.C Briand and Y. Labiche. A uml-based approach to system testing. In *Proceedings of the 4th International Conference on The Unified Modeling Language, Modeling Languages, Concepts, and Tools*, pages 194–208, London, UK, 2001. Springer-Verlag.
4. A. Cockburn. *Writing Effective Use Cases*. Addison-Wesley Professional, 2001.
5. A.L.L. de Figueiredo, W.L. Andrade, and P.D.L. Machado. Generating interaction test cases for mobile phone systems from use case specifications. *SIGSOFT Softw. Eng. Notes*, 31(6):1–10, 2006.
6. EPCGlobal. EPC Radio-Frequency Identity Protocols Class-1 Generation-2 UHF RFID Protocol for Communications at 860 MHz 960 MHz, 1.0.9.
7. A. Fantechi, S. Gnesi, G. Lami, and A. Maccari. Application of Linguistic Techniques for Use Case Analysis. In *Requirements Engineering, 2002. Proceedings. IEEE Joint International Conference on*, pages 157–164, 9-13 Sept. 2002.
8. Centre for Language Technology. Controlled Natural Languages, 2007.
9. M. Friske and H. Schlingloff. Von use cases zu test cases: Eine systematische vorgehensweise. 2005.
10. P. Fröhlich and J. Link. Automated test case generation from dynamic models. In *ECOOP '00: Proceedings of the 14th European Conference on Object-Oriented Programming*, pages 472–492, London, UK, 2000. Springer-Verlag.
11. J. Hartmann, C. Imoberdorf, and M. Meisinger. Uml-based integration testing. In *ISSTA '00: Proceedings of the 2000 ACM SIGSOFT international symposium on Software testing and analysis*, pages 60–70, New York, NY, USA, 2000. ACM.
12. S. Hudson. Cup - lalr parser generator for java, 2007.
13. Y. JinShan, L. Tun, and T. QingPing. The Use of UML Sequence Diagram for System-on-Chip System Level Transaction-based Functional Verification. In *Intelligent Control and Automation, 2006. WCICA 2006. The Sixth World Congress on*, volume 2, pages 6173–6177, 21-23 June 2006.
14. S. Kajtazovic, C. Steger, A. Schuhai, and M. Pistauer. Automatic generation of a verification platform for heterogeneous system designs. In *Advances in Design and Specification Languages for SoCs - Selected Contributions from FDL'05*, 2005.
15. S. Kansomkeat and W. Rivepiboon. Automated-generating test case using uml statechart diagrams. In *SAICSIT '03: Proceedings of the 2003 annual research conference of the South African institute of computer scientists and information technologists on Enablement through technology*, pages 296–300, , Republic of South Africa, 2003. South African Institute for Computer Scientists and Information Technologists.
16. Y.G. Kim, H.S. Hong, D.H. Bae, and S.D. Cha. Test cases generation from uml state diagrams. *Software, IEE Proceedings* -, 146(4):187–192, Aug 1999.
17. G. Klein. Jflex - the fast scanner generator for java, 2007.
18. Cadence Labs. The Transaction-Based Verification Methodology. Technical report, 2000.
19. Naumann and B.G. Lang. *Parsing*. 1994.
20. C. Norris and S. Swan. A tutorial introduction on the new systemc verification standard. Technical report, 2003.
21. A. Piziali. *Functional Verification Coverage Measurement and Analysis*. Kluwer Academic Publishers, 2004.
22. M. Riebisch and M. Hubner. Traceability-driven Model Refinement for Test Case Generation. In *Engineering of Computer-Based Systems, 2005. ECBS '05. 12th IEEE International Conference and Workshops on the*, pages 113–120, 4-7 April 2005.
23. Sun. Java architecture for xml binding (jaxb), 2003.
24. Q. Zhu, R. Oishi, T. Hasenawa, and T. Nakata. System-On-Chip Validation using UML and CWL. In *Hardware/Software Codesign and System Synthesis, 2004. CODES + ISSS 2004. International Conference on*, pages 92–97, 2004.

Analysis of Periodic Clock Relations in Polychronous Systems

Hugo Metivier, Jean-Pierre Talpin, Thierry Gautier, and Paul Le Guernic

Abstract The *polychronous* (synchronous, multiclocked) language Signal is used for the design and analysis of reactive systems. For the purpose of modeling event-driven systems, we consider an extension of the polychronous model of computation of Signal with periodic equations denoted by ultimately periodic infinite words. These equations express periodic constraints on the signals of programs, that can be used to enrich the existing *clock calculus* of Signal. Thanks to this more powerful clock calculus, the communications between processes using periodic equations can be analysed to guarantee their correctness. In particular, the maximal size of buffers is formally evaluated. We illustrate the design of so-defined periodic systems using a 4-stroke engine example.

1 Introduction

While synchronous programming has extensively been applied to the design of control-intensive software for event-driven embedded systems [3], recent work [11, 5] has investigated extensions to symbolic calculus for synchrony in the aim of analyzing periodic systems and communications between them. Synchronous languages are appropriate specification formalisms to address the design of such architectures, as the otherwise symbolic model of time they support can be equipped with ad-hoc program analysis techniques to perform needed timing evaluation. As an example, polychrony, the synchronous multi-clocked model of computation of the data-flow specification formalism Signal, is dedicated to the specification of concurrent event-driven embedded software and for the main purpose of architecture exploration. Polychrony provides a discrete and partially ordered model of time that differs from the classical *synchronous hypothesis* where time is abstracted by totally ordered symbolic clocks. For the purpose of modeling periodic systems, we

H. Metivier (University of Rennes) · J-P. Talpin · T. Gautier · P. Le Guernic (INRIA)
Campus de Beaulieu, 35 042 Rennes Cedex France
e-mail: firstname.lastname@irisa.fr

Please use the following format when citing this chapter:

Metivier, H., et al., 2008, in IFIP International Federation for Information Processing, Volume 271; *Distributed Embedded Systems: Design, Middleware and Resources*; Bernd Kleinjohann, Lisa Kleinjohann, Wayne Wolf; (Boston: Springer), pp. 45–56.

consider an extension of the polychronous MoC with periodic clocks denoted by ultimately periodic infinite words. This defines a compositional specification structure to express periodic relations between signals. Applications are the design of periodic systems and the analysis of communication resources.

Related work Many approaches have been investigated for the design of hybrid hardware/software, event-driven/time-triggered, synchronous/asynchronous, embedded systems. Most of them are based on the principles of process networks and inherit from the pioneering work of Kahn [7]. Many examples could be cited, the Ptolemy [4] project, the Yapi [8] project, etc. While symbolic reasoning on process networks has essentially been developed for the purpose of embedded, control-dominated, software design and in the context of synchronous programming languages [3], such as Esterel, Lustre and Signal, analytical reasoning has mainly been studied in the context of high-performance, data-dominated systems.

Some approaches have arisen to combine concepts of both domains. 1) The first one is, to our knowledge, the work of Smarandache [11]. It aims at combining the multi-clocked synchronous model of computation of the language Signal with a topological model of the Alpha specification formalism [6]. Alpha manipulates convex polyhedral domains to describe high-performance, massively parallel algorithms over multi-dimensional data. Signal-Alpha [11] proposes a calculus of affine clock relations, associating symbolic signal clocks with affine functions: two periodic signals x, y are said in $(n, m, q-p)$-affine relation iff their respective clocks $\hat{x}, \hat{y}$ can be expressed as functions $\hat{x} = \{n.t + p \mid t \in \hat{z}\}$ and $\hat{y} = \{m.t + q \mid t \in \hat{z}\}$ of a common reference of discrete time $\hat{z}$ (m, n, p, q are integers). This yields a very expressive calculus for the specification and the analysis of time-triggered systems, while in fact most of the decidable and algorithmically affordable analysis concerns $(1, m, n)$-affine relations. 2) More recently, Cohen et al. [5] propose *an algebra of ultimately periodic clocks* to interpret synchronization in the synchronous language Lucid-synchrone. This yields the capability to model process networks: synchronous functions networked by bounded-buffering communication mechanisms. The algebra of periodic clock relations under consideration consists of associating a signal with a period described by a binary word (e.g. (01)). In turn, this defines a rich algebra in which a clock is itself the generator of an ideal consisting of any possible stretch of the generator (e.g. (0101), etc.). 3) The UML profile for *Modeling and Analysis of Real-Time and Embedded systems* (MARTE [1]) provides a general model of time in different aspects : physical/logical, dense/discrete, single/multiple. It offers basic operators and relations to combine timed events and clocks : subclocking, periodicity, etc. The calculus we propose could be a way of solving MARTE clock relations (in particular, periodic ones) in the case of discrete multiple time.

Contribution The results described in this paper can be used for the design and analysis of periodic systems specified using the polychronous model. Our approach consists first in the design of a clock calculus that balances the tradeoff between decidability and compositionality pointed out earlier [11]. Just as for the affine clock relations, we define a calculus of periodic clock relations to support the compositional modeling of multi-rate systems. Like in [5], periods are expressed here using ultimately periodic infinite words. However, they are expressed using ternary logic instead of Boolean logic. The ternary logic allows to express periodicity on the values of boolean signals moreover periodicity on the presence/absence of signals. Our calculus corresponds to part of the domain of $(1,m,n)$-affine relations in [11], where most analyses are decidable and recasts these results in an extension of the algebra of [5] with ternary logic. Based on that algebra, we define a calculus of periodic clock relations to compositionally reason about real-time relations in multi-clocked and multi-rate systems. We provide a new Signal equation that allows the design of periodic processes. The clock calculus of Signal is extended to take it into account and an analysis can be applied on periodic processes to guarantee the communications using bounded buffers. The analysis gives as result the size of needed buffers.

Plan Section 2 gives a presentation of the polychronous language Signal. Section 3 presents our algebra of ultimately periodic words. Based on that calculus, section 4 defines a new Signal equation to write periodic processes using ultimately periodic infinite words; we illustrate this extension with a model of a 4-stroke engine. Section 5 describes the clock relation inference of Signal and its extension. Section 6 presents the analysis of periodic processes to guarantee communications using bounded buffers and the analysis is applied on the 4-stroke engine example.

2 Polychronous model of computation

We start with a definition of some required elements of the polychronous model of computation [9]. The set of *tags* $\mathscr{T}$ is the *discrete* time used in Signal and is partially ordered with the relation $t \leq u$. It stipulates that the tag t occurs before u. A *chain* $C \in \mathscr{C}$ is a subset of $\mathscr{T}$ which is totally ordered, $\mathrm{pred}_C(t)$ denotes the immediate predecessor tag in C. Signals, behaviors and processes are defined as follows :

- a *signal* $s \in \mathscr{S} = \mathscr{C} \to \mathscr{V}$ is a function from a *chain* of tags to a set of values,
- a *behavior* $b \in \mathscr{B} = \mathscr{X} \to \mathscr{S}$ is a function from a set of names x to signals, it represents a possible execution of a program.
- a *process* $p \in \mathscr{P}$ is a set of behaviors that have the same domain. This set represents all the possible executions of the program.

The set of possible values $\mathscr{V}$ is defined as union of sets of boolean values, integer values, etc. The type of a signal is that of its values. *Clock* signals take their values in the subset of $\mathscr{V}_B$ reduced to the $\{\ \mathsf{true}\ \}$ singleton. Type constraints are not described in this paper. We write $\mathrm{tags}(s)$ for the chain of tags of a signal s and $\min(\mathrm{tags}(s))$ for its first tag. We write $b|_X$ for the projection of a behavior b on a set of names X.

A Signal process consists of the synchronous composition of equations on signals. A signal x is an infinite flow of values that is discretely sampled according to the pace of its clock, noted $\hat{x}$. An equation partially relates signals with respect to an abstract timing model.

$$P ::= x = \mathsf{f}(y,z)\,|\,x = y\ \mathsf{pre}\ v\,|\,x = y\ \mathsf{when}\ z\,|\,x = y\ \mathsf{default}\ z\,|\,P\,|\,P$$

It is allowed to substitute a signal name by its definition to write concise processes. For example, $x = (y \neq z) \mid z = y \text{ pre true}$ may be written as $x = (y \neq (y \text{ pre true}))$.

Semantics of the Signal equations In the *functional equation* $x = \mathsf{f}(y,z)$, the signals x, y and z are assumed to be synchronous, (their sets of tags are equal). For each tag the signals are present, x holds the result of the function f applied on the values of y and z. f can be an arithmetic or boolean classical function ($+, \neq$, or ...).

The *delay equation* $x = y \text{ pre } v$ enforces the signals x and y to be synchronous too. The value of the signal x at a given tag is defined by the value of y from the previous tag in the chain. For its first tag, x holds the value v.

The *sampling equation* $x = y \text{ when } z$ defines x by y when z is true. It means that the output signal x is present and takes the value of y iff both input signals y and z are present, and z holds the value *true*. In the following definition, the notation $[z]$ represents the clock which is true when z is present and true, and absent otherwise.

The *merge equation* $x = y \text{ default } z$ defines x by y when y is present and by z otherwise. The signal x is present iff either of the signals y or z is present.

The *synchronous composition* $P \mid Q$ is defined by the simultaneous solution of the equations P and Q at all times. If we note $\text{vars}(P)$ the domain of a process P, it can be defined by the union $b \uplus c$ of behaviors that match on the interface $\text{vars}(P) \cap \text{vars}(Q)$ between P and Q.

$$[\![x = \mathsf{f}(y,z)]\!] = \left\{ b \in \mathscr{B}|_{x,y,z} \,\middle|\, \begin{array}{l} \text{tags}(x) = \text{tags}(y) = \text{tags}(z), \\ \forall t \in \text{tags}(x), b(x)(t) = \mathsf{f}(b(y)(t), b(z)(t)) \end{array} \right\}$$

$$[\![x = y \text{ pre } v]\!] = \left\{ b \in \mathscr{B}|_{x,y} \,\middle|\, \text{tags}(x) = \text{tags}(y) = C, b(x)(t) = \left| \begin{array}{ll} v & \text{if } t = \min(C) \\ b(y)(\text{pred}_C(t)) & \text{if } t \neq \min(C) \end{array} \right. \right\}$$

$$[\![x = y \text{ when } z]\!] = \{ b \in \mathscr{B}|_{x,y,z} \mid \text{tags}(x) = \text{tags}(y) \cap \text{tags}([z]), \forall t \in \text{tags}(x),\ b(x)(t) = b(y)(t) \}$$

$$[\![x = y \text{ default } z]\!] = \left\{ b \in \mathscr{B}|_{x,y,z} \,\middle|\, \begin{array}{l} \text{tags}(x) = C \\ = \text{tags}(y) \cup \text{tags}(z) \end{array}, \forall t \in C, b(x)(t) = \left| \begin{array}{l} b(y)(t) \text{ if } t \in \text{tags}(y) \\ b(z)(t) \text{ otherwise} \end{array} \right. \right\}$$

$$[\![P \mid Q]\!] = \{ b \uplus c \mid b \in [\![P]\!], c \in [\![Q]\!], b|_{\text{vars}(P) \cap \text{vars}(Q)} = c|_{\text{vars}(P) \cap \text{vars}(Q)} \}$$

3 An algebra of ultimately periodic infinite words

We now present an algebra of ultimately periodic infinite words used in our extension of Signal for the design and the analysis of periodic processes. We use the three-value logic induced by $\mathbb{Z}/3\mathbb{Z}$ to denote boolean or clock signals by using atoms $a \in \mathbb{Z}/3\mathbb{Z} = \{-1, 0, 1\}$. The absence is denoted by 0, false by -1 and true by 1. We introduce this algebra to represent periodicity over boolean and clock signals.

Ultimately periodic infinite words The ultimately periodic infinite words (called *words* further) noted w or $u(v)$ under consideration are composed of a prefix $u \in (\mathbb{Z}/3\mathbb{Z})^*$ and a period $v \in (\mathbb{Z}/3\mathbb{Z})^+$.

$$\mathbb{W} = \{ w = u(v) \mid u \in (\mathbb{Z}/3\mathbb{Z})^* \text{ and } v \in (\mathbb{Z}/3\mathbb{Z})^+ \}$$

A word $u(v)$ represents the infinite sequence of atoms composed by the sequence u followed by the sequence v repeated infinitely. Words that represent the same sequence of atoms are equal. We now present a few required notations:

- $|u|$ the length of a sequence $u \in (\mathbb{Z}/3\mathbb{Z})^*$
- $\langle u \rangle$ the number of non-zero atoms of a sequence $u \in (\mathbb{Z}/3\mathbb{Z})^*$
- w_n the nth atom of a word w
- $|w|_n^a$ the number of atoms a in the nth first atoms of w
- $w[n]$ the nth non-zero atom in the word w
- "." the classical operation of concatenation.
- $\langle w \rangle_n^a$ the position of the nth atom a in the word w

  i.e. $\langle a.w \rangle_1^a = 1 \quad \langle b.w \rangle_n^a = \begin{pmatrix} \langle w \rangle_n^a + 1 & \text{if } a \neq b \\ \langle w \rangle_{n-1}^a + 1 & \text{if } a = b \text{ and } n > 1 \end{pmatrix}$

  ex: $\langle 01(01\text{-}10) \rangle_1^1 = 2 \quad \langle 01(01\text{-}10) \rangle_2^1 = 4 \quad \langle 01(01\text{-}10) \rangle_2^{-1} = 9$

Operations and operators The partial order $w \sqsubseteq w'$ stipulates that the nth atom in w precedes the corresponding one in w', for all non-zero atoms. $w \sqsubseteq w'$ means that w' is stretched variant of w, since the non-zero atoms occur in the same order.

$$\forall n > 0, \forall a \neq 0, \quad w \sqsubseteq w' \Leftrightarrow \langle w \rangle_n^a \leq \langle w' \rangle_n^a \qquad a.w @ b.w' = \begin{pmatrix} 0.(a.w @ w') & \text{if } b \neq 1 \\ a.(w @ w') & \text{if } b = 1 \end{pmatrix}$$

We define the operator $w @ w'$ to resample a word w on an other one w'. The atoms of w being placed in correspondence with the atoms 1 of w', then the word $w @ w'$ has the corresponding atom of w when w' has the atom 1, and has the atom 0 otherwise. The @ operator distributes the values of the first stream to the positions where the second one holds the atom 1. This is an extension of the "w' on w" operator of [5]. This definition yields that $w \sqsubseteq w @ w'$ for all words w, w' and $(w @ w')_n = 0$ if $w'_n \neq 1$ and $w_{|w'|_n^1}$ if $w'_n = 1$.

Example 1. $\forall w \in \mathbb{W}$, $w @ (1) = w$ and $w @ (0) = (0)$

$(0\text{-}11) @ 0(1\text{-}1110) = 0(00\text{-}11)$

w'	0 1 -1 1 1 0 1 -1 1 1 0 ⋯ = 0(1-1110)
w	0 -1 1 0 -1 1 ⋯ = (0-11)
$w @ w'$	0 0 0 -1 1 0 0 0 -1 1 0 ⋯ = 0(00-110)

Remark 1. For any pair of words $u(v)$ and $x(y)$, it is always possible to build equivalent representations $u'(v') = u(v)$ and $x'(y') = x(y)$ such that $|u'| = |x'|$ and $|v'| = |y'|$ [5]. For example, 01(-11) and (-101) can be respectively rewritten as 01(-11-11-11) and -10(1-101-10). Such a rewriting is useful when pointwise operations have to be applied on words.

Synchronizable words

Definition 1. Two words w, w' are said *stretch-equivalent* if $\forall n > 0$, $w[n] = w'[n]$.

It means that the two stretch-equivalent words have the same order of non-zero atoms. Obviously, any two words the atoms of which take their values in $\{0, 1\}$ (called *binary words*) are stretch-equivalent.

In [5], it is shown that two binary words $u(v), u'(v')$ are *synchronizable* iff the lengths of their periods ($|v|$,$|v'|$) and their numbers of presence ($\langle v \rangle$,$\langle v' \rangle$) match $\langle v \rangle / |v| = \langle v' \rangle / |v'|$. This extends to stretch-equivalent ternary words.

Definition 2. Two stretch-equivalent ternary words w, w' are said *synchronizable*, written $w \sim w'$, iff there exists d, d' such that $w \sqsubseteq 0^d.w'$ and $w' \sqsubseteq 0^{d'}.w$.

The relation $w \sqsubseteq 0^d.w'$ means that we can delay the atoms of w' by d zero atoms so that the nth non-zero atom of w precedes the nth non-zero atom of w'. Then $w \sqsubseteq 0^d.w'$ (resp. $w' \sqsubseteq 0^{d'}.w$) implies that the distance between the nth non-zero value of w and the nth non-zero value of w' is bounded by d (resp. d'). This definition will be used to analyse the size of buffers required for communications (Section 6).

Property 1. Two stretch-equivalent words $u(v)$ and $u'(v')$ are synchronizable iff $\langle v\rangle/|v| = \langle v'\rangle/|v'|$. (the proof is similar to that of [5]).

4 Periodic processes

Periodic sampling equation We introduce a new operator in Signal, noted @, derived from the corresponding one defined on periodic words, in order to express periodic relations. A periodic sampling equation $x = w\,@\,y$ relates two (clock or boolean) signals x, y, with a word w. It defines x to hold the successive non-zero atoms of w when y takes the value true. We note $t_x[n]$ for the nth tag of a signal x.

$$[\![x = w\,@\,y]\!] = \left\{ b \in \mathscr{B}|_{x,y} \;\middle|\; \begin{array}{l} t \in \text{tags}(x) \Leftrightarrow \exists n > 0,\ t = t_y[n] \text{ and } w_n \neq 0 \\ \forall n > 0,\ b(x)(t_x[n]) = w[n] \end{array} \right\}$$

Example 2. $\forall w \in \mathbb{W}, x = (1)\,@\,y \Rightarrow x = [y]$, and $x = (0)\,@\,y \Rightarrow x$ is always absent. Recall that $[y]$ is a clock which is present iff the signal y is present and true.

$x = 0(10\text{-}1)\,@\,y$

y	1	-1	1	1	1	-1	1	1	-1	1	⋯
0(10-1)	0		1	0	-1		1	0		-1	⋯
x			1		-1		1			-1	⋯

Example 3. To outline the use of a periodic sampling equation in Signal, we consider the specification of a one-place buffer which is constrained to behave as a mailbox (every message has to be read once and only once before there is a new one). The process buffer uses two subprocesses, alternate and current. The process alternate stipulates that the signals x and y should have exclusive periods (01) and (10) with respect to the clock c. The process current stores the value of an input signal y and loads it into the output signal x upon request. The buffer has a main clock equivalence class $\hat{r} = c$ and two exclusive samples $\hat{x} = (01)\,@\,c$ and $\hat{y} = (10)\,@\,c$.

$$\begin{aligned} x = \mathsf{buffer}(y) &\overset{\text{def}}{=} (x = \mathsf{current}(y,c) \,|\, \mathsf{alternate}(x,y,c)) \\ \mathsf{alternate}(x,y,c) &\overset{\text{def}}{=} (\hat{x} = (01)\,@\,c \,|\, \hat{y} = (10)\,@\,c) \\ x = \mathsf{current}(y,c) &\overset{\text{def}}{=} (r = y \;\mathsf{default}\; (r \;\mathsf{pre}\; \mathit{initValue}) \,|\, x = r \;\mathsf{when}\; \hat{x} \,|\, \hat{r} = c) \end{aligned}$$

Use case In a 4-stroke engine, each cylinder performs a cycle with four phases: intake, compression, combustion and exhaust. During the intake phase, a blend of fuel and air is put in the cylinder, the compression compresses this blend, the combustion is the action of burning the blend because of an ignition and the exhaust evacuates the gas of the cylinder. To model this periodic system, like [2] we use a clock *clkShaft* which represents the rotation of the crankshaft. In figure 1, it appears that the crankshaft turns 720° for each cycle of the engine.

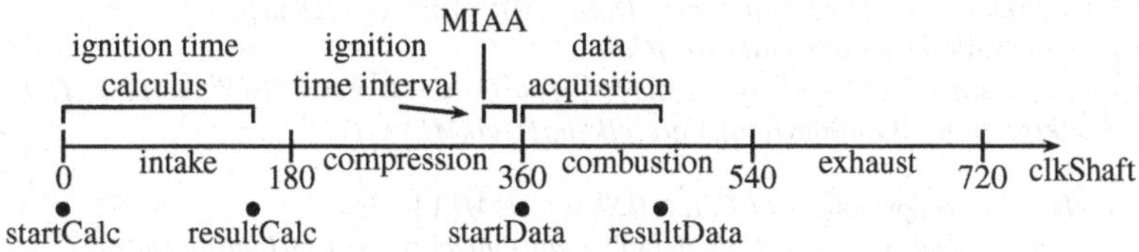

Fig. 1 4-stroke engine cycle for one cylinder

The date of ignition occurs during the 'ignition time interval' and must be computed for each cycle of the engine for a better efficiency. This date depends on several measures made during the combustion phase of the previous cycle. 'Data acquisition' is the period where the measures are done and 'ignition time calculus' is the one where the ignition date is calculated. The Maximal Ignition Advance Angle (MIAA) is the beginning of the 'ignition time interval'.

The process oneCylinder represents the model of a cylinder in Signal using periodic sampling equations. The signal *clkShaft* is a clock which is present each time the crankshaft turns one degree. The clocks *clkIntake, clkCompress, clkCombust, clkExhaust* represent the beginning of the four phases of the 4-stroke engine (1). For example, the equation $clkCompress = (0^{180}10^{539}) @ clkShaft$ constrains *clkCompress* to be present when *clkShaft* is present for the (181 modulo 720)th times that correspond to a turn of 180° from each beginning of a cycle. The clock *clkMIAA* corresponds to the MIAA.

We assume two external components represented by two processes: dataAcquisition for the acquisition of the data (2) and ignitionTime for the computation of the date of ignition (3). For each cycle, the beginning and the end of the running of the two processes are constrained by the periodic clocks of the signals *startData* and *resultData* for dataAcquisition and the signals *startCalc* and *resultCalc* for ignitionTime.

The ignition must occur at the MIAA plus a number of degrees contained in the result *resultCalc* of the process ignitionTime. The clock *clkIgnition* (4) is the result of the process Ignition (5) that computes this date. A buffer is needed to delay the acquisition of the data at the clock *resultData* to the use of this data at the clock $\widehat{startCalc}$ (in the next cycle of the engine). The management of the buffer to operate this delay is shown in the global process: 4cylinderEngine. The model of a four cylinder engine is a composition of four processes oneCylinder, the basic clocks of which are 'shifted' (6): the first cylinder starts running at the first presence of the clock *clk* of the crankshaft, the second cylinder starts with a delay of 180 degrees on the clock *clk*, the third one with a delay of 360 degrees and the fourth one with a delay of 540 degrees. The process bufferFIFO is a classical FIFO in which an element is added when one of the signals $d1, d2, d3$ or $d4$ (corresponding to the respective *resultData* signal of each cylinder) is present; an element is taken from the FIFO

$$\begin{array}{l}
\mathsf{oneCylinder}(clkShaft, resultData, startCalc) \stackrel{\text{def}}{=} \\
\left(\begin{array}{l} clkIntake = (1^{0}0^{719}) \mathbin{@} clkShaft \quad | clkCompress = (0^{180}1 0^{539}) \mathbin{@} clkShaft \\ | clkCombust = (0^{360}1 0^{359}) \mathbin{@} clkShaft \,|\, clkExhaust = (0^{540}1 0^{179}) \mathbin{@} clkShaft \\ | clkMIAA = (0^{330}1 0^{389}) \mathbin{@} clkShaft \end{array}\right) \quad (1) \\
| \left(\begin{array}{l} resultData = \mathsf{dataAcquisition}(startData) \\ | \hat{startData} = clkCombust \,|\, \hat{resultData} = (0^{470}1 0^{249}) \mathbin{@} clkShaft \end{array}\right) \quad (2) \\
| \left(\begin{array}{l} resultCalc = \mathsf{ignitionTime}(startCalc) \\ | \hat{startCalc} = 0^{720}(1 0^{719}) \mathbin{@} clkShaft \,|\, \hat{resultCalc} = 0^{720}(0^{150}1 0^{569}) \mathbin{@} clkShaft \end{array}\right) \quad (3) \\
| \; (\; clkIgnition = \mathsf{Ignition}(resultCalc, clkShaft, clkMIAA)) \quad (4)
\end{array}$$

$$\begin{array}{l}
clkIgnition = \mathsf{Ignition}(resultCalc, clkShaft, clkMIAA) \stackrel{\text{def}}{=} \\
\left(\begin{array}{ll} ignitionDelay = resultCalc \ \mathsf{default}\ (ignitionDelay \ \mathsf{pre}\ firstIgnitionDate) & \\ | i & = 0 \ \mathsf{when}\ clkMIAA \\ & \quad \mathsf{default}\ \text{-}1 \ \mathsf{when}\ (zi == ignitionDelay) \\ & \quad \mathsf{default}\ zi + 1 \ \mathsf{when}\ (zi \neq \text{-}1) \\ | zi & = i \ \mathsf{pre}\ \text{-}1 \quad | \quad \hat{i} = clkShaft \\ | clkIgnition & = \mathsf{true}\ \mathsf{when}\ (i == ignitionDelay) \end{array}\right) \quad (5)
\end{array}$$

$$\begin{array}{l}
\mathsf{4cylinderEngine}(clk) \stackrel{\text{def}}{=} \\
(6) \left(\begin{array}{l} \mathsf{oneCylinder}(clk, d1, c1) \\ | \mathsf{oneCylinder}(0^{180}(1) \mathbin{@} clk, d2, c2) \\ | \mathsf{oneCylinder}(0^{360}(1) \mathbin{@} clk, d3, c3) \\ | \mathsf{oneCylinder}(0^{540}(1) \mathbin{@} clk, d4, c4) \end{array}\right) \Bigg| \left(\begin{array}{l} add = d1 \ \mathsf{default}\ d2 \ \mathsf{default}\ d3 \ \mathsf{default}\ d4 \\ | take = \mathsf{bufferFIFO}(add) \\ | c1 \ = take \ \mathsf{when}\ \hat{c1} \,|\, c2 = take \ \mathsf{when}\ \hat{c2} \\ | c3 \ = take \ \mathsf{when}\ \hat{c3} \,|\, c4 = take \ \mathsf{when}\ \hat{c4} \end{array}\right) (7)
\end{array}$$

when one of the signals $c1, c2, c3$ or $c4$ (corresponding to the respective *startCalc*) is present (7). The analysis of the necessary size of this buffer is presented in Section 6. The figure 2 shows a chronogram of this model.

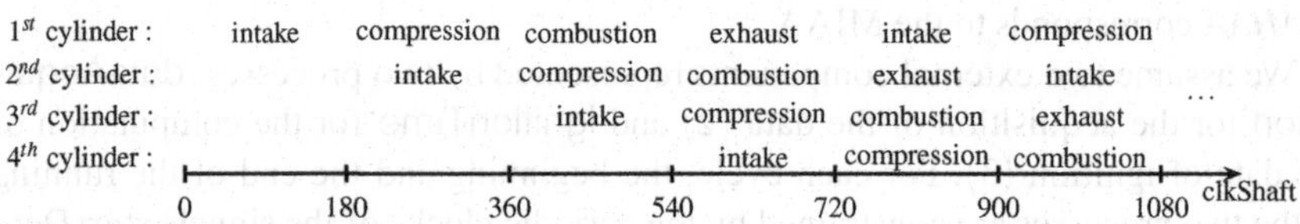

Fig. 2 a 4 cylinder engine chronogram

5 Inference of clock relations

In this section, we present the clock relations extracted from Signal equations and the associated clock calculus extended with the periodic sampling equation. In general, a clock c denotes a set of tags in the polychronous model of computation. The clock $\hat{x}$ of a signal x denotes the tags at which the signal x is present. The clock $[x]$ (resp. $[\neg x]$) denotes the tags at which a boolean signal x is present and true (resp. false). The intersection $\cap$, union $\cup$ and the complement $\setminus$ are the usual operators on sets applied on the sets of tags representing clocks. The expression $w \mathbin{@} c$ denotes the clock obtained by the periodic sampling defined in Section 4. When we are talking about clocks, all the words are binary words. Any Signal process P corresponds to a system of implicit clock relations C that denotes its implied timing structure.

$$c,d ::= \hat{x} \mid [x] \mid [\neg x] \mid c \cap d \mid c \cup d \mid c \setminus d \mid w @ c \qquad \text{(clock)}$$
$$C,D ::= c = d \mid C|D \qquad \text{(clock relation)}$$

The clock relations are specified by the inference system $P : C$ that is recursively defined by induction on the syntax of P. In a delay equation $x = y$ pre v, the signals are synchronous ($\hat{x} = \hat{y}$). In a sampling equation $x = y$ when z, the clock $\hat{x}$ is defined by the clock $\hat{y}$ at the sampling condition $[z]$. In a merge equation $x = y$ default z, $\hat{x}$ is present if either one of the clock y,z is. In a functional equation $x = \mathsf{f}(y,z)$ the signals x,y,z are synchronous. In a periodic sampling equation $x = w @ y$, x is defined by the atoms of w when y is true. The rule for composition $P \,|\, Q$ is defined to be $C \,|\, D$ and by induction on the deductions $P : C$ and $Q : D$ made on its sub-terms.

$$\begin{array}{ll} x = y \;\mathsf{pre}\; v & : (\hat{x} = \hat{y}) \\ x = y \;\mathsf{when}\; z & : (\hat{x} = \hat{y} \cap [z]) \\ x = y \;\mathsf{default}\; z & : (\hat{x} = \hat{y} \cup \hat{z}) \end{array} \qquad \begin{array}{l} x = w @ y : (\hat{x} = w^2 @ [y] \quad (*) \\ \qquad\qquad \mid [x] = [w] @ [y] \\ \qquad\qquad \mid [\neg x] = [\neg w] @ [y]) \end{array} \qquad \frac{P:C \quad Q:D}{P|Q : C|D}$$

(*) w^2, $[w]$ and $[\neg w]$ are binary words respectively defined by

$$(a.w)^2 = \begin{pmatrix} 1, a = 1 \\ 1, a = \text{-}1 \\ 0, a = 0 \end{pmatrix} .w^2 \quad [a.w] = \begin{pmatrix} 1, a = 1 \\ 0, a = \text{-}1 \\ 0, a = 0 \end{pmatrix} .[w] \quad [\neg a.w] = \begin{pmatrix} 0, a = 1 \\ 1, a = \text{-}1 \\ 0, a = 0 \end{pmatrix} .[\neg w]$$

Intuitively, the binary words w^2, $[w]$ and $[\neg w]$ are used to represent respectively presence, presence and true, presence and false of a boolean signal constrained by a periodic sampling equation using a word w.

Property 2. Let c,d and e be clocks of a process P and w and w' two binary words, $P : (c = w @ d \mid d = w' @ e) \Rightarrow P : c = (w @ w') @ e$

Proof : *We know that the operator* $@$ *is associative for binary words [5].*
$c = w @ (w' @ e) \Longrightarrow c = (w @ w') @ e$.

6 Communication analysis

Most of reactive systems use communications between their different components. In safety-critical domains, like car industry, there is a need for guaranteeing bounded communications. In the particular case of reactive systems described with our model of periodic processes, we provide a formal analysis allowing to determine minimal buffer size required for communications.

Buffer size analysis We consider a definition of periodically equivalent clocks based on the definition of synchronizable words (definition 2). Two clocks c and d are periodically equivalent if there exists a clock r such that the tags of c and d are included in the set of tags of r, and there are constraints $c = w_c @ r$, $d = w_d @ r$ where

w_c, w_d are synchronizable. It means that the difference of the number of presence of the clocks c and d is bounded all times the clock r is present.

Definition 3. Two clocks c,d are periodically equivalent in P, noted $c \sim d$, iff $\exists r$ a clock, such that $P : (c = w_c @ r, \ | \ d = w_d @ r)$ and $w_c \sim w_d$

From this definition, we define the synchronization of a clock c on another clock d, noted $c \succ d$. It constrains the nth occurrence of the clock c to precede the corresponding one of the clock d for all $n > 0$. c and d must be periodically equivalent. The operator $\succ$ on the clocks is not commutative.

Definition 4. A clock c is synchronizable on a clock d in P, noted $c \succ d$, iff
1. $c \sim d$, (i.e. $\exists r$ a clock, such that $P : (c = w_c @ r, \ | \ d = w_d @ r)$, $w_c \sim w_d$)
2. $w_c \sqsubseteq w_d$

When a clock c is synchronizable on a clock d, it means that values can be delayed from the clock c to the clock d using a bounded buffer. The maximal size of the buffer used by the delay can be computed. We thus obtain the minimal size of the buffer to delay a signal of clock c for its use on clock d.

Property 3. Minimal buffer size to guarantee the communication between two synchronizable clocks c and d in a process P.
From definition 4, we have $c \succ d \Leftrightarrow P : (c = w_c @ r, \ | \ d = w_d @ r)$, $w_c \sim w_d$ and $w_c \sqsubseteq w_d$. The minimal size of the buffer to guarantee the delay from the clock c to the clock d is : $size(c,d) = \max_{n>0}(|w_d|_n^1 - |w_c|_n^1)$
The $size(c,d)$ is the maximal difference between the numbers of presence of the clocks d and c. This size is computable thanks to remark 1 (section 3).

Analysis of the minimal buffer size required for the process bufferFIFO The inference system $(P : C)$ defined in Section 5 applied on the process 4cylinderEngine gives the following relations:

4cylinderEngine: $(add = 0^{291}(0^{179}1) @ clk \mid take = 0^{541}(0^{179}1) @ clk)$

The two clocks *add* and *take* are periodically equivalent (definition 3) and synchronizable (definition 4). So we can calculate the size of the buffer needed to delay values from the clock *add* to the clock *take* : $size(add, take) = 2$. The communications between the acquisition of the data from the previous cycle of the engine to the computation of the ignition date are guaranteed with a two place buffer.

Analysis of the number of components used for the computation of the ignition date. In the 4cylinderEngine process, each process oneCylinder uses a ignitionTime process to compute its ignition date. But this process could be shared between several oneCylinder processes (ignitionTime is only running during the intake phases). Just like for the above analysis of the minimal size of the FIFO buffer, the same kind of analysis can be done to calculate the number of ignitionTime processes required for the overall application. The ignitionTime process is running between an occurrence of the *startCalc* signal to the next occurrence of the *resultCalc* signal. The *size* function (between the clocks corresponding to the start and the end of the running of the ignitionTime process) can be used here to determine the maximal number of ignitionTime processes running at the same time.

$(\bigcup startCalc = 0^{541}(0^{179}1) @ clk \mid \bigcup resultCalc = 0^{690}(0^{179}1) @ clk)$

The result is $size(\bigcup startCalc, \bigcup resultCalc) = 1$. Therefore one single component can be used for the computation of the ignition date of the four processes oneCylinder. The previous computation is always finished when a new computation starts.

Applying the same analysis for a 4-stroke engine with 6 cylinders defined on a similar model than the 4cylinderEngine (with a delay of 120 degrees between the clocks *clkShaft*) gives a result size of 2, so that two components are needed for the computation of the ignition date of the six processes oneCylinder.

7 Conclusion

We have presented an extension of the polychronous model of computation of the Signal formalism with a periodic sampling equation using ultimately periodic infinite words. We have shown that periodic clock relations provide a calculus to compositionally reason about real-time relations in multi-clocked systems. Our main contributions are the adaptation of periodic relations of [5] to $\mathbb{Z}/3\mathbb{Z}$ and their handling in the clock calculus associated with the polychronous model. This extension is used for the design of periodic systems in Signal and we illustrated it with an example of a 4-stroke engine. We gave an analysis allowing to guarantee the communications using bounded buffers; the maximal size of buffers is formally evaluated.

The work that has been done allows to analyse periodic systems that are designed using the new specific periodic sampling equation introduced in Signal. A further study would be to define a static analysis that would extract periodic relations from implicit periodicities of the systems. This will allow to analyse a greater set of periodic systems.

References

1. C. André, F. Mallet, R. de Simone. Modeling time in UML. Research report ISRN I3S/RR-2007-16-FR, I3S Laboratory, 2007.
2. C. André, F. Mallet, M-A. Peraldi. A multiform time approach to real-time system modeling. SIES, 2007.
3. A. Benveniste, P. Caspi, S. Edwards, N. Halbwachs, P. Le Guernic, and R. de Simone. The Synchronous Languages Twelve Years Later. *Proceedings of the IEEE*. IEEE, 2003.
4. J. Buck, S. Ha, E. Lee, D. Messerschmitt. Ptolemy: a framework for simulating and prototyping hetrogeneous systems. *International Journal in Compuer Simulation*, v4(2), 1994.
5. A. Cohen, M. Duranton, C. Eisenbeis, C. Pagetti, F. Plateau, and M. Pouzet. N-synchronous Kahn networks: a relaxed model of synchrony for real-time systems. In *POPL*. ACM, 2006.
6. C. Dezan, P. Quinton. Verification of regular architectures using Alpha. In *Adaptative Sensor Array Processing Workshop*. IEEE Press, 1994.
7. G. Kahn. The semantics of a simple language for parallel programming. *Information Processing*, North Holland, 1974.
8. E. Kock, et al. Yapi: Application modeling for signal processing systems. *Design Automation Conference*. ACM, 2000.
9. P. Le Guernic, J.-P. Talpin, and J.-C. Le Lann. Polychrony for system design. In *Journal for Circuits, Systems and Computers*. World Scientific, 2003

10. H. Marchand, E. Rutten, M. Le Borgne and M. Samaan. Formal Verification of programs specified with Signal : application to a power transformer station controller. In *Science of Computer Programming*. Elsevier, 2001.
11. I. Smarandache, T. Gautier, P. Le Guernic. Validation of mixed Signal-Alpha real-time systems through an affine calculus on clock synchronization constraints. In *Formal Methods Europe*. Springer, 1999.

Formal Correctness of an Automotive Bus Controller Implementation at Gate-Level

Eyad Alkassar, Peter Böhm, and Steffen Knapp

Abstract We formalize the correctness of a real-time scheduler in a time-triggered architecture. Where previous research elaborated on real-time protocol correctness, we extend this work to gate-level hardware. This requires a sophisticated analysis of analog bit-level synchronization and message transmission. Our case-study is a concrete automotive bus controller (ABC). For a set of interconnected ABCs we formally prove at gate-level, that all ABCs are synchronized tight enough such that messages are broadcast correctly. Proofs have been carried out in the interactive theorem prover Isabelle/HOL using the NuSMV model checker. To the best of our knowledge, this is the first effort formally tackling scheduler correctness at gate-level.

1 Introduction

As more and more safety-critical functions in modern automobiles are controlled by embedded computer systems, formal verification emerges as the only technique to ensure the demanded degree of reliability. When analyzing correctness, as a bottom layer, often, only some synchronous model of distributed electronic control units (ECUs) sharing messages in lock-step is assumed. However, such models are im-

Eyad Alkassar[1] · Steffen Knapp[1]
Saarland University, Dept. of Computer Science, 66123 Saarbrücken, Germany
e-mail: {eyad, sknapp}@wjpserver.cs.uni-sb.de

Peter Böhm[1]
Oxford University Computing Laboratory, Wolfson Building, Oxford, OX1 3QD, England
e-mail: peter.boehm@comlab.ox.ac.uk

[1] Work partially funded by the German Research Foundation (DFG), by the German Federal Ministry of Education and Research (BMBF), and by the International Max Planck Research School (IMPRS).

Please use the following format when citing this chapter:

Alkassar, E., Böhm, P. and Knapp, S., 2008, in IFIP International Federation for Information Processing, Volume 271; *Distributed Embedded Systems: Design, Middleware and Resources*; Bernd Kleinjohann, Lisa Kleinjohann, Wayne Wolf; (Boston: Springer), pp. 57–67.

plemented at gate-level as highly asynchronous time-triggered systems. Hence it can not suffice to verify certain aspects of a system, as algorithms or protocols only.

In this paper we examine a distributed system implementation consisting of ECUs connected by a bus. Our study has to combine arguments from three different areas: (i) asynchronous bit-level transmission, (ii) scheduling correctness, and (iii) classical digital hardware verification at gate-level.

Our contribution is to show, by an extended case-study, how analog, real-time and digital proofs can be integrated into one pervasive correctness statement.

The hardware model has been formalized in the Isabelle/HOL theorem prover [11] based on boolean gates. It can be translated to Verilog and run on a FPGA. All lemmata relating to scheduling correctness have been formally proven in Isabelle/HOL. We have made heavy use of the model checker NuSMV [5] and automatic tools, e.g. IHaVeIt [18], especially for the purely digital lemmata. Most lemmata dealing with analog communication (formalized using reals) have been shown interactively.

Overview. The correctness of our gate-level implementation splits in two main parts: (i) the correctness of the transmission of single messages and (ii) the correctness of the scheduling mechanism initiating the message transmission and providing a common time base. Next we outline these two verification goals in detail.

The verification of asynchronous communication systems must, at some point, deal with the low-level bit transmission between two ECUs connected to the same bus. The core idea is to ensure that the value broadcast on the bus is stable long enough such that it can be sampled correctly by the receiver. To stay within such a so-called sampling window, the local clocks on the ECUs should not drift apart more than a few clock ticks and therefore need to be synchronized regularly. This is achieved by a message encoding that enforces the broadcast of special bit sequences to be used for synchronization. The correctness of this low-level transmission mechanism cannot be carried out in a digital, synchronous model. It involves asynchronous and real-time-triggered register models taking setup and hold-times of registers as well as metastability into account. Our efforts in this respect are based on [3, 8, 16].

Ensuring correct message transmission between two ECUs is only a part of the overall correctness. Let us consider a set of interconnected ECUs. The scheduler has to avoid bus contention, i.e. to ensure that only one ECU is allowed to broadcast at a time and that all others are only listening. For that, time is divided into rounds, which are further subdivided into slots. A fixed schedule assigns a unique sender to a given slot number. The gate-level implementation of the scheduler has to ensure that all ECUs have roughly the same notion of the slot-start and end times, i.e. they must agree on the current sender and the transmission interval. Due to drifting clocks some synchronization algorithm becomes necessary. We use a simple idea: A cycle offset is added at the beginning and end of each slot. This offset is chosen large enough to compensate the maximal clock drift that can occur during a full round. The local timers are synchronized only once, at the beginning of each round. This is done by choosing a distinguished master ECU, being the first sender in a round.

The combination of the results into a lock-step and synchronous view of the system is now simple. The scheduler correctness ensures that always only one ECU is sending and all other ECUs do listen. Then we can conclude from the first part that the broadcast data is correctly received by all ECUs.

Organization of the paper: In the remainder of this section we discuss the related work. In Section 2 we introduce our ABC implementation. Our verification approach is detailed in Section 3. Finally we conclude in Section 4.

Related Work. Serial interfaces were subject to formal verification in the work of Berry *et al.* [1]. They specified a UART model in a synchronous language and proved a set of safety properties regarding FIFO queues. Based on that a hardware description can be generated and run on a FPGA. However, data transmission was not analyzed.

A recent proof of the Biphase-Mark protocol has been proposed by Brown and Pike [4]. Their models include metastability but verification is only done at specification level, rather than at the concrete hardware. The models were extracted manually.

Formal verification of clock synchronization in timed systems has a long history [9, 12, 17]. Almost all approaches focused on algorithmic correctness, rather than on concrete system or even hardware verification. As an exception Bevier and Young [2] describe the verification of a low-level hardware implementation of the Oral Message algorithm. The presented hardware model is quite simplified, as synchronous data transmission is assumed.

Formal proofs of a clock-synchronization circuit were reported by Miner [10]. Based on abstract state machines, a correctness proof of a variant of the Welch-Lynch algorithm was carried out in PVS. However, the algorithm is only manually translated to a hardware specification, which is finally refined semi-automatically to a gate-level implementation. No formal link between both is reported. Besides, low-level bit transmission is not covered in the formal reasoning.

The formal analysis of large bus architectures was tackled among others by Rushby [15] and Zhang [19]. Rushby worked on the time-triggered-architecture (TTA), and showed correctness of several key algorithms as group membership and clock synchronization. Assuming correct clock synchronization, Zhang verified properties of the Flexray bus guardian. Both approaches do not deal with any hardware implementation. The respective standard is translated to a formal specification by hand.

In [14] Rushby proposes the separation of the verification of timing-related properties (as clock synchronization) and protocol specifications. A set of requirements is identified, which an implementation of a scheduler (e.g. in hardware) has to obey. In short (i) clock synchronization and (ii) a round offset large enough to compensate the maximum clock drift are assumed. The central result is a formal and generic PVS simulation proof between the real-time system and its lock-step and synchronous specification. Whereas the required assumptions are similar to ours, they have not been discharged for concrete hardware.

In [12] Rushby's framework is instantiated with the time triggered protocol (TTP). Pike [13] corrects and extends Rushby's work, and instantiates the new framework with SPIDER, a *fly-by-wire* communication bus used by NASA. The time-triggered model was extracted from the hardware design by hand. But neither approaches proved correctness of any gate-level hardware.

2 Automotive Bus Controller (ABC) Implementation

We consider a time-triggered scenario. Time is divided into so-called rounds each consisting of *ns* slots. We uniquely identify slots by a tuple consisting of a round-number $r \in \mathbb{N}$ and a slot-number $s \in [0 : ns-1]$. Predecessors $(r,s)-1$ and successors $(r,s)+1$ are computed modulo *ns*.

The ABC is split in four main parts: (a) the host-interface provides the connection to the host, e.g. a microprocessor, and contains configuration registers (b) the send-environment performs the actual message broadcast and contains a send-buffer (c) the receive-environment takes care of the message reception and contains a receive-buffer (d) the schedule-environment is responsible for the clock synchronization and the obedience to the schedule.

Configuration Parameter. Unless synchronization is performed, slots are locally T hardware cycles long. A slot can be further subdivided into three parts; an initial as well as a final offset (each *off* hardware cycles) and a transmission window (*tc* hardware cycles). The length of the transmission window is implicitly given by the slot-length and the offset. Within each slot a fixed-length message of ℓ bytes is broadcast.

The local schedule *sendl*, that is implemented as a bit-vector, indicates if the ABC is the sender in a given slot. Intuitively, in slot *s*, if $sendl[s] = 1$ then the ABC broadcasts the message stored in the send-buffer. Note that the ABC implementation is not aware of the round-number. It simply operates according to the slot-based fixed schedule, that is repeated time and again.

The special parameter *iwait* indicates the number of hardware cycles to be awaited before the ABC starts executing the schedule after power-up.

All parameters introduced so far are stored in configuration registers that need to be set by the host (we support memory mapped I/O) during an initialization phase. The host indicates that it has finished the initialization by invoking a *setrd* command. We do not go into details here, the interested reader may consult [7,8].

Message Broadcast. The send-environment starts broadcasting the message contained in the send-buffer *sb* if the schedule-environment raises the *startsnd* signal.

The receive-environment permanently listens on the bus. At an incoming message, indicated by a falling edge (the bus is high-active), it signals the start of a reception to the schedule-environment by raising the *startedrcv* signal for one cycle. In addition it decodes the broadcast frame and writes the message into the receive buffer *rb*.

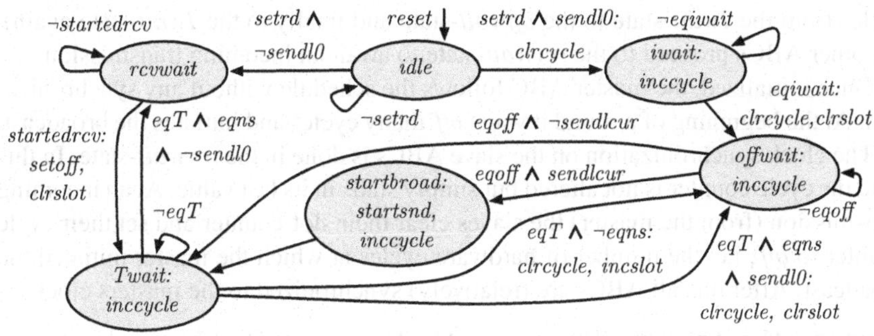

Fig. 1 Schedule Automaton

Scheduling. The schedule-environment maintains two counters: The cycle counter *cy* and the current slot counter *csn*. Both counters are periodically synchronized at the beginning of every round. All ECUs except the one broadcasting in slot 0 (we call the former *slaves* and the latter *master*) synchronize their counters to the incoming transmission in slot 0. Hence, the *startedrcv* signal from the receive environment is used to provide a synchronized time base (see below). Furthermore, the schedule-environment initiates the message broadcast by raising the *startsnd* signal for one cycle.

The schedule environment implements the automaton from Fig. 1. The automaton takes the following inputs: The *startedrcv* signal as described above. The signal *setrd* denotes the end of the configuration phase. The signal *sendl0* indicates if the ECU is the sender in the first slot and thus the master. Three signals are used to categorize the cycle counter; *eqiwait* indicates if the initial *iwait* cycles have been reached, similar to *eqoff* and *eqT*. The signal *eqns* indicates that the end of a round has been reached, i.e. that the slot counter equals $ns-1$. Finally *sendlcur* indicates if the ABC is the sender in the current slot, i.e. $sendlcur = sendl[csn]$.

The automaton has six states and is clocked each cycle. Its functionality can be summarized as follows: If the *reset* signal is raised (which is assumed to happen only at power-up) the automaton is forced into the *idle*-state. If the host has finished the initialization and thus invoked *setrd* we split cases depending on the *sendl0* signal. If the ABC is the master, i.e. if *sendl0* holds, the ABC waits first *iwait* hardware cycles (in the *iwait*-state), then an additional *off* cycles (in the *offwait*-state) before it starts broadcasting the message (in the *startbroad*-state) and proceeds to the *Twait*-state.

If the ABC is a slave ($sendl0 = 0$), it waits in the *rcvwait*-state for an active *startedrcv* signal and then proceeds to the *Twait*-state. There all ABCs await the end of a slot indicated by *eqT*. Then we split cases if the round is finished or not. If the round is not finished yet (indicated by ¬*eqns*), all ABCs proceed to the *offwait*-state. Furthermore, the sender in the current slot (indicated by *sendlcur*) proceeds to the *startbroad*-state, initiates the message broadcast and then proceeds to the *Twait*-state; all other ABCs skip the *startbroad*-state and proceed directly to the *Twait*-state. At the end of a round, the master simply repeats the 'normal' sender cycle (from the *Twait*-state to the *offwait*-state and finally to the *Twait*-state again). All other ABCs proceed to the *rcvwait*-state to await an incoming transmission.

Once initialized, the master ABC follows the schedule without any synchronization. At the beginning of a round it waits *off* many cycles and initiates the broadcast.

The clock synchronization on the slave ABCs is done in the *rcvwait*-state. In this state the cycle counter is not altered but simply stalls in its last value. At an incoming transmission (from the master) the slaves clear their slot-counter and set their cycle counter to *off*, i.e. the number of hardware cycles at which the master initiated the broadcast. After this all ABCs are (relatively) synchronized to the masters clock.

Hardware Construction. The number of ECUs connected to the bus is denoted *ne*. Thus an ECU number is given by $u \in [0 : ne-1]$. We use subscript ECU numbers to refer to single ECUs.

We denote the hardware configurations of ECU_u by h_u. If the index u of the ECU does not matter, we drop it. The hardware configuration is split into a host configuration and an ABC configuration. Since we do not go into details regarding the host, we stick to h to denote the configuration of our ABC. Its essential components are:

- Two single bit-registers, one for sending and one for receiving. Both are directly connected to the bus. We denote them $h.S$ and $h.R$.
- A second receiver register, denoted $h.\hat{R}$, to deal with metastability (see Sect. 3).
- Send buffer $h.sb$ and receive buffer $h.rb$ each capable of storing one message.
- The current slot counter $h.csn$ and the cycle counter $h.cy$.
- The schedule automaton is implemented straight-forward as a transition system on an unary coded bit-vector. We use $h.state$ to code the current state (see Fig. 1).
- Configuration registers.

The configuration registers are written immediately after reset / power-up. They contain in particular the locally relevant portions of the scheduling function.

To simplify arguments regarding the schedule we define a global scheduling function *send*. Given a slot-number s it returns the number of the ECU sending in this slot. Let $sendl_u$ denote the local schedule of ECU_u, then $send(s) = u \Leftrightarrow sendl_u[s] = 1$. Note that this definition implicitly requires a unique sender definition for each slot. Otherwise correct message broadcast becomes impossible due to bus contention.

Thus if ECU_u is (locally) in a slot with slot index s and $send(s) = u$ then ECU_u will transmit the content of the send buffer $h.sb$ via the bus during some transmission interval. A serial interface that is not actively transmitting during slot (r,s) puts by construction the idle value (the bit 1) on the bus.

If we can guarantee that during the transmission interval *all* ECUs are locally in slot (r,s), then transmission will be successful. The clock synchronization algorithm together with an appropriate choice of the transmission interval will ensure that.

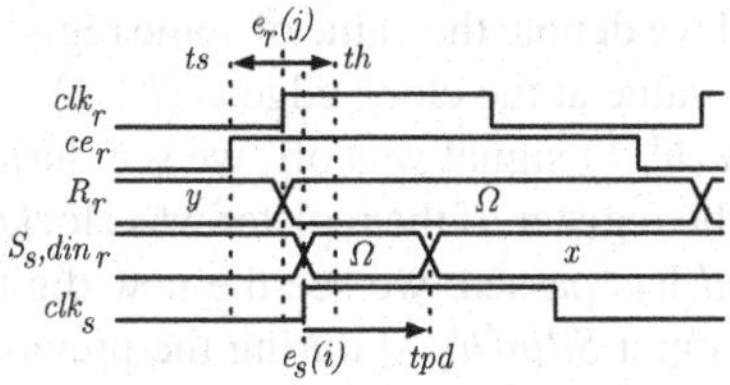

Fig. 2 Clock Edges

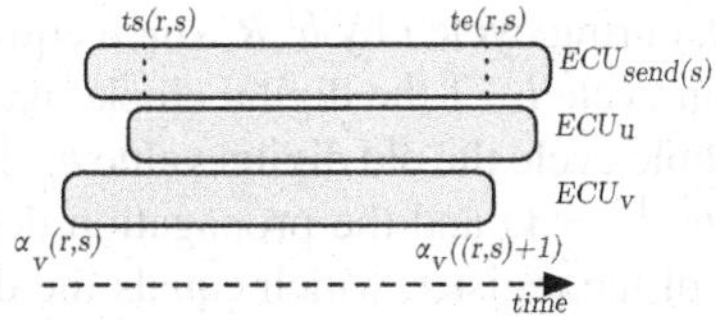

Fig. 3 Schedule

3 Verification

To argue about asynchronous distributed communication systems we have to formalize the behavior of the digital circuits connected to the analog bus. Using the formalization of digital clocks we introduce a hardware model for continuous time. In the remainder of this section we sketch the message transmission correctness, detail the scheduling correctness and combine both into a single correctness statement.

Clocks. The hardware of each ECU is clocked by an oscillator having a nominal clock period of τ_{ref}. The individual clock period τ_u of an ECU_u is allowed to deviate by at most $\delta = 0.15\%$ from τ_{ref}, i.e. $\forall u.\ |\ \tau_u - \tau_{ref}\ | \leq \tau_{ref} \cdot \delta$. Note that this limitation can be easily achieved by current technology.

Thus the relative deviation of two individual clock periods compared to a third clock period is bounded by $|\ \tau_u - \tau_v\ | \leq \tau_w \cdot \Delta$ where $\Delta = 2\delta/(1-\delta)$.

Given some clock-start offset $o_u < \tau_u$ the date of the clock edge $e_u(i)$ that starts cycle i on ECU_u is defined by $e_u(i) = o_u + i \cdot \tau_u$.

In our scenario all ECUs are connected to a bus. The sending ECUs broadcasts data which is sampled by all other ECUs. Due to clock drift it is not guaranteed, that the timing parameter of the sampling registers are obeyed. This problem is solved by serial interfaces. To argue formally we first introduce a continuous time model for bits being broadcast.

Hardware Model with Continuous Time. The problems solved by serial interfaces can by their very nature not be treated in a standard digital hardware model with a single digital clock *clk*. Nevertheless, we can describe each ECU_u in such a model having its own hardware configuration h_u.

To argue about the sender register $h.S$ of a sending ECU transmitting data via the bus to a receiver register $h.R$ of a receiving ECU, we have to extend the digital model.

For the registers connected to the bus –and only for those– we extend the hardware model such that we can deal with the concepts of propagation delay (tpd), setup time (ts), hold time (th), and metastability of registers. In the extended model used near the bus we therefore consider time to be a real valued variable t.

Next we define in the continuous time model the output of the sender register $h_u.S$ during cycle i of ECU_u, i.e. for $t \in (e_u(i) : e_u(i+1)]$. The content of $h_u.S$ at time t is denoted by $S_u(t)$. In the digital hardware model we denote the value of some register, e.g. R, during cycle i by $h^i.R$ which equals the value at the clock edge $e_u(i+1)$.

If in cycle $i-1$ the digital clock enable $Sce(h_u^{i-1})$ signal was off, we see during the whole cycle the old digital value $h_u^{i-1}.S$ of the register. If the register was clocked ($Sce(h_u^{i-1}) = 1$) and the propagation delay tpd has passed, we see the new digital value of the register, which equals the digital input $Sdin(h_u^{i-1})$ during the previous cycle (see Fig. 2). Otherwise we cannot predict what we see, which we denote by Ω:

$$S_u(t) = \begin{cases} h_u^{i-1}.S & : Sce(h_u^{i-1}) = 0 \wedge t \in (e_u(i) : e_u(i+1)] \\ Sdin(h_u^{i-1}) & : Sce(h_u^{i-1}) = 1 \wedge t \in [e_u(i) + tpd : e_u(i+1)] \\ \Omega & : \text{otherwise} \end{cases}$$

The bus is an open collector bus modeled as the conjunction over all registers $S_u(t)$ for all t and u.

Now consider the receiver register $h_v.R$ on any ECU_v. It is continuously turned on; thus the register always samples from the bus. In order to define the new digital value $h_v^j.R$ of register R during cycle j on ECU_v we have to consider the value of the bus in the time interval $(e_v(j) - ts, e_v(j) + th)$. If during that time the bus has a constant digital value x, the register samples that value, i.e. $\exists x \in \{0,1\}.\ \forall t \in (e_v(j) - ts, e_v(j) + th).\ bus(t) = x \Rightarrow h_v^j.R = x$. Otherwise we define $h_v^j.R = \Omega$.

We have to argue how to deal with unknown values Ω as input to digital hardware. We will use the output of register $h_u.R$ only as input to a second register $h_u.\hat{R}$ whose clock enable is always turned on, too. If Ω is clocked into $h_u.\hat{R}$ we assume that $h_u.\hat{R}$ has an unknown but digital value, i.e. $h_u^j.R = \Omega \Rightarrow h_u^{j+1}.\hat{R} \in \{0,1\}$.

In real systems the counterpart of register $\hat{R}$ exists. The probability that R becomes metastable for an entire cycle *and* that this causes $\hat{R}$ to become metastable too is for practical purposes zero.

Continuous Time Lemmata for the Bus. Consider ECU_s is the sender and ECU_r is a receiver in a given slot. Let i be a sender *cycle* such that $Sce(h_s^{i-1}) = 1$, i.e. the output of S is not guaranteed to stay constant at time $e_s(i)$. This change can only affect the value of register R of ECU_r in cycle j if it occurs before the sampling edge $e_r(j)$ plus the hold time th, i.e. $e_s(i) < e_r(j) + th$. The first cycle that is possibly being affected is denoted by $cy_{r,s}(i) = \min\{j \mid e_s(i) < e_r(j) + th\}$.

In what follows we assume that all ECUs other than the sender unit ECU_s put the value 1 on the bus and keep their Sce signal off (hence $bus(t) = S_s(t)$ for all t under consideration). Furthermore, we consider only one receiving unit ECU_r. Because the indices r and s are fixed we simply write $cy(i)$ instead of $cy_{r,s}(i)$.

Theorem 1 (Message Broadcast Correctness). *Let the broadcast start in sender-cycle i. The value of the send buffer of $ECU_{send(s)}$ is copied to all receive buffers on the network side within tc sender cycles, i.e.* $\forall u.\ h_u^{cy(i+tc)}.rb = h^i_{send(s)}.sb$.

This theorem is proven by an in-depth analysis of the send-environment and the receive-environment. For details see [8]. We do not go into details regarding the message transmission here. Instead we focus on the scheduling correctness.

Scheduling. We assume w.l.o.g. that the ECU with number 0 is the master, i.e. $send(0) = 0$. Let p_u be the point in time when ECU_u is switched on. We assume that at most cp_{max} hardware cycles have passed on the master ECU from the point in time it was switched on until all other ECUs are switched on, too. Thus $\forall u. \mid p_u - p_0 \mid \leq cp_{max} \cdot \tau_0$.

Once initialization is done, all hosts invoke a *setrd* command. The master ECU waits *iwait* hardware cycles before it starts executing the schedule. We assume that that there exists a point in time denoted I_{max} at which all slaves have invoked the *setrd* command and await the first incoming message. This assumption can be easily discharged by deriving an upper bound for the duration of the initialization phase, say i_{max} hardware cycles in terms of the master ECU, and choosing *iwait* to be $cp_{max} + i_{max}$. The upper bound can be obtained by industrial worst case execution time (WCET) analyzers [6] for the concrete processor and software.

We introduce some notation to simplify the arguments regarding single slots. The start time of slot (r,s) on an ECU_u is denoted by $\alpha_u(r,s)$. Initially, for all u we define $\alpha_u(0,0) = I_{max}$. To define the slot start times greater than slot $(0,0)$ we need a predicate *schedexec* that indicates if the schedule automaton is in one of three *executing* states, i.e. $schedexec(h_u^i) = h_u^i.state \in \{offwait, Twait, startbroad\}$. Let c be the smallest local hardware cycle such that $e_u(c)$ is greater than $\alpha_u((r,s)-1)$, $schedexec(h_u^c)$ holds, $h_u^c, cy = 0$, and $h_u^c.csn = s$. Moreover let c' be the smallest cycle sucht that $e_u(c')$ is greater than $\alpha_u((r,s)-1)$ and $h_u^{c'}.state = rcvwait$.

$$\alpha_u(r,s) = \begin{cases} e_u(c) & : u = 0 \vee s > 0 \\ e_u(c') & : \text{otherwise} \end{cases}$$

Using the definition of a clock edge we obtain the hardware cycle corresponding to $\alpha_u(r,s)$, denoted by $\alpha t_u(r,s)$.

The local timers are synchronized each round. Next we define the point in time when the synchronization is done in round r. The synchronization end time of round r on ECU_u, denoted by $\beta_u(r)$, is defined similar to the slot start time. Let c be the smallest hardware cycle such that that $schedexec(h_u^c)$ holds, $cycle_u^c = off$, and $slot_u^c = 0$. Then $\beta_u(r)$ is defined by $e_u(c)$.

Lemma 1 (Synchronization Times Relation). *For all u the synchronization of ECU_u to the master is completed within the adjustment time $ad = 10$ cycles relative to an arbitrary clock period τ_w, i.e. $\beta_0(r) = \alpha_0(r,0) + off \cdot \tau_0$ and $\beta_u(r) < \beta_0(r) + 10 \cdot \tau_w$*

The proof of this lemma is split in two parts. First, an analysis of the sender bounds the delay between an active *startsnd* signal and the actual transmission start. Second, we need to bound the delay on the receiver side until the *startedrcv* signal is raised after an incoming transmission plus an additional cycle to update the counters and the schedule control automaton. Next we relate the start times of slots on the same ECU.

Lemma 2 (Slot Start Times Relation). *The start of slot (r,s) on the master ECU depends only on the progress of the local counter, i.e. $\alpha_0(r,s) = \alpha_0((r,s)-1) + T \cdot \tau_0$. The start of slot (r,s) on all other ECUs is given by:*

$$\alpha_u(r,s) = \begin{cases} \beta_u(r) + (T - off) \cdot \tau_u & : s = 1 \\ \alpha_u((r,s)-1) + T \cdot \tau_u & : s \neq 1 \end{cases}$$

Proof by induction on r and s using arguments for the concrete hardware.

The transmission is started in slot (r,s) by $ECU_{send(s)}$ if the local cycle count equals *off*. This point in time is denoted by $ts(r,s) = \alpha_{send(s)}(r,s) + off \cdot \tau_{send(s)}$. According to Theorem 1 the transmission ends at time $te(r,s) = ts(r,s) + tc \cdot \tau_{send(s)} = \alpha_{send(s)}(r,s) + (off + tc) \cdot \tau_{send(s)}$.

The schedule is correct if the transmission interval $[ts(r,s), te(r,s)]$ is contained in the time interval, when all ECUs are in slot (r,s), as depicted in Fig. 3.

Theorem 2 (Schedule Correctness). *All ECUs are in slot (r,s) before the transmission starts. Furthermore, the transmission must be finished before any ECU thinks it is in the next slot, i.e. $\alpha_u(r,s) < ts(r,s)$ and $te(r,s) < \alpha_u((r,s)+1)$*

This theorem is proven by a case split on (r,s) using Lemmata 1 and 2. Now we can state the overall transmission correctness in the digital hardware model:

Theorem 3 (Overall Transmission Correctness). *Consider slot (r,s). The value of the send buffer of $ECU_{send(s)}$ at the start of slot (r,s) is copied to all receive buffers by the end of that slot, i.e. $\forall u.\ h_u^{\alpha t_u((r,s+1))-1}.rb = h_{send(s)}^{\alpha t_{send(s)}(r,s)}.sb$*

To prove this theorem we combined Theorem 1 and Theorem 2. According to Theorem 1 the actual broadcast is correct if the transmission window $[ts(r,s), te(r,s)]$ is big enough. The latter is proven by Theorem 2.

4 Conclusion

In this paper we present a formal correctness proof of a distributed automotive system at gate-level (Sect. 3) along with its hardware implementation (Sect. 2). The hardware model has been formalized in Isabelle/HOL on boolean gates.

While a simple version of the message transmission correctness has already been published before [8,16], in this new work, we have formally analyzed the scheduler itself and have integrated both results into a single correctness statement. All lemmata relating to scheduling correctness have been formally proven in Isabelle/HOL which took about one person year.

We used automatic tools as the symbolic, open source model checker NuSMV, to discharge properties related to bit-vector operations and the schedule automaton of the hardware. With our implementation heavily using bit-vectors, we ran into the infamous state explosion problem. By resorting to IHaVeIt (a domain-reducing preprocessor for model checkers) we were able to cope with this problem. However, missing support for real-linear arithmetic in the automatic tool landscape, made the verification of the analog and timed models tedious. Yet the integration of decision procedures of dense-order logic would be helpful. In short: automatic tools took a heavy burden from us in the digital world but were almost useless for continous-timed analysis.

Summing up, our work provides a strong argument for the feasibility of formal and pervasive verification of concrete hardware implementations at gate-level.

References

1. Berry, G., Kishinevsky, M., Singh, S.: System level design and verification using a synchronous language. In: ICCAD, pp. 433–440 (2003)
2. Bevier, W., Young, W.: The proof of correctness of a fault-tolerant circuit design. In: Second IFIP Conference on Dependable Computing For Critical Applications, pp. 107–114 (1991)
3. Beyer, S., Böhm, P., Gerke, M., Hillebrand, M., In der Rieden, T., Knapp, S., Leinenbach, D., Paul, W.J.: Towards the formal verification of lower system layers in automotive systems. In: ICCD '05, pp. 317–324. IEEE Computer Society (2005)
4. Brown, G.M., Pike, L.: Easy parameterized verification of biphase mark and 8N1 protocols. In: TACAS'06, *LNCS*, vol. 3920, pp. 58–72. Springer (2006)
5. Cimatti, A., Clarke, E.M., Giunchiglia, E., Giunchiglia, F., Marco Pistore, M.R., Sebastiani, R., Tacchella, A.: NuSMV 2: An open source tool for symbolic model checking. In: CAV '02, pp. 359–364. Springer-Verlag (2002)
6. Ferdinand, C., Martin, F., Wilhelm, R., Alt, M.: Cache Behavior Prediction by Abstract Interpretation. Sci. Comput. Program. **35**(2), 163–189 (1999)
7. Hillebrand, M., In der Rieden, T., Paul, W.: Dealing with I/O devices in the context of pervasive system verification. In: ICCD '05, pp. 309–316. IEEE Computer Society (2005)
8. Knapp, S., Paul, W.: Realistic Worst Case Execution Time Analysis in the Context of Pervasive System Verification. In: Program Analysis and Compilation, *LNCS*, vol. 4444, pp. 53–81 (2007)
9. Lamport, L., Melliar-Smith, P.M.: Synchronizing clocks in the presence of faults. J. ACM **32**(1), 52–78 (1985)
10. Miner, P.S., Johnson, S.D.: Verification of an optimized fault-tolerant clock synchronization circuit. In: Designing Correct Circuits. Springer (1996)
11. Nipkow, T., Paulson, L.C., Wenzel, M.: Isabelle/HOL: A Proof Assistant for Higher-Order Logic, *LNCS*, vol. 2283. Springer (2002)
12. Pfeifer, H., Schwier, D., von Henke, F.W.: Formal verification for time-triggered clock synchronization. In: DCCA-7, vol. 12, pp. 207–226. IEEE Computer Society, San Jose, CA (1999)
13. Pike, L.: Modeling Time-Triggered Protocols and Verifying Their Real-Time Schedules. In: FMCAD'07, pp. 231–238 (2007)
14. Rushby, J.: Systematic formal verification for fault-tolerant time-triggered algorithms. IEEE Transactions on Software Engineering **25**(5), 651–660 (1999)
15. Rushby, J.: An overview of formal verification for the time-triggered architecture. In: FTRTFT'02, *LNCS*, vol. 2469, pp. 83–105. Springer-Verlag, Oldenburg, Germany (2002)
16. Schmaltz, J.: A Formal Model of Clock Domain Crossing and Automated Verification of Time-Triggered Hardware. In: FMCAD'07, pp. 223–230. IEEE/ACM, Austin, TX, USA (2007)
17. Shankar, N.: Mechanical verification of a generalized protocol for byzantine fault tolerant clock synchronization. In: FTRTFT'92, vol. 571, pp. 217–236. Springer, Netherlands (1992)
18. Tverdyshev, S., Alkassar, E.: Efficient bit-level model reductions for automated hardware verification. In: TIME 2008, to appear. IEEE Computer Society Press (2008)
19. Zhang, B.: On the Formal Verification of the FlexRay Communication Protocol. Automatic Verification of Critical Systems (AVoCS'06) pp. 184–189 (2006)

Unifying HW Analysis and SoC Design Flows by Bridging Two Key Standards: UML and IP-XACT

Sebastien Revol, Safouan Taha, François Terrier, Alain Clouard, Sébastien Gerard, Ansgar Radermacher, and Jean-Luc Dekeyser

Abstract In order to save time and improve efficiency, all SoC development processes are separated into many parallel flows. These flows should keep a strong communication to avoid redundancy and incoherency. We distinguish two main trends. One aims at designing and implementing hardware when the other focuses on its functional description that may serve to software architecturing, analysis and allocation. Even if both are newly using UML, no connections have been made to synchronize them. The goal of this work is then to bridge permanently the gap between those two hardware design trends by unifying their corresponding model-based standards: UML and IP-XACT.

1 Introduction

Many initiatives are working on adapting the Unified Modelling Language (UML), for Hardware design in order to benefit from model driven development, reuse, refinement and complexity management. In electronics system design, depending on the modelling purpose, we can distinguish two main trends. One aims to implement hardware, describing circuits (structure and behaviour) using UML techniques [8][9][10][11]. The other trend focuses on functional description of hardware for analysis and allocation purposes [1][2]. These two approaches have never been efficiently unified, keeping the two modelling flows separated.

The number of the various UML diagrams enables to address many different aspects of a system. Moreover UML offers specialization mechanism for specific

Sebastien Revol · Alain Clouard
STMicroelectronics, e-mail: firstname.lastname@st.com

Safouan Taha · François Terrier · Sébastien Gerard · Ansgar Radermacher
CEA LIST, e-mail: firstname.lastname@cea.fr

Jean-Luc Dekeyser
INRIA-DaRT, e-mail: dekeyser@lifl.fr

Please use the following format when citing this chapter:

Revol, S., et al., 2008, in IFIP International Federation for Information Processing, Volume 271; *Distributed Embedded Systems: Design, Middleware and Resources*; Bernd Kleinjohann, Lisa Kleinjohann, Wayne Wolf; (Boston: Springer), pp. 69–78.

domains, namely the UML profile capability. An UML profile is a set of stereotypes that extend UML concepts, and bring them a specialized semantics. It is the standard way to tune this general purpose language for a particular domain.

In the domain of System on Chip (SoC) design, different initiatives worked on defining profiles, having in mind a code generation purpose and using UML as a hardware design language. The UML SoC profile [10], standardized by the OMG (Object Management Group), proposes a graphical description of the SoC structure and permits SystemC[1] code generation. Likewise, the UML profile for SystemC [12] is a one-to-one transcription in UML context of all SystemC concepts including behaviour aspects. However, those profiles are often too close to the implementation languages and this has for effect to extend UML with implementation semantics. To resolve this point, our strategy was to get inspired from the IPXACT[2] concepts. This standard, widespread in the electronics community, is defined by the SPIRIT consortium with the objective to factorize in an XML grammar the hardware concepts, and to clearly dissociate the structural characteristics of a component (interfaces, registers etc.) from the way they are implemented. At STMicroelectronics we developed the ESL (Electronic System Level) profile that extends UML with IP-XACT concepts, allowing interoperability between them as well as the derivation of these formalisms into specific implementation languages.

In parallel to the hardware implementation flow, it is a common practice to specify functional, abstracted and understandable hardware models in order to communicate design intends and study interdependencies between hardware and software. Software design, allocation and analysis (e.g schedulability) require a high level description model of the hardware architecture in terms of number of processors, amount of memory Several profiles were also developed to define functional models of hardware like SPT [1] and AADL [2]. They classify resources whether if they are for computing, storage, communication and so on. These profiles are only introducing generic concepts and they are really lacking details and specific embedded systems properties. As a part of the new OMG standard MARTE [3] (Modelling and Analysis of Real-Time and Embedded systems), we developed in CEA LIST the HRM [4][5] (Hardware Resource Model) profile that is an open framework for UML-based hardware modelling. It provides many functional views and covers many detail levels.

The reason behind the separation between implementation models and functional ones, is the inadequacy between their levels and nature of details. This separation leads to redundancy and incoherency between these parallel flows. Implementation models are considered as very low level specification that cant serve for functional description. In this paper, we demonstrate that HRM profile is enough detailed, and ESL profile is enough abstracted to be able to define bridges between a functional description and an implementation one. Relying on the UML capability to provide different views of the same model, we succeeded to unify both profiles, so that they

[1] Open SystemC Initiative, www.systemc.org

[2] The Spirit Consortium: www.spiritconsortium.org

can be applied on an unique model, serving both for analysis and implementation concerns.

In the following sections, we will first present the HRM profile, its concepts and the way they can be used. Then we will introduce the ESL profile and its interoperability with IP-XACT. Last we will describe the unification process and illustrate it within a small example.

2 MARTE standard: Hardware Resource Model

The new OMG standard MARTE is proposed to replace the UML profile for Schedulability, Performance and Time (SPT). It handles the heterogeneity of embedded systems by adopting the Y-model [6] which consists of three models represented by different colours within Figure 1:

- Application model of the system tasks.
- Resource model of the execution platform, which is, in turn, composed of:
  - Software Resource Model describes the software execution platform (e.g. an operating system, drivers).
  - Hardware Resource Model.
- Allocation model that maps the application onto resources.

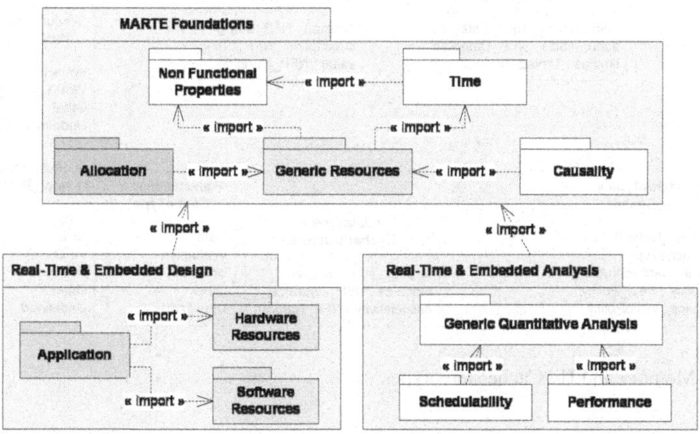

Fig. 1 MARTE structure

MARTE extends UML with a detailed Hardware Resource Model (HRM). This latter is intended to serve for functional description of hardware platforms, through different views and detail levels [4]. The Hardware Resource Model is grouping most of hardware concepts under a hierarchical taxonomy with several categories depending on their nature, functionality, technology and form. It is composed of two subprofiles, a logical one that classifies hardware resources depending on their functional properties, and a physical profile that focuses on their physical properties. HRM exploits particularly the Non-Functional Properties (NFP) package of MARTE [7] that allows quantitative annotations with measurement units and provides a rich UML library of basic types like Duration, Data Transmission Rate, Data Size and Power.

In this paper we will focus on the logical part of HRM that classifies hardware resources depending on their functional properties. The objective is then to provide a functional taxonomy of hardware resources, whether if they are computing, storage, communication, timing or auxiliary devices. This classification is mainly based on services that each resource offers. A big amount of stereotypes are introduced within HRM, they are rigorously specified and organized under a tree of successive inheritances from generic stereotypes to specific ones, no stereotype is orphan because a particular care has been made to explicit semantic relations and links among all the needed concepts. This is the reason behind the ability of the HRM profile to cover many abstraction levels. Another feature of the HRM is support of most hardware concepts thanks to a big range of stereotypes and once more its layered architecture. If no specific stereotype corresponds to a particular hardware component, a generic stereotype may match. This is appropriate to support new hardware components and new technologies. Finally, HRM includes many notations, and there is an appropriate icon for each logical stereotype.

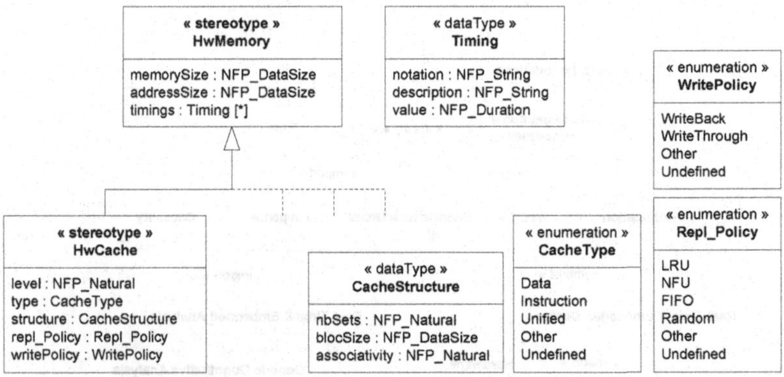

Fig. 2 HwMemory and HwCache stereotypes

In Figure 2 we extracted a part of the memory package from the logical subprofile of HRM. HwCache is a processing memory where frequently used data can be stored for rapid access. HwCache may vary depending on its level, type and structure. The cache structure is organized under sets of blocks, where associativity value is the number of blocks within one set.

In order to maximize flexibility, HRM stereotypes extend most UML structural concepts, allowing the use of the profile within any structural UML diagram. However, we provide in [5], a specific methodology to guide the hardware designers within an incremental process of successive compositions. It helps to resourcefully use HRM and benefit from its features. Finally, notice that we provide the XMI of the profile. This enables using XML-based technologies like model transformation and code generation for analysis, allocation or simulation of hardware models.

3 Electronic System Level Profile

The objective of the ESL profile is to provide a first view of the hardware architecture as a starting point of the refinement flow toward implementation, just after hardware software partitioning. Since this partitioning often leads to the reuse of existing components as well as the definition of new components, the goal of our profile is to provide both a strong IP interconnection mechanism and a way to ex-press the specifications permitting to quickly derive the implementation of new components. The following figure illustrates the role of ESL in the workflow.

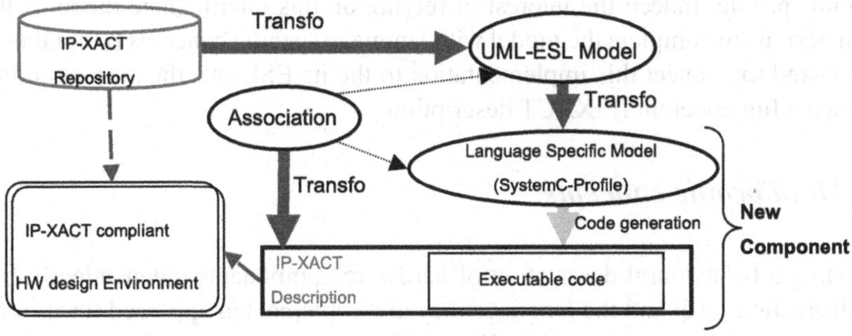

Fig. 3 Transformations workflow around the ESL profile

3.1 *Positioning the profile*

Regarding other initiatives, our objectives may seem similar to the OMGs SoC profile. However, the analysis of this profile led us to conclude that its semantics was very close to the old 2.0 version of SystemC. Particularly, the interconnection semantics, based on *soc_port* that can be *in*, *out* or *inout* and must be connected to *soc_interface* implementations, really constrains the SoC description to the SystemC coding-style (with *sc_in*, *sc_out*, *sc_inout* ports and *sc_interface*). This way to proceed does not provide an efficient way to describe a connection such as a master bus interface, which may be later implemented with a set of *in* and *out* ports. Moreover, the register memory map description of a component is an important concept when describing an IP, being at the frontier of the structure and the functionality of the component (since a register is a structural feature that may influence the way a component will work). This notion unfortunately does not appear in the SoC profile (neither in SystemC).

On the other side, the goal of IP-XACT is to provide a standard XML abstraction of HW components implementation files, whatever the language is (VHDL, Verilog, SystemC, etc.). Hence, they can be handled with standard compliant EDA tools, to favor the reuse of IPs. To do so, the members of the SPIRIT consortium realized a big effort to identify the concepts that represent the characteristics of a component from those that are specific to a particular implementation. Our approach was to select in the IP-XACT grammar the concepts that could be useful in an UML flow, not in order to replace IP-XACT with UML, but to provide a way to use them complementarily. Indeed, UML better fits for the definition of new components, whereas IP-XACT provides specific mechanisms for their instantiation.

The introduction of IP-XACT concepts into UML positions the ESL profile as a pivot language. As illustrated in figure 3, it enables the translation between a IPX-ACT models an UML ones. Moreover, the structural information contained in an ESL model can then be used to transform this model into a specific implementation, either directly to code, either to intermediate language specific profiles, such as the SystemC profile. Indeed the interest of relying on this intermediate model is then that it permits to complete the model with language specific concepts (including behavior) and to connect this implementation to the its ESL specification in order to generate a full coherent IP-XACT description.

3.2 Main profile concepts

Providing a behavioural description of hardware components independently from the abstraction level and the language they are implemented appeared for us a real challenge (that is not addressed by IP-XACT). Consequently, we had to focus and started by the structural description. The concepts we defined can be grouped into three main categories: the identification, the interconnections mechanisms and the register memory map.

The reuse of existing components implies to identify them clearly. To do this, IP-XACT provides the HW component with a unique identifier, based on the four attributes that are: the Vendor name, the Library to which it belongs, the Name of the component, and its last Version (VLNV). It is translated by extending the UML StructuredClass metaclass with a HWComponent stereotype, owning three tagged values (Vendor, Library and Version, the name of the component being mapped on the name attribute of the Class).

IP-XACT interconnection mechanisms is translated to UML using the port and provided/required interface UML concepts. However, IP-XACT introduces the Bus-Definition principle, which defines compatibility rules to connect together master and slave BusInterfaces. Instead of dealing only with in and out ports, the BusInterface represents a connection point of the component defined by a protocol (BusDefinition). We mainly distinguish two types of connection points: a Master- BusIf which initiates communication transactions and a SlaveBusIf that only answers them. The protocol type was expressed with the UML Interface concept, which also has to be uniquely identified with a VLNV. So, we used the provided and required interface mechanisms to express that a MasterBusIf requires the interface and must be only connected to a SlaveBusIf providing it.

The register map description relies on the Definition/Instantiation mechanism provided by the Class/Property couple. As illustrated in Figure 4, a component can instantiate several register maps that are defined by the RegisterMapDef. The latter can instantiate, in turn, several registers, characterized by several attributes such as their address offset, bit-width, multiplicity, access type (read-only, readwrite, write-only) and so on. By the same way, a register definition instantiate fields (set of bits in a register), also characterized by the same kind of attributes. Each definition concept is then mapped on a Class stereotype with the tagged values corresponding to its respective attributes, whereas each instance concept is mapped on a property stereotype, also accompanied of its tagged values.

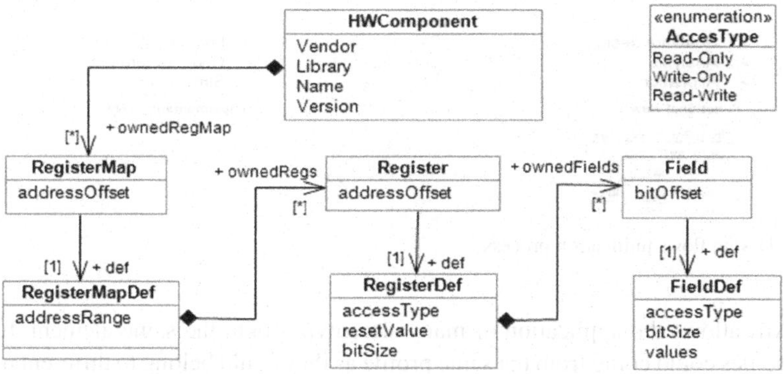

Fig. 4 Register map model

4 Unification of both approaches

Both HRM and ESL profiles permit to describe the structure of a hardware platform. In practice, they are used on the same kind of diagrams: the class diagram for the definition of components, and the composite structure diagram to describe module interconnections, and the hierarchical structure of the IP. However the concepts added to UML via the stereotypes of each profiles are not conflicting, but rather complementary. Whereas HRM brings to the model some information about the functionality of the IP, the ESL profile focuses on the way it will be implemented. On one hand, HRM introduces many stereotypes for each hardware function when ESL profile has a unique HWComponent concept permitting to identify components. On the other hand, HRM does not provide a strong interconnection semantics, with only a single stereotype to describe a connection point (HwEndPoint) when the ESL profile provides stronger connection rules distinguishing different kinds of connection points. The ESL profile also provides a fine grain description of the IP internal structure (e.g. registers) that is not addressed at all by HRM.

HRM will be useful for platform architects who want to analyse the characteristics of the system under construction, and study the mapping of an application on this platform. The ESL profile will then be used to specify and realize this platform, containing enough information to generate a big part of its implementation.

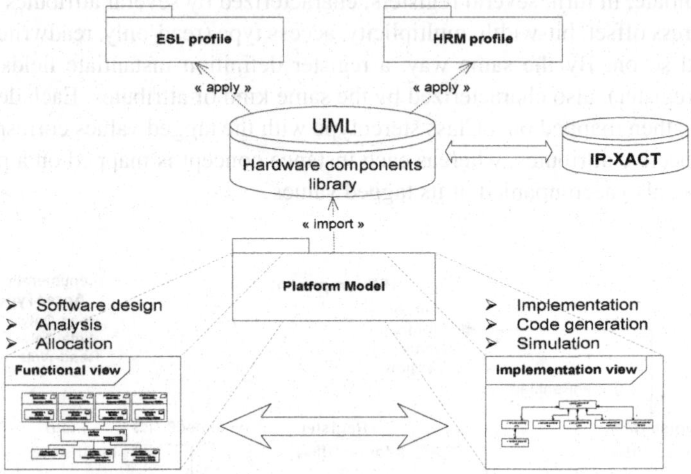

Fig. 5 Design flows unification process

UML allows the application of many stereotypes onto the same element, these stereotypes could come from the same profile as they could belong to different ones. In the first case, it means that the resource is playing many roles in the domain specified with the corresponding profile. While in the second case, it is an adequate way to merge concepts coming from different domains in the same model. In fact, we will unify different concerns that are defined in unconnected profiles into one complete hardware model, by means of multi-profile application.

The Figure 5 illustrates the development process we propose to manage the unification of design flows. First, we defined an UML library of hardware components on which we applied both ESL and HRM profiles. Each component is annotated with many stereotypes (as shown on Figure 7), there is at least one stereotype from ESL for implementation semantics and one stereotype from HRM for functional ones. This way we are filling a library of models that is conform to IP-XACT. Then, importing this library, the hardware designer may build its hardware platform by arranging and connecting components in an adequate way thanks to ESL stereotypes. Once the platform model is built and thanks to UML, we automatically provide two projections of the platform, one for implementation that only extracts the ESL annotations from the library, and one for functional purposes (e.g. software architecturing) that is HRM-based.

Therefore, two development flows are separated but keep sharing the same model, which means that they keep a strong communication between each-other. Suppose that in an incremental or refinement process, one of the design flows changed the hardware platform model, it will be automatically mirrored on the other flows view.

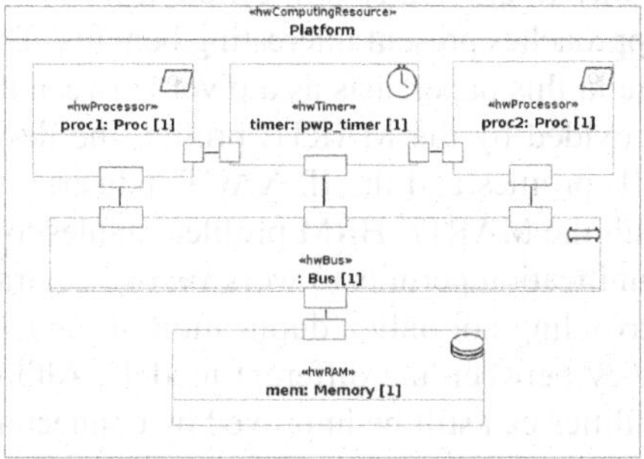

Fig. 6 Hardware platform functional view

Lets do a simple example, we create an SMP hardware platform where two processors proc1 and proc2 are sharing one system bus and the same main RAM memory mem. Figure 6 is a typical functional view of such platform model. It is used by software developers to take into account the multiprocessing aspect by designing a multi-tasks application. This view is also used by system designers for allocation or schedulability analysis, who may map each application task on one of the two processors depending on their strategy criteria and then test the adequation.

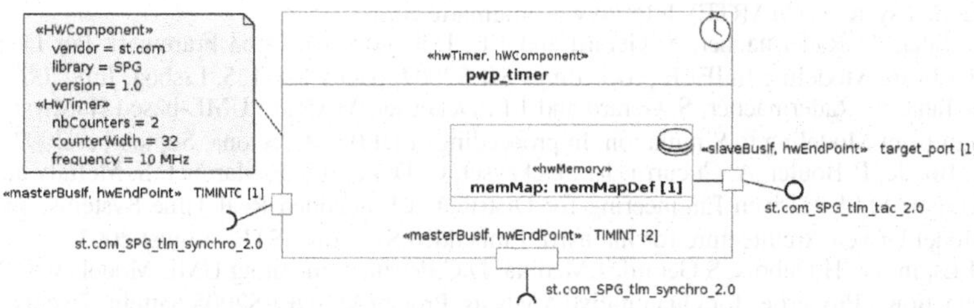

Fig. 7 The hardware component *pwp_timer*

Lets assume that the architectural study led to define a new timer component. The ESL profile will permit to specify its interfaces as well as its register map (Figure 7). The model transformation we developed enables the generation of more than 80% of its UML-SystemC implementation model, including base class inheritance, ports and registers declarations. It also generates the address decoding algorithms in the read/write communication API, containing meaningful debugging messages and taking into account the access type of each registers. After this step, the designer can complete its model, adding the missing behavioural features with for instance the state machines of the SystemC-profile, and generate both the full executable code and the coherent IP-XACT description. The latter allows handling this new IP in any IP-XACT compliant CAD tools.

5 Conclusion

We have presented a way to efficiently join different flows of the SoC design for which model-based approaches present interesting benefits. The ESL profile, introduced for the first time in this paper, acts as a pivot between three key aspects: the functional analysis provided by the MARTE profile, the design approaches with language-specific UML profiles and the IP-XACT industrial standard. Its level of details, compatible with the MARTE-HRM profile, enables to use both of them on a single model. This unification permits to work on one central model where three were needed before, avoiding not only a duplication of modelling efforts, but also the risk of inconsistency between the different models. Although we believe that the automation possibilities can still be improved by connecting our approach with higher level specifications processes, the efficient integration of different industrial standards we have presented in this paper let us foresee a soon adoption of this approach in a real industrial context.

References

1. Object Management Group, UML profile for Schedulability, Performance and Time (SPT), Version 1.1. OMG Document, 05-01-02.
2. Avionics Architecture Description Language Standards Document (AADL), http://www.aadl.info.
3. Object Management Group, UML profile for Modeling and Analysis of Real-Time and Embedded systems (MARTE), http://www.omgmarte.com.
4. S. Taha, A. Radermacher, S. Gerard and J-L. Dekeyser. An Open Framwork For Detailed Hardware Modeling In IEEE proceedings SIES2007, pages 118-125, Lisboa, July 2007.
5. S. Taha, A. Radermacher, S. Gerard and J-L. Dekeyser. MARTE: UML-based Hardware Design from Modeling to Simulation. In proceedings FDL07, Barcelona, September 2007.
6. L. Bonde, P. Boulet, A. Cucurru, J-L. Dekeyser, C. Dumoulin, P. Marquet, S. Meftaly and M. Samyn, Model Driven Engineering for Distributed Embedded Real-Time Systems, chapter Model Driven Architecture for Intensive Embedded Systems, ISTE, August 2005.
7. H.Espinoza, H.Dubois, S.Gerard, J.Medina, D.C.Petriu. Annotating UML Models with Non-Functional Properties for Quantitative Analysis, Proc of MODELS2005 Sattelite Events, Lecture Notes in Computer Science, Springer, 2006.
8. Y. Wang, X.G. Zhou, B. Zhou, L. Liang and C.-L. Peng. A MDA based SoC Modeling Approach using UML and SystemC. Proceedings of the Sixth IEEE International Conference on Computer and Information Technology (CIT'06)
9. T. Schattkowsky, J. Hendrik Hausmann, G. Engels. Using UML Activities for System-on-Chip Design and Synthesis, In proceedings of MoDELS 2006, Genova, Italy October 2006
10. Q. Zhu, R. Oishi and T. Hasegawa, T. Nakata, Integrating UML into SoC Design Process, DATE '05: Proceedings of the conference on Design, Automation and Test in Europe
11. W. Mueller, A. Rosti, S. Bocchio, E. Riccobene, P. Scandurra, W. Dehaene, Y. Vanderperren, UML for ESL design: basic principles, tools, and applications, ICCAD '06: Proceedings of the 2006 IEEE/ACM international conference on Computer-aided design
12. Riccobene, E; Scandurra, P.; Rosti, A.; Bocchio, S., A model-driven design environment for embedded systems, Design Automation Conference, 2006

Expressing Environment Assumptions and Real-time Requirements for a Distributed Embedded System with Shared Variables

Simon Tjell and João M. Fernandes

Abstract In a distributed embedded system, it is often necessary to share variables among its computing nodes to allow the distribution of control algorithms. It is therefore necessary to include a component in each node that provides the service of variable sharing. For that type of component, this paper discusses how to create a Colored Petri Nets (CPN) model that formally expresses the following elements in a clearly separated structure: (1) assumptions about the behavior of the environment of the component, (2) real-time requirements for the component, and (3) a possible solution in terms of an algorithm for the component. The CPN model can be used to validate the environment assumptions and the requirements. The validation is performed by execution of the model during which traces of events and states are automatically generated and evaluated against the requirements.

1 Introduction

In this paper, we describe an approach to requirements engineering using Colored Petri Nets that has been devised during an industrial case study concerning an automated hospital bed. A control system allows the bed to be adjusted into different positions by moving the sections on which the mattress rests. The control system depends on transparent sharing of variables among a group of embedded nodes. For this purpose, a communication component has been developed and, in this paper, we focus on the documentation and validation of the requirements for this component.

Fig. 1 shows a simplified overview of the control system. The system consists of a collection of autonomous embedded nodes, connected by a communication bus. Each node is physically connected to a collection of actuators ($A_{1...3}$) and sensors

Simon Tjell
Department of Computer Science, University of Aarhus, Denmark

João M. Fernandes
Departamento de Informática, Universidade do Minho, Portugal

Please use the following format when citing this chapter:

Tjell, S. and Fernandes, J.M., 2008, in IFIP International Federation for Information Processing, Volume 271; *Distributed Embedded Systems: Design, Middleware and Resources*; Bernd Kleinjohann, Lisa Kleinjohann, Wayne Wolf; (Boston: Springer), pp. 79–88.

($S_{1...2}$) that are controlled and monitored by local applications ($App_{1...5}$). The control system is distributed, because an application running in one node is able to monitor sensors and control actuators connected to any node with the limitation that each actuator is controlled by exactly one application. Remote monitoring and control is made possible by a collection of shared variables. A variable value can be used for (1) the current reading of a sensor (e.g. an angle or a push button), (2) the current output for an actuator (e.g. the displacement of a linear actuator), or (3) a link between two applications. Two kinds of variable instances exist: originals and copies. A variable original exists in the node where new values to the variable is written by a locally running application. One example could be that App_2 in $Node_1$ periodically reads a current from the S_1 sensor and writes the measurement to the Var_2 variable original. In $Node_2$, the application App_3 relies on the readings of S_1 for its task of controlling the A_2 actuator. For this reason, $Node_2$ houses a variable copy instance of Var_2 that is kept updated to have the same value as the variable original and thus providing the input from S_1 to App_3.

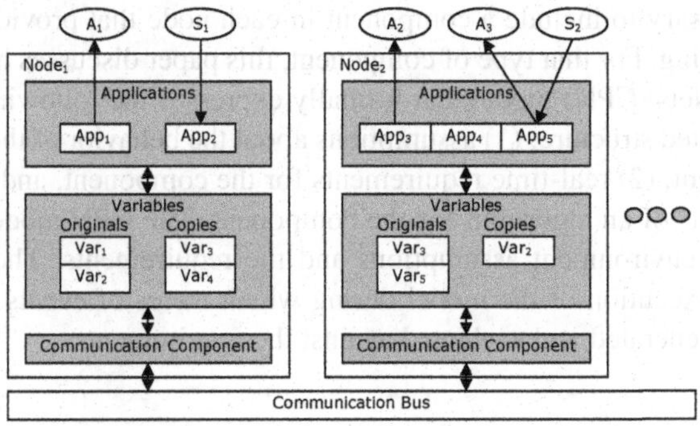

Fig. 1 Informal system overview

The task of keeping variable copies updated with the values of their matching variable originals is handled by the communication component that exists in each node. Messages about variable values are exchanged among the communication component instances through the communication bus. The work presented in this paper focuses on the requirements for the communication component. The approach we present allows a collection of requirements to be represented formally in combination with formal representation of the behavioral assumptions about the environment of the system. We will use the following requirement (Req. 1) as an example: *For any variable copy* v_C *related to a variable original* v_O*, the following must be satisfied if a warm-up period of 10000 ms. since system start has passed: if the value of* v_O *has been stable (i.e. the same) for a coherent period of least 50 ms.,* v_C *must have the same value. The maximum delay allowed before the value of* v_C *reflects that of* v_O *is 500 ms.*

2 The CPN Model

This section presents an approach to developing a CPN model that contains a formal representation of (1) the assumed behavior of the environment of the communication component, (2) the real-time requirements, and (3) a possible solution satisfying the requirements (i.e. an initial design for the communication component). The approach extends previous work [3, 10, 11] by the introduction of explicitly expressed real-time requirements and validation of these.

CPN is a formal modeling language with a graphical representation. It is a high-level extension of standard Petri Nets to which it adds: complex data types for token values (allowing distinction of tokens and modeling of data manipulation), a programming language for guard expression and data manipulation, hierarchical constructs, and real-time modeling through timestamps on tokens. The CPN language is supported by CPN Tools [1], which provides a graphical modeling environment where models are developed and experimented with through simulation and state space analysis. The main concepts of the modeling language will be introduced in the description of the CPN model in this section. Further details are found in [7].

The CPN model presented here is hierarchical and has the structure of a tree in which the nodes are modules and the edges are connections between modules. The root node is called the top module and is shown in Fig. 2. The module contains four *substitution transitions* (double-edged rectangles) connected by arcs to four places (ellipses) through which interaction and observation is possible. Both the arcs and the places carry inscriptions. A substitution transition represents an instance of a module which may be found in multiple instances throughout the model. A module is itself a CPN structure that may contain further levels of substitution transitions which allows the model to be structured using many hierarchical levels. In the top module, the substitution transitions represent domains. The places represent collections of shared phenomena about which the domains communicate. A shared phenomenon is either a state or an event, which is controlled by exactly one domain but may be observed by multiple domains. A domain controls a phenomenon if it causes it to happen in the case of an event or cause it to change in the case of a state.

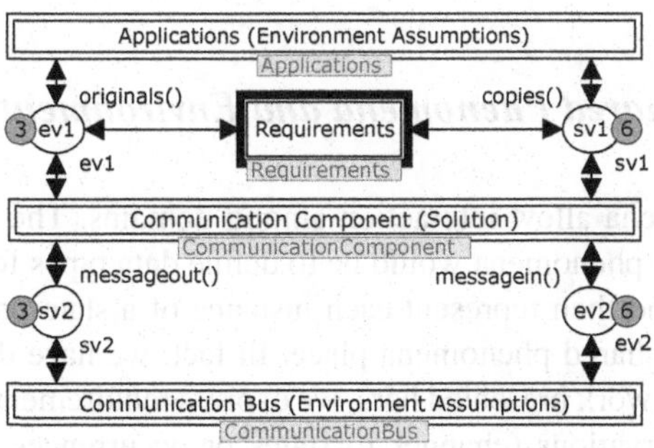

Fig. 2 The top module

The shared phenomena places carry two kinds of inscriptions: color set definitions (`ev1`, `sv1`, `ev2`, and `ev2`) and initial markings (`originals()`, `copies()`, etc.). The color set definition of a place specifies the data type of the tokens that are allowed to exist in the place. The names of the color sets match those defined in the reference model introduced in [4]: the color sets `ev1` and `ev2` contain visible phenomena controlled by the environment (variable originals and incoming messages from the bus respectively) while the color sets `sv1` and `sv2` contain those controlled by the communication component (variable copies and outgoing messages from the nodes respectively). In addition to the visible/shared phenomena, all domains contain collections of hidden and locally controlled phenomena. The initial marking definition of a place tells which tokens will exist in a place in its initial state - for state phenomena, this initialization value will be the initial value of the state and for event phenomena it will typically be a token value representing the information that no events of a given type have been generated before the initial state of the model. The actual contents of these phenomena places will be introduced in Section 2.1.

The top module captures a description of how we have chosen to structure our assumptions about the environment in which our problem and its possible solution is found. The top level module is structured in the same way as a Jackson Problem Diagram [6] and can be described in the following way: *the problem is to develop a communication component that, given the environment assumptions about the behavior of the applications and the communication bus, performs the task of keeping the variable copies updated to match the changing values of the variable originals in a way that satisfies the requirements.*

The top module contains a representation of the requirements connected to two shared phenomena places (`ev1` and `sv1`). This connection implies that the requirements be expressed in terms of the phenomena found in `ev1` and `sv1` - the variable originals and copies. Implicitly, this tells us that requirements cannot be expressed in terms of messages being exchanged through the communication bus since the substitution transition has no connection to these phenomena places. The top module represents the structure of the domains seen from one node and the modeling language allows us to use this structure to represent the behavior of a parameterized number of concurrently operating nodes.

2.1 Modeling Shared Phenomena and Environment Assumptions

The shared phenomena allow interaction among domains. The trivial approach to modeling the shared phenomena would be to define data types for events and states of different kinds and then represent each instance of a state or an event as an individual token in a shared phenomena place. In fact, we have done so in previous works [3, 10]. In the work presented here, we express requirements over timed traces of phenomena observations (changes to states or occurrences of events) and we therefore need a slightly richer representation of shared phenomena in the places, namely one that preserves the history of phenomena observations rather than just

Listing 1 Definition of the `Trace` color set

```
colset NodeID = int with 1..NumberOfNodes;
colset State =
 union VariableOriginalValue:VariableValue+VariableCopyValue:VariableCopyValue;
colset Event =
 union MessageInValue:VariableValue + MessageOutValue:VariableValue;
colset PhenomenonID = union
 VariableOriginalID:VariableID + VariableCopyID:VariableID +
 MessageOutID:VariableID + MessageInID:VariableID;
colset Phenomenon = union State:State + NewEvent:Event + OldEvent:Event;
colset TimedPhenomenon = product Phenomenon *  Timestamp;
colset Phenomena = list TimedPhenomenon;
colset Trace = product NodeID * PhenomenonID * Phenomena timed;
```

snapshots. For this purpose, the `Trace` color set has been defined (Listing 1). This listing is an example of declarations in the CPN model expressed in terms of the built-in functional language CPN ML - a variant of Standard ML. The `Trace` color set is a superset of all the color sets found in Fig. 2 (`ev1`, `sv1`, etc.).

The listing contains the definitions of the two kinds of phenomena (states and events), introduces timestamped phenomena, and defines a trace to be a triple containing (1) the identity of a node, (2) the identity of a phenomenon, and (3) a list of timestamped phenomena occurrences/changes. The `PhenomenonID` color set is a union type of a collection of different identifiers. This is practical since some phenomena may need to be identified using an index and a name, while others may be more appropriately identified using an enumerated value or a string. The union type approach is also used for the phenomenon values: this is again practical because it makes it possible to use different data types of varying complexity to represent different phenomena. An event is either old or new: a `NewEvent` element is used to represent an event that has occurred but has not yet been observed while an `OldEvent` represents an event that has been observed. This makes it possible to ensure that the occurrence of an event is only detected once in each observing node. When an observable phenomenon occurs in a domain, this is recorded by adding an element to one or more trace tokens (one token exists per observing node).

The addition of elements to traces is performed using two functions `state` and `event`. In the case of the occurrence of an event, a `NewEvent` element is added. In the case of a state change, a new element is only added if the state indeed changed to a new value. In both cases, the new element is associated with a timestamp indicating the model time at which the phenomenon occurred.

Following the structure found in Fig. 2, the environment of the communication component consists of the applications and the communication bus. The communication component interfaces with these two domains through phenomena related to the variables (originals and copies) and messages (outgoing and incoming) respectively. A description of the structure of the environment is captured in the top module (Fig. 2), while description of the assumed behavior of the domains environment is found in the `Applications` and `CommunicationBus` modules.

The `Applications` module (not shown) describes assumptions about how the applications in the nodes write new values to local variable originals and about the timing of these write operations. The `CommunicationBus` module (Fig. 3) describes assumptions about how messages are exchanged between nodes with potential loss of messages in the case of physical connection problems. The module is connected to the top module through the places marked by I/O labels. These places are connected to the places with matching names in the top module. In this way, it is possible to describe the details of the communication bus inside the module while avoiding too many possibly confusing details in the top module. Whenever a message is sent by a node (modeled in the `Communication Component` module), a `NewEvent` element is added to a trace token found in the `sv2` place. The `NodeID` in this trace token matches that of the sending node. When the element is added to the trace token, it becomes visible to the `CommunicationBus` module through the `sv2` place.

The semantics of CPN is based on the notions of *enabling* and *occurrence*. For example, the `Detect Message` transition (Fig. 3) is said to be enabled whenever its input place (`sv2`) contains a token that satisfies the constraints of the transition: (1) the pattern expression in the input arc, and (2) the guard expression. The guard expression is seen in brackets in the left-hand side of the transition and it specifies that the transition can only become enabled if the trace contains a new (not yet observed) event. When the transition is enabled it may occur (or *fire*) causing the consumption of one token from the input place (`sv2`) and the production of a collection of tokens in the output places (`sv2` and `Outgoing`). The trace token is updated and placed back in the `sv2` place. The update consists in using the `oldevent` function to change the type of the observed message event from a `NewEvent` to an `OldEvent` element (preserving the parameter values). The consumption and production of the token to the `sv2` place can be seen as a data manipulation operation. In the `Outgoing` place, a collection of tokens is produced by the `broadcast` function: one token representing a message for each receiving node - all with the same variable value information. From the `Outgoing` place, tokens can be consumed individually by either the `Loose Message` transition (modeling a physical connection being unavailable) or the `Transmit Message` transition (modeling a message being successfully delivered to a receiving node). In the later case, the `event` function is used to add a `NewEvent` element containing the variable information to the trace related to the node in which the message is received.

The `CommunicationBus` module also shows an example of how assumptions about the timing properties of the environment are modeled: the `Transmit Message` transition carries a delay inscription (`@+MessageDelay`) indicating that each successful transmission of a message takes `MessageDelay` time units. In this case, the

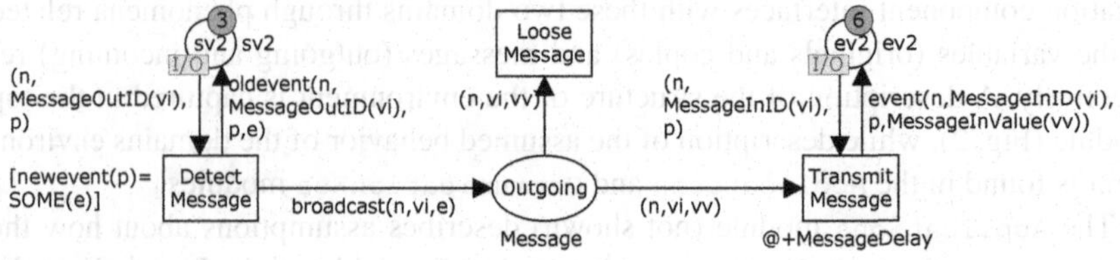

Fig. 3 Environment assumptions expressed in the `CommunicationBus` module

delay is a constant (the average assumed delay), but for a more detailed modeling of this assumption, a stochastic distribution function could have been applied.

The modules described here explicitly represent our assumptions about the behavior and structure of the environment in which the communication component must provide a solution to the problem of maintaining the consistency between the variables.

2.2 Expressing Requirements

In the introduction, Req. 1 was informally presented. Here, we will give an example of how this requirements has been formally expressed in the CPN model using the concepts of Duration Calculus [12]. As seen in Fig. 2, the model contains a `Requirements` module (shown in Fig. 4). This module contains the expression of all requirements about the communication component. The requirement transitions are connected to the phenomena places using double-headed arcs. Informally, this means that the transitions are observing but not modifying the contents of the phenomena places - i.e. the requirements are expressed using transitions that monitor the traces of the shared phenomena (in this case the variables).

The `Requirements` module contains the `Requirements Satisfied` place that initially holds three tokens identifying three requirements (`Req1`, `Req2`, and `Req3`) of which the first was described informally in the introduction. The module also has three transitions with guards containing negations of the three requirements. If a requirement is *not* satisfied, the respective transition will become enabled. If a requirement transition occurs during the execution of the CPN model, the token identifying the requirement is removed from the `Requirements Satisfied` place. By monitoring the contents of this place after or during execution, we are able to detect situations in which the solution fails to satisfy the requirements. We briefly discuss how execution of the CPN model is used for experimenting with a possible solution in Section 2.3.

As described in Section 2.1, the phenomena are recorded in traces in which the elements carry timestamps that record when the phenomena happened - i.e. when a state changed or when an event occurred. The requirements are expressed about the

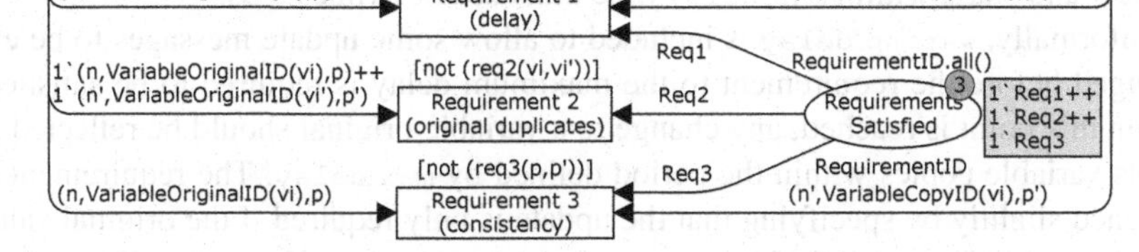

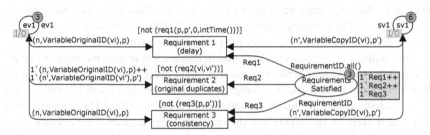

Fig. 4 The `Requirements` module

Listing 2 The `requirement1` function

```
1  fun req1(trace1,trace2,t1,t2) =
2  let val original_trace = intervals(t1,t2,trace1)
3  val copy_trace = intervals(t1,t2,trace2)
4  val max_delay = 500   val min_length = 50   val warmup_delay = 10000
5  in forall original_trace (fn(t1,t2,v) =>
6    implies(t2>warmup_delay andalso t2-t1>=min_length
7          andalso upper_bound(copy_trace)>t2+max_delay,
8      exists copy_trace (fn(t1',t2',v')=>
9      (t1'>t1 andalso v'=v andalso t1'-t1<max_delay))
10 )) end;
```

variable copies and originals. For this reason, the transitions in the `Requirements` module are connected to the phenomena places holding the traces about variable copies and originals through interface places.

We now focus on the definition of Req. 1 seen in Listing 2. The `req1` function is used as a guard expression for the matching requirement transition in Fig. 4. The function returns *true* if and only if Req. 1 is satisfied for a trace of a specific variable original (`trace1`) and a trace of a matching variable copy (`trace2`) within a timespan (`t1`...`t2`). Fig. 4 shows how pattern matching in the input arcs to the `Requirement 1` transition is applied to specify that the variable ID of the traces for the variable original and the variable copy should match (bound to the variable `vi`) while the node IDs (bound to `n` and `n'`) and the traces (bound to `p` and `p'`) may (and will) differ. The satisfaction of Req. 1 is evaluated by comparing the trace of a variable original to one trace representing a matching variable copy. For a given variable ID, there is only one trace for a variable original while multiple traces representing variable copies may exist (one per reading node). The evaluation is performed one copy trace at a time and each evaluation is performed using the `req1` function (Listing 2). Line 1 gives the signature of the function. In lines 2 and 3, the `intervals` function is used to generate lists of intervals based on the traces for easier traversal. Line 4 defines constants used in the representation of the requirement found in lines 5-10. The `forall` function is used for universal quantification over the `original_trace` (line 5). This value is a list of intervals defined by triples: start time of an interval (`t1`), end time of the interval (`t2`), and the state value within the interval (`v`). For all intervals (elements), the `implies` function is used to require that if the interval ends after a `warmup_delay` and is longer that `min_length` and the last interval of the copy trace ends after `t2+max_delay` (lines 6-7), then there should exist an interval in the copy trace (`(t1',t2',v')`) that starts after `t1` and has the value `v` and starts within `max_delay` time units after `t1` (lines 8-9).

Informally, `warmup_delay` is included to allow some update messages to be exchanged before the requirement to the maximum delay is required to be satisfied. When this point is reached, any change to a variable original should be reflected in all its variable copies within the period defined by `max_delay`. The requirement is softened slightly by specifying that the update is only required if the original value remains stable for a period of at least `min_length` time units. Hence, transient values of an original are not required to be reflected in all matching copies.

2.3 Experimenting with Possible Solutions

Until now, following the suggestions of [5], we have deliberately avoided discussing any concrete approaches to solving the problem of maintaining consistency throughout the variables. Instead, we have focused on the environment assumptions and the real-time requirements - i.e. constraints that apply to any possible solution we can think of. Now, we will briefly discuss how the fact that the CPN model is executable makes it possible to experiment with explicitly expressed solutions while monitoring the satisfaction of the requirements through the effects on (part of) the environment. A possible solution is expressed in the `CommunicationComponent` module of the CPN model (Fig. 2). The details of this module are not shown.

The overall purpose of the communication component is to handle the task of maintaining consistency between variable originals and their copies by exchanging messages through the communication bus. Basically, two alternative approaches are possible: event- and time-triggered communication. In an event-triggered approach, the communication component transmits a message containing a new value whenever the value of a variable original is changed by a local application. In a time-triggered approach, the communication component periodically transmit messages containing the current values of local variable originals. In both cases, the values of local variable copies are updated with the values found in incoming broadcast messages received by the communication components.

We have experimented with a solution based on the principles of *Soft State Signaling* [9] that combines a time-triggered messaging scheme with special validity tags on the variables copies. A variable copy is tagged *invalid* if the periodic update messages are not received for a predefined period of time.

In CPN Tools, the CPN model can be executed in an interactive manner - i.e. allowing the user to select transitions to occur and their parameters. The model can also be executed more freely in which case the tool will make free and fair choices of transitions to simulate different scenarios. In addition to this, the *monitor* mechanism can be applied to give an alert (stop simulation) if a global state of the model is reached where the `Requirements Satisfied` place (Fig. 4) does not contain all requirement ID tokens. This is useful, because such a situation would indicate that one or more of the requirement transitions have fired, meaning that a requirement was not found to be satisfied in a state reached during the simulation of the model. Whenever a requirement is found not to be satisfied during a simulation, the task is to investigate whether the cause is to be found in the environment assumptions (or their descriptions), too strict requirements, the proposed solution, or a combination.

3 Conclusions and Future Work

Several authors have already proposed the adoption of Petri Nets for modeling the structure and behavior of distributed embedded systems, and in particular for verifying real-time requirements. For example, [2] discusses a Petri Net-based approach to verification of embedded systems and introduces a systematic procedure to translating the descriptions into linear hybrid automata in order to use existing model checking tools. A complete design flow based on high-level Petri Nets for real-time embedded systems for modeling both discrete and continuous parts of the systems by the event-based Petri net semantics is presented in [8]. The Petri Net model is used for formal verification and hardware/software partitioning purposes. This paper extends (and generalizes) the results presented in [11] and also suggests the use of a unique language based on Petri Nets for modeling the system and its environment, but the focus is on validating the real-time requirements expressed in terms of the required effects on the environment caused by the system.

Future work includes making the structuring approach introduced here more generally applicable by formally defining it as a structural subclass of CPNs with unmodified semantics. Such a definition could also serve as a foundation for the definition of refinement operations that could be used for refining requirements into specifications taking the environment assumptions into account. It would also be interesting, for example, to look at how environment entities could be modeled using CPN representations of differential equations based on the principles of [8].

References

1. CPN Tools. `http://daimi.au.dk/CPNTools`.
2. L. A. Cortés, P. Eles, and Z. Peng. Verification of Embedded Systems Using a Petri Net Based Representation. In *ISSS 2000*.
3. J. M. Fernandes, J. B. Jørgensen, and S. Tjell. Requirements Engineering for Reactive Systems: Coloured Petri Nets for an Elevator Controller. In *APSEC 2007*.
4. C. A. Gunter, E. L. Gunter, M. Jackson, and P. Zave. A Reference Model for Requirements and Specifications. *IEEE Software*, 17(3), 2000.
5. I. J. Hayes, M.A. Jackson, and C.B. Jones. Determining the Specification of a Control System from that of its Environment. In *FME 2003*.
6. M. Jackson. *Problem Frames — Analyzing and Structuring Software Development Problems*. Addison-Wesley, 2001.
7. K. Jensen, L. M. Kristensen, and L. Wells. Coloured Petri Nets and CPN Tools for Modelling and Validation of Concurrent Systems. *STTT*, 9(3-4), 2007.
8. B. Kleinjohann, J. Tacken, and C. Tahedl. Towards a Complete Design Method for Embedded Systems Using Predicate/Transition-Nets. In *CHDL 1997*.
9. S. Raman and S. McCanne. A Model, Analysis, and Protocol Framework for Soft State-Based Communication. In *SIGCOMM 1999*.
10. S. Tjell. Distinguishing Environment and System in Coloured Petri Net Models of Reactive Systems. In *SIES 2007*.
11. S. Tjell. Model-Based Analysis of a Windmill Communication System. In *DIPES 2006*.
12. C. Zhou, C. A. R. Hoare, and A. P. Ravn. A Calculus of Durations. *Inf. Process. Lett.*, 40(5), 1991.

The Components Data Flow Machine: An Intermediate Modeling Format to Support the Design of Automobiles E/E Systems Architectures

Augustin Kebemou and Ina Schieferdecker

Abstract The design of the architectures of automobiles E/E (Electric/Electronic) systems consists in the allocation of the hardware platform and the distribution of the computing and the communication loads of the application software within the allocated hardware. This operation is called the partitioning. Following the actual model-driven design schemes, the input of the partitioning is generally a functional specification of the system under development in the form of communicating software components that must be mapped on the allocated hardware platform. However, even though these models are sufficient to describe the structure of a system, they are not good enough to support a CAD-supplied partitioning. They lack the facilities needed to support the analysis of the data flow and to investigate the closeness between the elements of the specification, thus to support the mapping. In this paper, we define the Components Data Flow Machine (*CDFM*), a modeling format that is defined to support the design of automobiles E/E systems architectures. The *CDFM* defines the semantics of a synthesis model that results from a transformation of standard models like SysML, EAST ADL or AUTOSAR models.

Key words: automotive systems, architecture, design, partitioning, mapping

1 Introduction

With the increasing demand for electronic-actuated features in automobiles, two solutions are broadly proposed to optimize the cost of new vehicles. The first solution

Augustin Kebemou
Fraunhofer Institute for Software and Systems Engineering (ISST)
Mollstrasse 1, 10178 Berlin, Germany

Ina Schieferdecker
Fraunhofer Institute for Open Communication Systems (FOKUS)
Kaiserin-Augusta-Allee 31, 10589 Berlin, Germany

Please use the following format when citing this chapter:

Kebemou, A. and Schieferdecker, I., 2008, in IFIP International Federation for Information Processing, Volume 271; *Distributed Embedded Systems: Design, Middleware and Resources*; Bernd Kleinjohann, Lisa Kleinjohann, Wayne Wolf; (Boston: Springer), pp. 89–100.

proposes to develop flexible and particularly portable automotive software components. The second solution is to reduce the amount of hardware in automobiles' E/E systems. In reality, these two options are complementary since the efficient usage of the hardware resources is achieved by both a goal-oriented definition of the architecture of the E/E system and an advantageous resource allocation policy. This is the duty of the partitioning. The optimal partitioning must minimize the quantity of processing units, memories and cables that are needed to execute the functionality of the system, to store its data and its software code and to realize the inter-device communication. The partitioning involves three activities: The allocation, the mapping and the deployment. The allocation is concerned with the design of the physical configuration of the system. This consists in the definition of the number of devices (ECUs, sensors, actuators, gateways), the definition of their individual equipments (processing units, memories, internal buses, etc.), their positioning within the physical system (i.e. the topology of the system) and the choice of the communication media and protocols for the inter-device communications. The mapping deals with the distribution of the working load of the system's application among the available devices while the deployment is the task of distributing the individual computation power of the devices among the tasks and assigning the available memory space and the intra-devices communication bandwidths to the system's data. During the mapping, each functional component of the system is assigned to one or several devices depending on the required redundancy grade of its implementation. Two functional components that are assigned to different devices must communicate through the inter-devices communication channels. As these are mostly bus systems running frame-oriented communication protocols like CAN, MOST, FlexRay, LIN, etc., the mapping must also pack the inter-devices communication data in the communication frames in the most economical way.

Thus, a good partitioning must assign closely related components, e.g. highly communicating components, to the same device in order to minimize the inter-devices communication and maximize the hardware sharing [1]. Currently, this is done manually by highly experienced system architects. They usually add the new software components on the existing system without changing the precedent contents of the devices. When the existing devices are overloaded, they generally decide to add new devices. This optimistic approach of the partitioning is justified by the fact that the existing systems are well-functioning and reliable configurations with stable communication matrices. A new design of the system's architecture is practically equivalent to a design from scratch, economically unsupportable in this fast evolving industry where the time to market is vital for each OEM. But, the direct consequence of this practice is the excessive number of buses and processors installed in the vehicles. Moreover, without efficient CAD techniques to support the partitioning, unexperienced designers cannot expect to design good systems. A CAD-supported partitioning will allow automotive systems architects to investigate and compare different architectural options. This necessitates a global view of the system's specification and a reasonable degree of portability of the software components at the system-level. With the implementation of the concepts developed within the AUTOSAR[2], standard and platform-independent software components will enlarge the solution space of the partitioning of automobiles' E/E systems and thus, will allow the consideration of much more architectural options and enable the design of more cost-sensitive E/E systems than today. The E/E design can take advantage of this only if it is provided CAD-support for the partitioning.

2 Problem Presentation

However, a CAD-supplied partitioning tool needs a model that can enable the analysis of the data flow and highlight the closeness between the elements of the specification. This is not provided by the mostly used modeling formats, e.g. SysML[3], EAST ADL[4] and AUTOSAR[5] models. Although these prominent meta-models optimally describe the logical structure of E/E systems, they cannot be used to synthesize the inter-components communication or to determine the closeness between the elements of a model as it is needed to make the mapping decisions. For example, there are generally multiple connectors and interfaces joining two communicating components, making the tracing of the communication paths extremely difficult for a computer system. To solve this problem, we defined a modeling solution called the *FN* -for "Functional Network"- that copes with the deficits of the usual automotive modeling solutions concerning the requirements for a CAD-supplied partitioning such as the screening of the communication paths and the traceability of the communication data. The *FN* is an intuitive modeling solution that inherits the concepts of interconnected software components with ports and interfaces from UML, SysML and EAST ADL, plus the atomicity and portability principles defined within the AUTOSAR. But, in contrast to an AUTOSAR VFB (Virtual Functional Bus), the *FN* interfaces allow clear screening of the communication paths and an easy tracing of the data flowing on each connector by transforming for example the branched connectors found in a VFB into single P2P connectors.

Each *FN* model can be formally defined with a quintuple $\langle F,R,P,I,C\rangle$ as follows: F (Functions) is the set of all the behavioral components in the model, i.e. $F = \{F_1,F_2,...,F_f\}$ where each F_i represents a functional component, $i,f \in \mathbb{N}$; R (Repositories) is the set of all the data components in the specification, i.e. $R = \{R_1,R_2,...,R_r\}$ where each R_i represents a data component, $i,r \in \mathbb{N}$; P (Ports) is the set of input and output ports, i.e. $P = \{P_1,P_2,...,P_p\}$ $i,p \in \mathbb{N}$ with $P = IPorts \oplus OPorts$ (i.e. Input ports $\oplus$ Output ports); I (Interfaces) is the set of all the port interfaces in the specification, i.e. $I = \{I_1,I_2,...,I_p\}$ where each I_i represents the interface of the port i, $i,p \in \mathbb{N}$; C (Connectors) is the set of all the connectors in the specification, i.e. $C = \{C_1,C_2,...,C_l\}$ where each C_i represents a connector, $i,l \in \mathbb{N}$; Each component F_i or R_i is defined by its internal behavior *beh* and its interface *Int*, i.e. each component is completely defined by a tuple $< beh,Int >$ with $Int \subseteq P$ and *beh* is defined by the runnables and the RTEEs (Runtime Environment Events); Each port P_i is defined by its behavior *beh* and its interface *Int*, i.e. $P_i =< beh,Int >$ with $P_i.Int \in I$; For each connector C_i, $\exists src \in OPort$, $dst \in IPort$ and *Int* so that $C_i =< src,dst,Int >$ where $C_i.src$ is the port source of the connector C_i, $C_i.dst$ is the port destination of the connector C_i and $C_i.Int$ is the set of the data that might flow on C_i; $C_i.Int = C_i.src.Int \cap C_i.dst.Int$.

Due to its P2P conception of ports inter-connections, the *FN* enables the production of specifications that are more compliant with the requirements of an automatic partitioning than the standard modeling solutions. Nevertheless, the *FN* does not provide any advanced feature to synthesize the communication and extract the closeness values between the elements of a specification. This can be achieved with a formal representation format on which efficient mathematical tools can be used to analyze and quantify the relationships between the elements of the functional specification of a system. We call our solution the "Components Data Flow Machine (*CDFM*)". The *CDFM* is a synthesis model that enables the automatic analysis of the inter-components communication, the determination of the closeness values between them and the assignment of the exchanged data to the communication frames. A more detailed specification of the requirements for such a synthesis model concerning the partitioning of automobiles E/E systems is given in section 3. Then, the *CDFM* and the rules that govern the translation of *FN* models into *CDFM* models are defined in section 4 and illustrated in section 7 while the annotations of *CDFM* models and their formal definition are presented respectively in section 5 and section 6.

3 Requirements for the synthesis model

The usefulness of a synthesis model is given by its ability to support the intended design task, in the present case, the partitioning. This includes the ability to reflect the system architecture as given in the *FN* input model, the ability to specify the information that is needed for the partitioning and the ability to enable rapid estimation of the partitioning metrics, in particular the closeness between the components. Reflecting the system architecture requires that the synthesis model must be at least at the same level of granularity with the input model. Enabling rapid metrics estimations requires that as much information as possible is known before the partitioning begins. Depending on the type of representation used, the formal representations that meet the requirements for the synthesis model can be roughly classified in two groups: Those based on FSMs or Petri nets and those based on graphs. In contrast to graph-based representations that consider a unique system state, FSMs [6] and Petri nets-based representations [7] are powerful in modeling and verifying the dynamics of a system. But, they are obviously not the best representation forms when the architecture of the system is important. The main kinds of architecture-oriented forms of FSMs used in the design of embedded systems include the FSM with data paths (FSMD) [8] and the FSM with Coprocessors (FSMC) [9]. Even these forms cannot reproduce the system's architecture in a useful way. Moreover, they considerably suffer from the state explosion problem.

The most usual graph-based systems representations include data flow graphs (DFG)[10], control flow graphs (CFG), data control flow graphs (DCFG)[11] and task graphs. DFGs are well-featured to describe the data dependencies. CFGs are well-suited to model control-oriented systems, but they provide restricted facilities for the data flow analysis. CDFGs extend the DFG with control nodes. They provide good models for data flow oriented applications whose the control information is important. Task graphs are similar with DFGs in their structure. But, in opposition to DFGs, special types of task graphs may be cyclic or undirected [10, 12]. Like in [13], various special task graph-based modeling formats have been used for problems that are similar to the one presented in this work. In [14], a directed task graph, called access graph, is used to model the accesses (i.e. data exchange) between the functional components of the system, while a similar, but undirected graph, called communication graph is used in [15] to model the communication between a set of tasks. These solutions yield static models that however effectively reproduce the structure and the communication of a system, providing a good basis for our synthesis model.

4 The *CDFM*

The synthesis model is intended to specify the components of a system, their communication and every relevant relationships between them. We defined it as a task graph (V, E, Ω, S) in with each node $v_i \in V$ represents a behavioral or a data component of the corresponding *FN* model. In contrast to *FN* models, it exists only one edge between two nodes of a *CDFM* model. Each edge $e_{ij} = (v_i, v_j) = (v_j, v_i) \in E$ materializes the communication between the *FN* components represented by v_i and v_j. The semantic of such a node is reduced to: "These connected nodes exchange data in some way" , i.e. the direction is ignored by the edge itself. However, transforming multiple and oppositely directed connectors into a single undirected link introduces two problems: Firstly, we need a convenient interpretation of the original connections that will allow to properly capture the data shared between the connected nodes. Secondly, as the edges are undirected, the direction of the communication must be specified somewhere else.

We solved this problem by introducing the concept of tokens in the *CDFM*. A token models a data object that is exchanged between the nodes of a *CDFM* model. The set of the tokens flowing around the graph is Ω. A token $T_{ij}^k \in \Omega$ represents the data object k that is exchanged between two nodes v_i and v_j. A token is unbounded in the dimension and is not supposed to contain any additional information such as the beginning of the token or the end of the token. Independently of the connector through which a data object k is exchanged within a *FN* model, the corresponding token T_{ij}^k is associated with the edge e_{ij} that connects the nodes v_i and v_j. Thus, the set of the tokens associated with an edge models the intensity of the communication between the two nodes. As the edges are undirected, we model the direction of the communication in the tokens, i.e. the direction of a token defines the sense of its transfer. This definition of the *CDFM* leads to the following straightforward transformation of *FN* models into the corresponding synthesis models:

- Each component of a FN model is transformed into a node,
- Each connection of a FN model is transformed into an edge and
- Each data object exchanged between two components of a FN model is transformed into a token.

Note that several mechanisms can be used on this basic modeling format to describe the data exchange procedure. For example, a node can send data by placing it on the dedicated edge, i.e. the token is addressed exclusively to the node connected at the other end of this edge, or the sender can just put the token on its output where it will be collected by the destination node. These two mechanisms are fundamentally different concerning the resulting behavior of the system. The first one processes a peer-to-peer communication while the second one, if not enhanced with restrictive routing rules, is merely adapted to realize broadcast communication since each component that is related with the sender can access the data that is on the sender's output port. Note that it is also conceivable that the sender node pushes the data to the destination and so synchronous and asynchronous communication schemata can be designed. Defining such mechanisms would introduce a dynamical dimension in the specification of the communication in $CDFM$ models. But, as the $CDFM$ is yet not intended to support the simulation, the dynamics of the data exchange and the routing mechanisms will not be discussed in this paper. However, we agree that a token is created as soon as the corresponding data object is emitted. We then say that the token is available. Thus, a token is available at the date of its creation. Note that a token is available solely means that the token can be transfered. However, the date at which a token is sent is not absolutely the date at which it is available. Depending on its freshness requirements, a very hasty token must be transfered as soon as it is available while the transfer date of a less hasty token can be delayed. These concepts are introduced in the $CDFM$ to support the scheduling of the communication and to control the occupation of the communication buses.

In addition to the technical factors of cost optimization such as the communication and the resource usage, the design of an E/E system typically underlies a full range of constraints and strategic concerns that arise from the commercial, the technological, the organizational circumstances of the design as well as the procurement, the production issues, etc. Consequently, some components of the functional model might be required to run on the same device while others are required to run on different devices, e.g. for safety reasons. These relationships between the components typically have heavy consequences on the partitioning and must be specified in the synthesis model. We model them by means of *needs* and *excludes* relations:

- Two nodes v_i and v_j are in a *needs* relationship, i.e. $needs(v_i,v_j)$ is TRUE, if v_i and v_j must be implemented on the same device;
- Two nodes v_i and v_j are in an *excludes* relationship, i.e. $excludes(v_i,v_j)$ is TRUE, if it is forbidden to implement v_i and v_j on the same device.

The *needs* and *excludes* relationships are also defined between the tokens. Note that several similar relationships can be defined on $CDFM$ models. They are managed within the set S. So defined, the $CDFM$ enables the synthesis of the communication, but it does not yet contain the information required to guide the partitioning, i.e. the information on the basis of which the clustering decisions must be made during the mapping and those through which the cost and the quality of the resulting partition can be investigated. This is provided by means of attributes.

5 Annotations for the *CDFM*

Annotations for the nodes: The performance and the cost of a node are determined by its execution time, the frequentness of its execution, the size of the resulting software code or the size of the hardware that should be needed to implement the component. Assuming that a particular hardware unit or a family of hardware units have been identified to implement or to store each component so that the memory needs for the code size and for the stacks or the heaps of its runnables are known (or can be estimated), the attributes of the nodes of a *CDFM* model include:

– The software size (swSize): The total amount of memory required to store the code and the data of the corresponding *FN* component when implemented in software.

– The hardware size (hwSize): The total amount of hardware components that would be used to implement the function of the corresponding component.

– The execution rate (eR): The maximum of the execution rates of the runnables of the corresponding component. The execution rate of a runnable is the mean number of times that it is executed during an activation time of the system.

– The priority (prio): The priority order of the most prioritized runnable of the corresponding component.

– The execution time (eT): The "sum" of the execution times of the runnables of the corresponding component.

Annotations for the edges: The attributes of the edges of a *CDFG* model include:

– The weight (T): The set of tokens that flow over it during an activation period of the system.

– The access frequency (accFreq): The access frequency of the most accessed connector within the corresponding *FN* connection.

– The constraints (cons): Are given by all the consistent sets of all the constraints on the connectors of the corresponding *FN* connection. This include e.g. the latency, the reliability, the security, the safety constraints, etc.

Annotations for the tokens: The most relevant attributes of the tokens include:

– The direction (dir): It defines the sense in which the token is transferred. It is given by the source and the destination nodes of the token.

– The resolution or dimension (res): The number of bits that is needed to encode the corresponding data object.

– The frequency (freq): The mean frequency of emission of the corresponding data object.

– The priority (prio): The priority level that the corresponding data object enjoys in the occupation of a given communication channel.

– The date of occurrence (occur): The date at which the token is available.
– The freshness requirements (fresh): Determine the latest date at which the token must be sent.

– The constraints (cons): The data objects, thus the tokens, may underly some constraints concerning for example their freshness, their safety, their security level, etc.

6 Formal definition of the *CDFM*, model transformation

Given a *FN* model $A = \langle F, R, P, I, C \rangle$ of the functionalities of a E/E system with the components $M = \{M_1, M_2, ..., M_k\} = F \cup R$, the corresponding synthesis model is a graph $G = (V, E, \Omega, S)$, where $V = M$ is the set of the nodes, E is the set of the edges $e_{ij} = (v_i, v_j) = (v_j, v_i)$, Ω is the set of the tokens and S is the set of the relationships induced by the constraints and the strategic concerns of the design over the set of the nodes and the set of the tokens, i.e.

- for each $M_i \in M$ there is a corresponding node $v_i \in V$,
- for each data object k exchanged between two components M_i and M_j there is a corresponding token T_{ij}^k or $T_{ji}^k \in \Omega$,
- each relation between two components (resp. two data objects) also exists between the corresponding nodes (resp. the corresponding tokens), and:

- Each node $v_i = \langle swSize, hwSize, eR, prio, eT \rangle$ where $v_i.swSize$ (resp. $v_i.hwSize$) is the software (resp. the hardware) size of v_i, $v_i.eR$ is the execution rate of v_i, $v_i.prio$ is the priority of v_i, $v_i.eT$ is the execution time of v_i.
- Each edge $e_{ij} = e_{ji} = \langle T, accFreq, cons \rangle$ where $e_{ij}.T = T_{ij} \cup T_{ji}$ is the weight of the edge e_{ij}, i.e. of the edge e_{ji}, where $T_{ij} = \left\{ T_{ij}^k, k \in \mathbb{N} \right\}$ is given by the set of the tokens transferred from node v_i to node v_j and $T_{ji} = \left\{ T_{ji}^k, k \in \mathbb{N} \right\}$ is given by the set of the tokens transferred from node v_j to node v_i (note that $e_{ij}.T = e_{ji}.T$ for all $i, j \in \mathbb{N}$ but $T_{ij} \neq T_{ji}$ for each given pair of nodes i, j), $e_{ij}.accFreq$ is the access frequency of the edge e_{ij}, i.e. of e_{ji} and $e_{ij}.cons$ is the set of constraints on the edge e_{ij}, i.e. on e_{ji}.
- Each token $T_{ij}^k = \langle dir, res, freq, prio, occur, fresh, cons \rangle$ where $T_{ij}^k.dir$ is the direction in which T_{ij}^k flows, (the direction is also given by the foot notation ij of the token), $T_{ij}^k.res$ is the resolution of the token T_{ij}^k, $T_{ij}^k.freq$ is the emission rate of the token T_{ij}^k, $T_{ij}^k.prio$ is the priority of the token T_{ij}^k, $T_{ij}^k.occur$ is the date of occurrence of the token T_{ij}^k, $T_{ij}^k.fresh$ are the freshness requirements on the token T_{ij}^k, $T_{ij}^k.cons$ is the set of the constraints and requirements on the token T_{ij}^k.

The metric that is used to determine the weight of the edges of *CDFM* models is defined as follows: Given a *FN* model A and its corresponding *CDFM* model G, consider the operator $width_{ij}$ that defines the set of connectors of A that are represented by the edge e_{ij} in G (i.e. these are the connectors that relate A_i with A_j). Assume that the operator $srcConnectors(A_i)$ returns the set of connectors for which A_i is the source and the operator $dstConnectors(A_i)$ returns the set of connectors for which A_i is the destination, i.e.:

$srcConnectors(A_i) = \{c \in C | c.src \in A_i.Int\}$ and

$dstConnectors(A_i) = \{c \in C | c.dst \in A_i.Int\}$, then

$width_{ij} = srcConnectors(A_i) \cap dstConnectors(A_j)$ and thus, given two nodes v_i and v_j of G, the weight of e_{ij} (i.e. the set of tokens transferred over the edge e_{ij}) is:

$$e_{ij}.T = T_{ij} \cup T_{ji} = \bigcup_{c \in width_{i,j}} c.Int$$

7 Applications

The figures 1 and 2 illustrate the results of the transformation of FN models into $CDFM$ models. Figure 1 shows a part of the FN model of the ACC (active cruise control) functionality and figure 2 shows the corresponding $CDFM$ model. In the $CDFM$ version, the relationships between the components are clearly identifiable. Each connection is materialized by a single edge and the exchanged data objects are specified in terms of tokens associated each with the corresponding edge so that the magnitude of the communication between the components can be easily estimated and compared with each other.

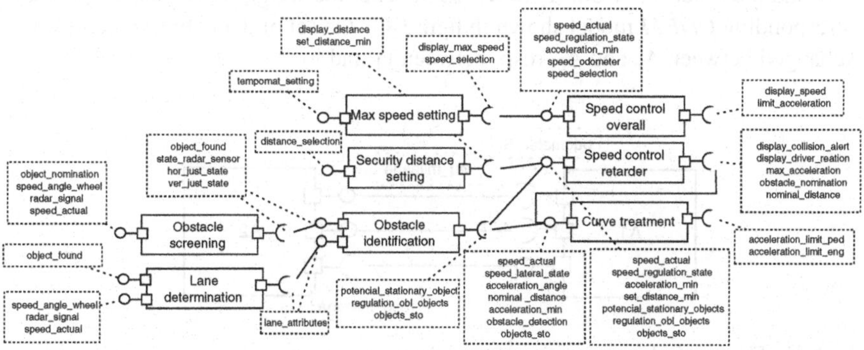

Fig. 1 The ACC *FN* model

The following simplified example illustrates the transformation of a FN connection in a $CDFM$ edge. Suppose that two FN components are connected with a sender-receiver port interface, i.e. an interface through which they can exchange data elements, and a client-server interface, i.e. an interface through which operation calls can be initiated. Every 10 seconds, the first component A_1 sends for example the actual distance covered since the very first starting of the system (as read from the odometer) to the second component A_2. This is done through the sender-receiver

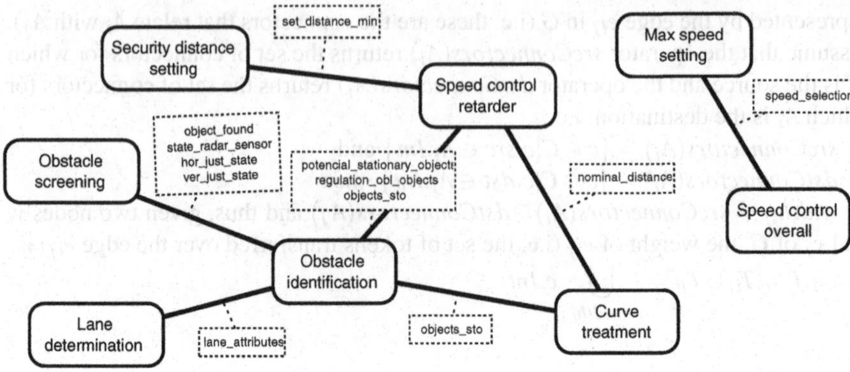

Fig. 2 The corresponding *CDFM* model

interface. Then following a time interval of 1 minute, A_1 triggers A_2 periodically to calculate the total mileage, i.e. the total distance that has been covered by the vehicle since the beginning of the actual trip. The mileage is communicated to A_1 that displays it to inform the user. This is done through the client-server interface. In an AUTOSAR model, these two communication interfaces would be specified by means of one sender-receiver and one client-server interface. But, in a *FN* model, they are specified with three connectors as shown in figure 3. In fact, following the semantics of the *FN*, as A_1 must receive the result of the mileage computation done by A_2, the client-server interface will be modeled by two connectors, one from A_1 to A_2 and the other one from A_2 to A_1. In the end, the weight of the edge e_{12} in the corresponding *CDFM* model shown in figure 4 is the set of data objects, i.e. tokens, exchanged between A_1 and A_2, resp. between v_1 and v_2.

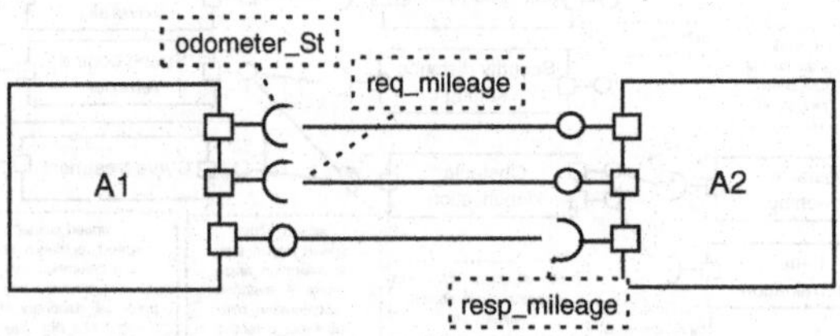

Fig. 3 The FN graphical representation of the mileage inquiry

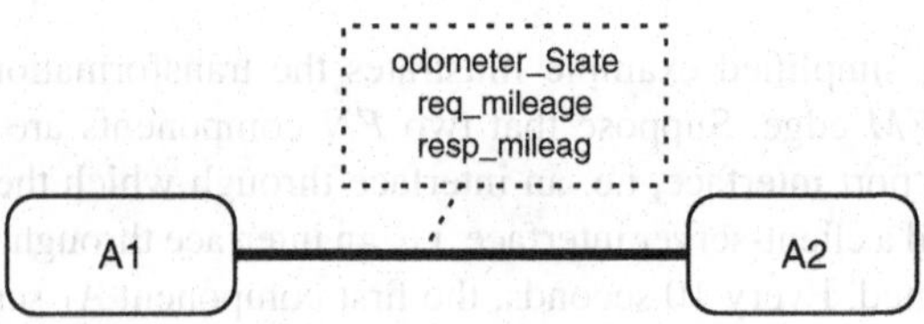

Fig. 4 Graphical representation of the corresponding CDFM

8 Conclusion

The *CDFM* provides a powerful modeling format for the design of E/E systems architectures. It is featured to support the analysis, the synthesis and the measurement of the data flow for the mapping in very complex E/E system specifications at the hight level. The representation of the components interconnections through single unified edges with the corresponding data flow simplifies the measurement and the comparison of the communication between the system components. The graph formulation of *CDFM* models enables the application of usual graph partitioning algorithms to realize the clustering. Due to the concept of directed tokens, the *CDFM* is well-adapted to support the frames packing problem that is inherent to the resource allocation in automotive communication networks such as CAN, MOST, LIN, etc. Furthermore, *CDFM* models are obtained from a simple and straightforward transformation of *FN* models that allow the implementation of CAD system to support the transformation of *FN* into *CDFM* models. Thereto, the *CDFM* format allows the design of flexible models, since *CDFM* models scalable and do not underly any restriction on the granularity of their elements (nodes and tokens). They can easily be enhanced to support the simulation.

References

1. A. Kebemou, "Partitioning Metrics for improved Performance and Economy of Distributed Embedded Systems," *IESS proceedings on IFIP TC10 Working Conference, pp 289-300*, Aug. 15-17 2005.
2. AUTOSAR, "www.autosar.org."
3. *Systems Modelling Language (SysML) Specification, OMG document: ad/2006-03-01; version 1.0 Draft.*
4. EAST-EEA, " Embedded Electronic Architecture. Definition of Language for Automotive Embedded Electronic Architecture v. 1.02," ITEA, Tech. Rep., 30.06.2006.
5. *UML Profile for AUTOSAR; V1.0.0; AUTOSAR Adminstration web content, 28.04.2006.*
6. M. von der Beeck, "A Comparison of Statecharts Variants," in *Proceedings of the Third International Symposium Organized Jointly with the Working Group Provably Correct Systems on Formal Techniques in Real-Time and Fault-Tolerant Systems ; pp 128 - 148*, 1994.
7. M. Varea, "Modelling and Verification of Embedded Systems based on Petri Net oriented Representations," Ph.D. dissertation, University of Southampton, United Kingdom, Sep 2003.
8. D. D. Gajski and L. Ramachandran, "Introduction to High-Level Synthesis," in *IEEE Design and Test of Computers, Vol. 11, No. 4, pp. 44-54*, Dec, 1994.
9. A. Jerraya, H. Ding, P. Kission, and M. Rahmouni, "Behavioral Synthesis and Component Reuse with VHDL," *Kluwer Academic Publishers, Boston/ London / Dortrecht*, 1996.
10. E. A. Lee and D. G. Messerschmitt, "Static Scheduling of Synchronous Data Flow Program for Digital Signal Processing," in *IEEE Transactions on Computers, 75(9):1235-1245*, Jan. 1987.
11. J. H. D. Herrmann, J. Henkel, and R. Ernst, "An Approach to the Adaptation of Estimated Cost Parameters in the COSYMA System," in *Proceedings of the 3 rd International Workshop on Hardware /Software Codesign - CODES/CASHE '94, pp 100–107,*, 1994.
12. S. S. Bhattacharyya, P. K. Murthy, and E. A. Lee, *Software Synthesis from Dataflow Graphs*, M. Norwell, Ed. Kluwer Academic Publishers, 1996.

13. K. Koutsougeras, C. A. Papachristou, and R. R. Vemuri, "Data Flow Graph Partitioning to Reduce Communication Cost," in *Proceedings of the 19th annual workshop on Microprogramming; pp 82 - 91*, 1986.
14. F. Vahid and D. D. Gajski, "SLIF: A Specification-Level Intermediate Format for System Design," in *1995 European Design and Test Conference (ED&TC '95)*, 1995.
15. P. Arato, Z. A. Mann, and A. Orban, " Algorithmic Aspects of Hardware/Software Partitioning," in *ACM Transactions on Design Automation of Electronic Systems, Vol. 10, Nr. 1, pp 136-156*, Jan 2005.

On the Use of Software Quality Metrics to Improve Physical Properties of Embedded Systems

Ricardo M. Redin, Marcio F. S. Oliveira, Lisane B. Brisolara, Julio C. B. Mattos, Luis C. Lamb, Flávio R. Wagner, and Luigi Carro

Abstract As software production achieves a growing importance in the embedded systems world, quality evaluation of embedded software and its impact on physical properties of embedded systems becomes increasingly relevant. Although there are tools for embedded software design that improve software specification and verification, we are still short of a tool that supports the designer's decisions on the best design strategy regarding low level, physical characteristics like performance, energy, and memory footprint, which are critical in the embedded domain. In this paper, we provide an analysis of the correlation between software quality metrics and physical metrics for embedded software. By means of experiments, we investigate the impact of software engineering best practices on embedded software and show that software quality metrics can be used to guide design decisions toward improving physical properties of embedded systems.

Key words: embedded software, software engineering, measurement, quality metrics

1 Introduction

Software engineers have been improving the software design process, and new methods have been proposed for all software development steps, from requirements specification to testing. New programming paradigms have arisen, such as Object-Orientation (OO) and Aspect-Orientation (AO), as well as new development methods such as Model-Driven Engineering. A key factor of any engineering process is the measurement and assessment of its characteristics; thus different metrics to gauge and improve the quality of software products have been also proposed. Such

Ricardo M. Redin · Marcio F. S. Oliveira · Lisane B. Brisolara · Julio C. B. Mattos · Luis C. Lamb · Flávio R. Wagner · Luigi Carro
Institute of Informatics, Federal University of Rio Grande do Sul (UFRGS), Brazil

Please use the following format when citing this chapter:

Redin, R.M., et al., 2008, in IFIP International Federation for Information Processing, Volume 271; *Distributed Embedded Systems: Design, Middleware and Resources*; Bernd Kleinjohann, Lisa Kleinjohann, Wayne Wolf; (Boston: Springer), pp. 101–110.

metrics have been designed to evaluate concepts such as reuse, abstraction, cohesion, coupling, and other software attributes.

In the case of embedded systems, differently from the traditional software domain, the main metrics currently in use are the physical ones, such as performance, memory, energy, power, size, and weight, guided by design constraints. Other important and related metrics are reuse, time-to-market, and price. Although many methodologies extract the physical metrics by proposing estimation or simulation tools, the reuse and time-to-market factors are approached only through design methods without direct or indirect evaluation.

However, the hard constraints typically found in embedded systems do not allow the embedded system community to benefit from the advances in traditional software methodologies As a result, the most critical challenge for Systems-on-Chip (SoC) design is the software development process, which now accounts for 80% of the cost of embedded system development. Notwithstanding the growth in the use and application of software engineering methodologies in embedded software development, the current practice of embedded software development is still unsatisfactory, in particular in industry .

Traditional (or classical) quality metrics provided by software engineers have been successfully applied to improve the software quality for general-purpose systems, leading to improvements in reuse and time-to-market. Traditionally, these metrics help designers to increase properties such as abstraction and reuse, which are good for time-to-market and maintainability. However, some best design practices for conventional software cannot be applied to embedded software because they can cause a negative impact on the physical metrics.

In this work, we investigate the relationship between traditional (classical) software quality metrics and the relevant physical metrics for embedded systems. Different design decisions over the application model influence these metrics, thus we intend to find out which software quality metrics are relevant for embedded software design. Moreover, we show that the best design practices of traditional software can negatively impact the physical properties of embedded systems, which implies that some sacrifices in terms of reuse or maintainability are required to achieve a better performance. Finally, we propose to use the knowledge about the relationship between quality and physical metrics to suggest modifications in the modeling solution that will improve this solution regarding the physical metrics.

The remaining of this paper is organized as follows. Section 2 presents related background work. Section 3 describes the software quality metrics selected for our analysis. Section 4 presents the experiments conducted and our main results. Section 5 concludes the paper and points out directions for future work.

2 Related work

There are several proposals of metric frameworks to evaluate the quality of the software products in the software engineering literature, see e.g.. In the case of object-oriented software, a well-known survey of quality metrics is. In a more recent empirical study of OO metrics, the authors apply several quality metrics to three different projects and study the relationship between these metrics .

However, only a few works relating software quality measures for embedded software products and physical metrics for embedded systems have been published so far. For instance, in the authors describe the results of an experiment where four different mobile devices running Role Playing Games applications are analyzed in terms of software quality metrics and performance. The study shows that the development effort can be greatly reduced without compromising the performance through the reuse of platform and/or software components.

Our work focuses on measuring the correlation between object-oriented quality metrics for traditional software design and physical metrics for embedded systems design. We aim at finding out how the correlation between these metrics can be used to aid a designer to improve the embedded software quality and still achieve better results in terms of performance, memory, and power consumption. Moreover, we show that one can use specific quality metrics as reliable predictors for the impact of software design decisions on the final system physical metrics.

3 Software metrics

As the key of any engineering process is measurement, research efforts have provided many measures and metrics to evaluate processes, software products, and projects in order to guide design decisions. A set of important metrics was selected from and. Since there is no well-defined or widely accepted metrics classification, we group these metrics by the attribute which the metric refers to, in order to facilitate the presentation. The classification and the used metrics are as follows.

Coupling: It measures the relationship between components, including calls, and number of instances. High values of these metrics lead to an application that is poor in encapsulation, reuse, and maintainability. The following metrics fit into this category: Afferent Coupling (Ca), Efferent Coupling (Ce), and Instability (I).

Cohesion: It measures the degree to which the elements of a scope are functionally related. The recommendation from software engineering is to use strongly cohesive modules, which implement functionality that is related to one feature of the software and requires little or no interaction with other modules. Lack of Cohesion of Methods (LCOM) is the cohesion metric used in this work.

Extensibility and reuse: These metrics evaluate the possible reuse of a scope and the capacity of it to be extended. Abstractness (A), Normalized Distance from Main Sequence (Dn), and Depth of Inheritance Tree (DIT) are metrics used in this work.

Population (or size) metrics: These metrics measure the system in terms of attributes, methods, and classes. They are also associated to complexity. In general, higher values of these metrics mean an increase in memory footprint, lower performance, and a more complex solution. Nevertheless, the distribution of the population metrics has more impact on the dynamic behavior of the application. Almost all population metrics count the number of a given structure inside the application code. The used population metrics are: Number of Attributes (NOA), Number of Classes (NOC), Number of Methods (NOM), Number of Packages (NOPK), Number of Parameters (NOP), Number of Static Attributes (NOSA), Number of Static Methods (NOSM), and Total Lines of Code (TLOC).

Complexity: These metrics measure the hardness to understand or express the problem/algorithm. They are related to alternative execution flows, element granularity/hierarchy, and nested execution. Metrics in this category are: McCabe Cyclomatic Complexity (VG), Method Lines of Code (MLOC), Nested Block Depth (NBD), and Weighted Methods per Class (WMC).

There is a large number of software metrics. We have selected this set of metrics because they are commonly and widely used in the software engineering domain and there are several tools to automatically extract them from source code or even from UML models. Surely, other metrics could be applied in this study, and other important metrics are planned for future experiments.

4 Experiments

We have carried out experiments aiming at: (1) verifying the correlation between software quality metrics and physical ones; (2) identifying the relevant quality software metrics for embedded software design; (3) measuring the impact of specification strategies by using software quality metrics. Furthermore, we show that these metrics can be used to improve embedded software with respect to its physical properties. We will also show that some sacrifices in terms of reuse or maintainability are required in order to achieve a hard constrained performance.

The analyzed applications are a wheelchair control and an MP3 player. The wheelchair control application consists of a real-time embedded system dedicated to the automation and control of an intelligent wheelchair that helps people with special needs. For this experiment, we have implemented only the wheelchair movement control, which is an essential use case of the system. The MP3 player is an application that is usually embedded in many consumer electronics systems, used to play music in a compressed data format. This application presents a dataflow processing channel in which many algorithms must be executed until the compressed data can be played.

Different solutions were developed for both applications. All solutions were implemented using Java for the target platform. For every alternative implementation, a synthesis tool was used to obtain the hardware description and the Java byte codes for the application. From the final implementation, in Java byte codes, we extracted the physical metrics by using a cycle-accurate simulation , while from the Java source code we extracted the software quality metrics by using the Eclipse Metrics plug-in.

The physical data from cycle-accurate simulation and software metrics from Eclipse Metrics were matched using the cross-correlation formula that measures the similarity of two arrays of data. Results obtained for both quality and physical metrics, including the cross-correlation between them, are presented in the following.

4.1 Experimental results

Firstly, we have analyzed the cross-correlation between these different metrics for a given application and afterwards among different applications to observe whether the achieved correlation is similar for all applications or not. A positive cross-correlation means that an increase on a given quality metric results in an increase on the related physical property. On the other hand, negative values translate to an inverse relationship.

In the MP3 player experiment three different solutions were analyzed. Sol-1 is object-oriented and follows as much as possible the recommendations of software engineering. Sol-2 is OO too, but much more concerned with physical proprieties of the final system. Sol-3 is entirely targeted at good values for physical proprieties of the resulting product and thus entirely static. Table 1 shows the physical properties obtained for each MP3 solution. Analyzing these results, one can observe that the best solution considering traditional software engineering paradigms (Sol-1) is the worst one regarding physical metrics.

Table 2 presents the quality metrics and the correlation between them and the physical properties. For all software metrics the maximum value or total is showed, except the metrics marked with an asterisk (*), for which we have used the average value because their total values just tell us where to look for bad code constructs. An average value, in turn, shows us how much a good or bad behavior is distributed across the entire application.

Table 1 Extracted physical metrics from the MP3 player.

Property	Sol. 1	Sol. 2	Sol. 3
Program memory	238,484	237,192	242,688
Data memory	146,812	117,756	324,733
Cycles	1,830,675,876	830,365,894	239,748,559
Energy (J)	79.8575	36.2221	21.9624

For the wheelchair experiment four solutions were analyzed. Sol-1 is the most concerned about performance, energy, and memory of the final system. All operating system services were implemented by the application, and only the required services are implemented. Sol-2, in turn, is the most concerned with the quality of the software product. It uses threads and an underlying platform that supports multithreading, among other features. Sol-3 and Sol-4 use the same platform as Sol-2 and differ from each other in design strategies. Table 3 summarizes the physical proprieties of the wheelchair solutions, and Table 4 shows the software metrics val-

Table 2 Extracted software quality metrics and its cross-correlation to physical metrics on MP3 Player.

Property	Sol. 1	Sol. 2	Sol. 3	Prog. Mem.	Data Mem.	Cycles	Energy
Abstractness	0.143	0	0.2	0.858	0.804	-0.132	0.005
Afferent Coupling	3	2	5	0.994	0.979	-0.536	-0.416
Depth of Inheritance Tree	2	1	2	0.682	0.608	0.147	0.281
Efferent Coupling	4	2	3	0.225	0.130	0.622	0.723
Instability	0.75	1	1	0.293	0.384	-0.930	-0.972
Lack of Cohesion of Methods*	0.655	0.42	0.245	-0.671	-0.740	0.998	0.980
McCabe Cyclomatic Complexity*	1.832	7.448	6.492	0.137	0.232	-0.860	-0.922
Method Lines of Code	4101	4618	5675	0.850	0.897	-0.942	-0.887
Nested Block Depth*	1.188	2.23	2.305	0.349	0.438	-0.951	-0.984
Normalized Distance*	0.707	0.556	0.626	0.184	0.088	0.654	0.752
N. of Attributes	186	112	6	-0.797	-0.852	0.969	0.926
N. of Children	106	22	4	-0.447	-0.531	0.978	0.997
N. of Classes	27	26	64	0.979	0.994	-0.769	-0.674
N. of Methods	463	85	47	-0.371	-0.458	0.957	0.988
N. of Packages	5	3	6	0.884	0.834	-0.185	-0.048
N. of Parameters	7	14	6	-0.761	-0.695	-0.033	-0.169
N. of Static Attributes	98	58	597	0.987	0.998	-0.740	-0.641
N. of Static Methods	127	2	71	0.283	0.189	0.574	0.681
Total Lines of Code	7891	6853	8423	0.887	0.838	-0.191	-0.055
Weighted methods per Class	1081	648	766	-0.030	-0.127	0.800	0.875

ues and the cross-correlation between software and physical metrics. In Table 3, BC identifies the metric value for the Best Case execution of the controller.

Table 3 Physical metrics obtained from the Wheelchair Movement Controller.

Property	Sol. 1	Sol.2	Sol. 3	Sol. 4
Program memory	2,063	6,248	5,208	5,094
BC Data memory	372	582	431	421
BC Performance	1,898	28,588	9,104	7,776
BC Energy	2,714,132	40,569,570	12,916,022	11,026,748

As one of the applications is dataflow and the other one is control flow, some correlations differ from one experiment to the other. As expected, performance and energy are highly-correlated physical properties. In all experiments these two metrics follow the same tendencies, and correlation between software metrics and each of them hardly differ significantly from the other.

4.2 Experimental results analysis

While some good practices of software engineering cause an overhead in the physical properties of embedded systems, other ones can help to design better products

Table 4 Extracted software quality metrics from the Wheelchair Movement Controller and its cross-correlation to physical ones.

Property	Sol. 1	Sol. 2	Sol. 3	Sol. 4	Prog. Mem.	Data Mem.	Cycles	Energy
Abstractness	0	0	0	0	0.000	0.000	0.000	0.000
Afferent Coupling	1	4	2	2	0.849	0.994	0.992	0.992
Depth of Inheritance Tree	1	2	2	2	0.958	0.584	0.572	0.571
Efferent Coupling	1	2	2	2	0.958	0.584	0.572	0.571
Instability	1	0.5	0.667	0.667	-0.995	-0.846	-0.837	-0.837
Lack of Cohesion of Methods*	0.71	0.639	0.51	0.519	-0.588	0.025	0.040	0.041
McCabe Cyclomatic Complexity*	1.238	1.312	1.261	1.25	0.773	0.995	0.996	0.996
Method Lines of Code	58	94	62	49	0.525	0.916	0.922	0.922
Nested Block Depth*	1.143	1.25	1.174	1.15	0.720	0.983	0.985	0.985
Normalized Distance*	0.5	0.567	0.583	0.583	0.885	0.419	0.405	0.404
N. of Attributes	0	22	20	17	0.988	0.710	0.700	0.699
N. of Children	0	0	0	0	0.000	0.000	0.000	0.000
N. of Classes	5	7	7	7	0.958	0.584	0.572	0.571
N. of Methods	2	29	20	17	0.982	0.883	0.876	0.875
N. of Packages	3	4	4	4	0.958	0.584	0.572	0.571
N. of Parameters	3	3	3	2	-0.163	0.224	0.234	0.234
N. of Static Attributes	20	28	17	19	0.408	0.864	0.870	0.871
N. of Static Methods	8	3	3	3	-0.958	-0.584	-0.572	-0.571
Total Lines of Code	146	283	190	170	0.782	0.996	0.996	0.996
Weighted methods per Class	26	42	29	25	0.629	0.962	0.966	0.966

without affecting physical properties or even improving them. In this section, we analyze our experimental results and show some tradeoffs between software engineering guidelines and code optimizations to improve as much as we can physical properties of the final system, looking for a good balance between both sides.

The best OO practices indicate that a reduced coupling is desired, so the coupling metrics Ca, Ce, and Instability should have small values. We observed that there is a high correlation (around 0.9) among the metric Ca and data and program memory, which suggests that this metric impacts on the memory footprint. This is confirmed, by the case studies, where Sol-1 of the wheelchair controller and Sol-2 of the MP3 player present the smallest Ca value and achieve the smallest memory size in comparison with the other solutions. Instability (I) indicates if a package is stable or not. A value of zero is required. A correlation around -0.9 was found between Instability and energy as well as between Instability and performance, showing that this quality metric has a negative impact on these physical metrics. It means that solutions with higher I values are the best ones in terms of performance/energy, as confirmed by our results.

The OO paradigm leads designers to build cohesive modules that require little or no interaction with other modules. It suggests that, in order to have components architecturally and logically well defined, smaller values for Lack of Cohesion (LCOM) are desired. We have observed that the best solution for the MP3 player in terms of energy/performance is Sol-3, which has the smallest LCOM value. The opposite situation is found for the wheelchair controller, where Sol-1 is the best solution for all physical properties and presents the highest LCOM. The reason for that is the fact that Sol-1 of the wheelchair controller has the smallest number of attributes (NOA), which is a metric strongly related to performance and energy.

High reuse is desired in all traditional software projects. High values for the metrics Abstractness (A) and Depth of Inheritance Tree (DIT) are thus required, because they indicate that the components are extensible and can be reused. Abstractness measures the number of abstract classes and has an impact on the memory footprint, as can be observed in the results for the MP3 player. For the wheelchair case study, no abstract class or interface is used. DIT measures the depth of inheritance tree, and high values for this metric lead to higher reuse. As expected, inheritance causes an overhead in memory, performance, and energy. The best solution for all of these physical aspects has the smallest DIT numbers.

Normalized Distance (Dn) is another reuse metrics, but numbers close to zero indicate a good packaging design. The best solutions for physical metrics in our experiments also show the smallest Dn values. However, the variation of Dn is too small in our experiments to consider it as an interesting correlation.

The quality of software is also evaluated using population metrics. However, there are no safe value ranges for these metrics because they depend on the size of the project. Since these population metrics also impact on the physical properties, we have also analyzed the correlation between them.

As expected, when the number of static attributes (NOSA) increases, the data memory also increases, which is confirmed by our results. Sol-3 of the MP3 player and Sol-2 of the wheelchair controller have the highest values for NOSA in comparison with the other solutions, and, consequently, these solutions are the less efficient regarding data memory.

A considerable high correlation among the number of attributes (NOA) and the performance and energy is found for both case studies. The solution with small NOA is the best one regarding performance and energy. As expected, the number of attributes impacts on the required data memory size. Sol-1 of wheelchair controller presents NOA equal to 0 and has the smallest data memory size. It is interesting to notice that Sol-3 of the MP3 player has the smallest number of attributes (NOA) but has the highest number of static attributes (NOSA). This shows that the designer of this solution decided to pay an overhead in memory footprint by the use of static attributes in order to improve the performance and energy metrics. The high correlation between the NOA and memory cannot be found in the MP3 player because of the strong correlation between NOA and NOSA. The reduction on the number of dynamic attributes (NOA) and the increase of static attributes (NOSA) lead to a better result in terms of performance and energy. This can be observed in Sol-4 of the wheelchair controller and in Sol-3 of the MP3 player.

It is known that the number of packages (NOPk) impacts the program memory size, and this has been observed in our experiments by the high correlation among these metrics and by the fact that the solutions with less NOPk present small program memories.

As expected, the number of methods (NOM) has a direct impact on the number of cycles and on the energy, as confirmed by the high correlation found among them.

The best solutions regarding performance and energy are those that have a small number of methods. However, in the OO paradigm using a small numbers of large methods is not a good practice.

Embedded software designers usually replace dynamic methods by static ones in order to reduce the overhead for method invocation. In the wheelchair controller case study, the results confirmed this statement, since the best solution in performance and energy is Sol-1, which has the highest number of static methods (NOSM). However, in the MP3 player case study, this is not found. For this case study, Sol-1 has the highest NOSM (127), but this solution is not the best one regarding performance/energy. The reason for this is that the number of methods (NOM) is strongly related to the NOSM and this solution has the highest (NOM) value (463), which causes a huge overhead in both performance and energy that was not compensated by the variation in NOSM values. Sol-3 is more efficient regarding performance and energy and has an intermediate (NOSM) value (71).

5 Conclusions and future work

We have presented an analysis of the relationship between software quality metrics and physical metrics for embedded systems. The experiments have shown that decisions on the software design phase can greatly impact on the physical properties of the final system. We have shown that it is also possible to use software quality metrics to help in design decisions in order to improve the physical properties of embedded systems. However, our experiments show that there are strong correlations between some quality metrics and, in this case, they cannot be separately analyzed.

Moreover, we have proposed the use of software quality metrics to indicate modifications that can be applied to a given modeling solution in order to obtain a better solution in terms of performance, energy, or memory footprint, with a small decrease, for instance, in code reuse. We are currently developing a tool to modify a modeling solution with respect to the quality metrics in order to find a sweet spot in the design space.

A large subset of the metrics used in this work can be measured directly on UML models. Using these metrics on UML models can help designers to early explore the solution space, looking for sweet spots without the use of a previously measured library of components directly in UML.

References

1. Aggarl, K. K. et al. Empirical Study of Object Oriented Metrics. Journal of Object Technology, v. 5, n. 8, 2006.
2. Beck, A.C. et al. CACO-PS: A General Purpose Cycle-Accurate Configurable Power Simulator. In: Proc. of Symposium on Integrated Circuits and Systems Design (SBCCI), 2003.

3. Graaf, B.; Lormans, M.; Toetenel, H. Embedded Software Engineering: the State of the Practice. IEEE Software, v. 20, n. 6, p. 61- 69, Nov. – Dec. 2003.
4. Henderson-Sellers, B. Object-Oriented Metrics, Measures of Complexity. Prentice Hall, 1996.
5. Henzinger, T.A.; Sifakis, J. The Discipline of Embedded Systems Design. IEEE Computer, v. 40, n. 10, p. 32-40, Oct. 2007.
6. Ito, S.; Carro, L.; Jacobi, R. Making Java Work for Microcontroller Applications. IEEE Design & Test of Computers, v. 18, n. 5, 2001.
7. Jerraya, A.A. et al. Embedded Software for SoC. Kluwer Academic Publishers, 2003.
8. Martin, R. Agile Software Development, Principles, Patterns and Practices. Prentice Hall, 2002.
9. Metrics. Eclipse Plug-in Available at: http://metrics.sourceforge.net/
10. Sommerville, I. Software Engineering, 7th ed. Pearson, 2004.
11. Xenos, M. et al. Object-oriented Metrics - A Survey. In: Proc. of the Federation of European Software Measurement Associations (FESMA), 2000.
12. Zhang, W.; Jarzabek, S. Reuse without Compromising Performance: Industrial Experience from RPG Software Product Line for Mobile Devices. In: LNCS, n. 3714, 2005.

Minimizing Leakage Energy with Modulo Scheduling for VLIW DSP Processors

Meng Wang, Zili Shao, Hui Liu, and Chun Jason Xue

Abstract As technology scaling approaches to the nanometer, leakage power has become a significant component of the total power consumption. In this paper, we develop a novel leakage-aware modulo scheduling algorithm to achieve leakage energy savings for DSP applications with loops on VLIW architecture. The proposed algorithm is designed to maximize the idleness of function units integrating with leakage management scheme [9], and reduce the number of transitions between active and sleep modes. We have implemented our technique into the Trimaran compiler [1] and conducted experiments using a set of benchmarks from DSPstone [11] and Mibench [7] on the VLIW simulator of Trimaran. The results show that our algorithm achieves significant leakage energy savings compared with the leakage-aware scheduling algorithm [8].

1 Introduction

As technology feature size continues to shrink, leakage power is becoming comparable to dynamic power in the current generation of technology [3, 6, 10], and it will further dominate the overall energy consumption in future technologies [4]. High performance DSP (Digital Signal Processing) needs to be performed not only with high data throughput but also with low power consumption in embedded sys-

Meng Wang · Zili Shao
Department of Computing, The Hong Kong Polytechnic University, Hong Kong
e-mail: csmewang, cszlshao@comp.polyu.edu.hk

Hui Liu
Software Engineering Institute, Xidian University, Xi'an, China
e-mail: liuhui@xidian.edu.cn

Chun Jason Xue
Department of Computer Science, City University of Hong Kong, Hong Kong
e-mail: jasonxue@cityu.edu.hk

Please use the following format when citing this chapter:

Wang, M., et al., 2008, in IFIP International Federation for Information Processing, Volume 271; *Distributed Embedded Systems: Design, Middleware and Resources*; Bernd Kleinjohann, Lisa Kleinjohann, Wayne Wolf; (Boston: Springer), pp. 111–120.

tems. VLIW (Very Long Instruction Word) architecture that has multiple functional units (FUs) and can process several instructions simultaneously is widely adopted in high-end DSP. While this multiple-FUs architecture can be exploited to increase instruction-level parallelism and improve time performance, it causes more leakage power consumption. Therefore, it becomes an important problem to reduce the leakage energy of a DSP application on VLIW architecture. Since loops are usually the most critical parts in a DSP application, we develop a loop scheduling technique to reduce the leakage energy of an application on VLIW architecture.

A lot of research efforts have been put to characterize cost models for analyzing static power [3] and evaluate techniques for leakage power reduction [9]. The architecture level model in [3] confirms that the functional units contribute to a noticeable fraction of leakage power despite having relatively fewer transistors compared to caches. A hardware based leakage energy management scheme is proposed in [9] for short idle periods. In their scheme, the dual-threshold domino logic with sleep mode that can transit between active mode and sleep mode is utilized.

Many techniques [8, 5] are proposed to reduce leakage energy consumption of functional units for VLIW architecture. Nagpal et al. [8] proposed a leakage-aware instruction scheduling algorithm for VLIW and clustered VLIW architectures to reduce leakage energy by exploiting the scheduling slacks of instructions. In most of the above work, the instruction scheduling for reducing leakage power is based on DAG (Directed Acyclic Graph) scheduling in which only intra-iteration dependencies are considered. In this paper, we show that we can significantly improve the leakage energy by carefully exploiting inter-iteration dependencies.

In this paper, we propose a leakage-aware modulo scheduling algorithm that assists the hardware based leakage energy management scheme [9] to achieve leakage savings for DSP applications in the context of VLIW architecture. Our basic idea is to schedule nodes into better locations in order to maximize the idleness of function units integrating with leakage reduction control, and reduce the number of transitions between active and sleep modes. We implement our technique into the Trimaran compiler [1] and conduct experiments on a set of benchmarks from DSPstone [11] and Mibench [7] based on the power model in [9]. The results show that our algorithm achieves significant leakage energy savings compared with the leakage-aware scheduling algorithm [8]. On average, our technique contributes to 14.73% reduction in the leakage energy consumption with only 1.74% decrement in the performance.

The rest of the paper is organized as follows. Motivational examples are shown in Section 2. The basic concepts are introduced in Section 3. The scheduling algorithm is proposed in Section 4. The experimental results and analysis are provided in Section 5, and the conclusion is given in Section 6.

2 Motivational Examples

In order to show how our approach works, we present an example in this section. We use Trimaran compiler [1] to generate the Data Flow Graph for this example and perform modulo scheduling on it. We compare the scheduling generated by the traditional modulo scheduling and our technique. The energy model to calculate the leakage energy is introduced in Section 3.2.

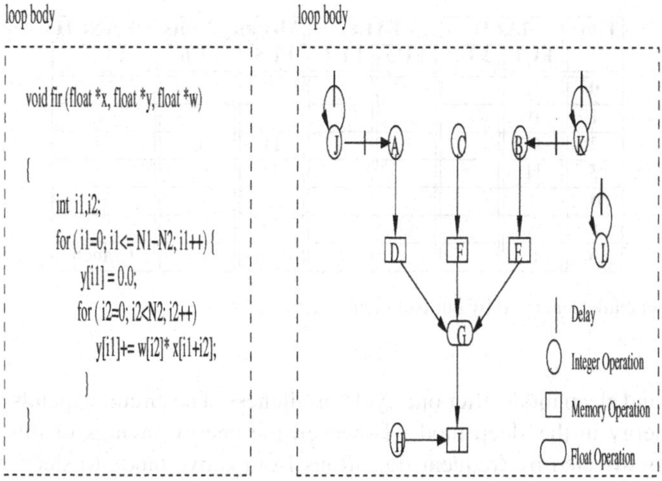

Fig. 1 The FIR program and its corresponding data flow graph.

A real DSP application, the FIR program and the Data Flow Graph of the innermost loop is shown in Figure 1. In the graph, each node denotes a computational task in the loop, and there are 7 integer ALU operations, 4 memory operations, 1 floating ALU operation and 1 branch for this particular example. The edge without delay represents the intra-iteration data dependency (e.g. $A \rightarrow D$), and the edge with delays represents the inter-iteration data dependency (e.g. $J \rightarrow A$ has an edge with one delay which is denoted by one bar), in which the number of delays represents the number of iterations involved.

Assume that we want to schedule the graph in Figure 1 to the VLIW architecture with 7 FUs which are fully pipelined. And let $FU1$ and $FU2$ be integer ALUs, $FU3$ and $FU4$ be floating-point ALUs, $FU5$ and $FU6$ be memory units and $FU7$ be the branch unit. Note that we assume the integer operations A, B, C, H, J, K, L take 1 cycle for execution, the load operations D, E, F take 2 cycles, the store operation I takes 1 cycle, and the floating multiplication node G takes 2 cycles to finish execution in this example.

The schedule generated by the traditional modulo scheduling is shown in Figure 2. Based on the power model in [9], for integer ALUs which are most heavily utilized, the dual-threshold domino logic with sleep mode can transit between ac-

Time	IALU		FALU		Memory Units		BRANCH
	FU1	FU2	FU3	FU4	FU5	FU6	FU7
0	A	B			I		
1	C	H			D	E	
2	J	K			F		
3	L						
4			G				
5							Branch

Fig. 2 The schedule generated by performance-oriented modulo scheduling.

Time	IALU		FALU		Memory Units		BRANCH
	FU1	FU2	FU3	FU4	FU5	FU6	FU7
0	A				I		
1	B						
2	C				D	E	
3	H				F		
4	J						
5	K		G				
6	L						Branch

Fig. 3 The schedule generated by our technique.

tive mode and sleep mode after one cycle of idleness. The circuit expends very little leakage energy in the sleep mode. However, the energy savings of this schedule are severely affected by frequent transitions from active mode to sleep mode and vice-versa because of many short idle periods.

The schedule generated by our technique is shown in Figure 3. For this example, the schedule generated by our technique has little performance loss than the traditional modulo scheduling algorithm. In this schedule, $FU2$ is totally unused, so we can put $FU2$ into the sleep mode before entering the loop body. Thus, our technique achieves big leakage savings compared with the performance-oriented modulo scheduling.

3 Basic Concepts

3.1 Modulo Scheduling Overview

The objective of modulo scheduling [2] is to engineer a schedule for one iteration of the loop such that when this same schedule is repeated at regular intervals, no intra- or inter-iteration dependence is violated, and no resource usage conflict arises between operations of either the same or distinct iterations. This constant interval between the start of successive iterations is termed the initiation interval (II). The repetitive portion can be re-rolled to yield a new loop which is termed the kernel.

The prologue is the code that precedes the repetitive part and the epilogue is the code following the repetitive part. The minimum initiation interval (MII) is a lower bound on the smallest possible value of II for which a modulo schedule exists. The MII must be equal to or greater than both the resource-constrained MII (ResMII) and the recurrence-constrained MII (RecMII). The candidate II is initially set to the MII and increased until a legal modulo schedule is found.

3.2 Energy Model

The energy model used in this paper is based on [9]. The total energy in a functional unit in this model is determined as follows:

$$E_{total} = Dyn\_Energy + Leak\_Energy + Trans\_Energy + Sleep\_Energy$$

$$E_{total} = n_A\ (\alpha E_A + (1\text{-}D)E_{S_1}) + (n_A D + n_{UI})(\alpha E_{S_0} + (1\text{-}\alpha)E_{S_1}) + M_Z((1\text{-}\alpha)E_A + E_{Sleep}) + n_Z E_{S_0}$$

Here, n_A is the number of active cycles, n_{UI} is the number of uncontrolled idle cycles, n_Z is the number of sleep mode cycles and M_Z is the number of transitions between different modes. E_{S_0} and E_{S_1} are low and high leakage energy consumption, respectively.

4 Leakage-Aware Modulo Scheduling Algorithm

In this section, we first propose the leakage-aware modulo scheduling algorithm in Sections 4.1. Then we discuss its key functions in Section 4.2.

4.1 The Proposed Algorithm

In the proposed algorithm, our basic idea is to schedule nodes of a loop to better locations in order to enlarge the idleness in FUs which can be exploited to apply leakage energy control mechanism. In most of the previous work, loop is modeled as the DAG part of a DFG in which only intra-iteration dependencies are considered. As shown in Section 2, by exploring inter-iteration dependencies, we can get more opportunities to schedule nodes of DFG to better locations in a schedule to achieve more leakage energy saving. The leakage-aware modulo scheduling algorithm is shown in Algorithm 4.1.

In the algorithm, G is the data flow graph of the loop, TC is the timing constraint and the *BudgetRatio* is the ratio of the maximum number of operation scheduling steps attempted before giving up to the number of operations in the loop. This parameter determines how hard the function IterativeSchedule() tries to find a legal

Algorithm 4.1 The leakage-aware modulo scheduling algorithm.

Require: The data flow graph G=⟨V, E, d, t⟩, the timing constraint TC, BudgetRatio.
Ensure: A schedule S with minimum leakage energy *Min_Energy*.

// Initialize the value of II to the Minimum Initiation Interval
II := MII();
Min_Energy $\leftarrow \infty$;
while II < TC **do**
  Budget := BudgetRatio * NumberofOperations;
  while IterativeSchedule(II, Budget)!= SUCCESS **do**
    II := II+1;
    // Calculate the leakage energy based on the power model [9]
    S' := The generated legal schedule;
    $E_{S'}$:= CalculateEnergy(S');
    if Min_Energy > $E_{S'}$ **then**
      $S \leftarrow S'$ and *Min_Energy* $\leftarrow E_{S'}$
    end if
  end while
end while

schedule for a candidate II before giving up. The output of the algorithm is a legal schedule S with minimum leakage energy *Min_Energy*.

In the algorithm, we first initialize the value of II to the minimum initiation interval. Then, function IterativeSchedule() is used to perform the actual scheduling as shown in Algorithm 4.2. After all operations have been scheduled and a legal schedule is generated, we record the energy of it and compare it with *Min_Energy*. The algorithm terminates when the timing constraint is achieved.

4.2 Function IterativeSchedule()

In function IterativeSchedule(), we first calculate the priority for each operation based on the height-based priority function ComputePriority() of modulo scheduling, and pick up the operation with highest priority to be scheduled. In function ComputePriority(), we calculate the longest path from the node to the end of the data flow graph. This function gives higher priority to operations on the critical path in order to achieve a good schedule.

Then, the schedule time bounds for the current operation are calculated according to the data dependence constraint. We use function FindTimeSlot() to find a legal time slot for the current operation within the range (*MinTime*, *MaxTime*). *MinTime* is the earliest start time for an operation as constrained by its dependences on its predecessors. *MaxTime* equals to $MinTime + II - 1$ since each iteration in modulo scheduling begins exactly II cycles after the previous one.

In function FindTimeSlot(), the goal is to find an empty block to put the operation *CurrOper* in. We first calculate the start time and the end time of each empty block in each functional unit.

Algorithm 4.2 Function IterativeSchedule().

Require: Graph G, the initiation interval II and the Budget.
Ensure: A schedule S or failure information.

```
    // Calculate the schedule time bounds for the current operation
ComputePriority();
while (the list of unscheduled operations is not empty) & (Budget > 0) do
    CurrOper = HighestPriority();
    // Calculate the schedule time bounds for the current operation
    (MinTime,MaxTime) = ComputeSlack(CurrOper);
    // Select the time slot for leakage energy optimization
    SchedSlot = FindTimeSlot(CurrOper,MinTime,MaxTime);
    // Perform the actual scheduling
    Schedule(CurrOper,SchedSlot);
    Budget–;
end while
if all operations are scheduled then
    return SUCCESS;
else
    return FAILURE
end if
```

In order to enlarge the idleness in FUs, we always start to search from FU_1 and try to find the earliest empty block on it. If we can not find an empty block in FU_1, FU_2 will be tried next time; then we try $FU_3, \cdots, FU_n$, until we can find such an empty block. In this way, we can schedule operations onto one functional unit as much as possible. And thus, we can enlarge the idleness of FUs and increase the number of unused FUs. The benefit is that we have more chance to put the total unused functional units into low leakage mode before entering the loop body. It is possible that we can not find any empty block to put the operation in. In this case, we employ the same backtracking method as that of Rau's modulo scheduling algorithm [2].

After finding the suitable empty block, we compare the earliest schedule time of the operation and the start time of the empty block in order to determine whether the operation should be scheduled at the beginning or at the end of this empty block. By scheduling the nodes into locations close to each other, we can maximize the consecutive idle period in functional units.

5 Experiments

We have implemented our technique into the Trimaran compiler [1] and conduct experiments using a set of benchmarks from DSPstone [11] and MiBench [7] on the cycle-accurate VLIW simulator of Trimaran. In this section, we first discuss the setup of our experiments in Section 5.1, and then present experimental results in section 5.2.

5.1 Experimental Environment

To compare our technique with the leakage-aware scheduling technique [8], we use the VLIW simulator of Trimaran [1] as our test platform. The configuration for the VLIW Trimaran simulator is shown in Table 1.

Table 1 The configurations of Trimaran.

Parameter	Configuration
Functional Units	4 integer ALU, 2 floating point ALU, 2 load-store units 1 branch unit, 5 issue slots
Instruction Latency	1cycle for integer ALU, 1 cycle for floating point ALU 2 cycles for load in cache, 1 cycle for store, 1 cycle for branch
Register file	32 integer registers, 32 floating point registers

5.2 Results and Discussion

In the experiment, we obtain the results of the leakage energy reduction of Integer ALUs and performance penalty on the code generated by our technique. We compare the energy results with that of the code generated by the leakage-aware scheduling algorithm [8] with leakage management scheme [9]. We compare the performance penalty results with that of the code generated by the modulo scheduling [2].

We assume that the technology is 65nm and 50% of the total energy of the VLIW processor is the leakage energy. In the following, we present and analyze the results in terms of leakage energy reduction and performance penalty.

5.2.1 Leakage Energy Reduction

We compare our algorithm with leakage-aware scheduling technique [8] in Trimaran [1], the percentage of reduction in the leakage energy consumption is shown in Figure 4. In Figure 4, the results for Nagpal's technique and our technique are presented in bars with different color, and the right-most bar "AVG." is the average result.

Our algorithm reduces leakage consumption in the functional units by scheduling operations using less functional units to maximize the idleness of the functional units. Moreover, in the loop-level granularity, our technique minimizes the number of transition time between low level and high level leakage mode by turning off the totally unused functional units before entering the loop body. The experimental results show that our algorithm significantly reduces the leakage energy of the processor. Compared with leakage-aware scheduling technique [8], on average, our algorithm achieves 14.73% reduction for the benchmarks.

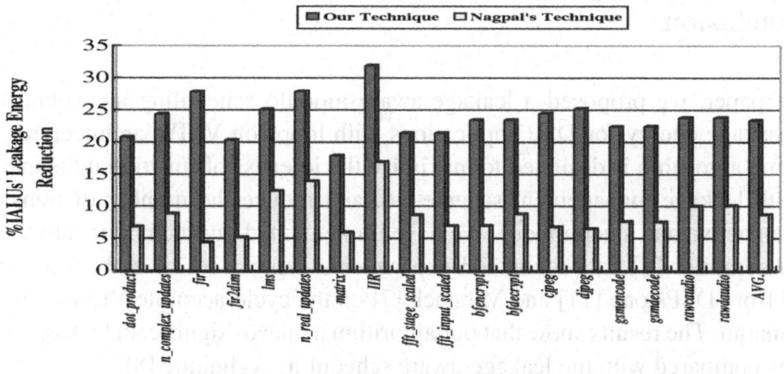

Fig. 4 Leakage energy reduction due to our leakage-aware scheduling algorithm compared with leakage-aware scheduling technique [8].

5.2.2 Performance Penalty

We compare our technique with the performance-oriented modulo scheduling [2], and the percentage of performance penalty is shown in Figure 5. On average, the results show that our technique leads to a 1.74% performance penalty for the benchmarks.

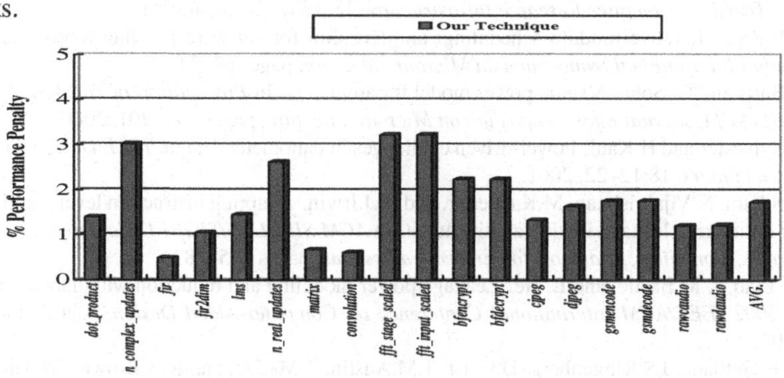

Fig. 5 Performance penalty.

The reason of the performance loss is that our technique may use less functional units to schedule the operations and try to schedule them close to each other. Thus, it may enlarge the schedule length to achieve the goal of maximizing the idleness of functional units. However, in our technique, the performance penalty is controlled by the timing constraint that determines whether employing our technique or not. In the experiment, the maximum number of delays is set as 1.3 * MII (Minimum Initiation Interval). Therefore, the performance penalty is very small. With such small performance loss, our technique is suitable for embedded systems.

6 Conclusion

In this paper, we proposed a leakage-aware modulo scheduling algorithm to reduce leakage energy for DSP applications with loops on VLIW architectures. The proposed algorithm is designed to maximize the idleness of function units integrating with leakage management scheme [9], and reduce the number of transitions between active and sleep modes. We have implemented our technique into the Trimaran compiler [1] and conducted experiments using a set of embedded benchmarks from DSPstone [11] and Mibench [7] on the cycle-accurate VLIW simulator of Trimaran. The results show that our algorithm achieves significant leakage energy savings compared with the leakage-aware scheduling technique [8].

Acknowledgements The work described in this paper is partially supported by the grants from the Research Grants Council of the Hong Kong Special Administrative Region, China (CERG 526007 (PolyU B-Q06B), and PolyU A-PA5X).

References

1. *The Trimaran Compiler Research Infrastructure*. http://www.trimaran.org/.
2. B.R.Rau. Iterative modulo scheduling: an algorithm for software pipeling loops. In *27th Annual International Symposium on Microarchitecture*, pages 63–74.
3. J. Butts and G. Sohi. A static power model for architects. In *Proceedings of The 33rd Annual IEEE/ACM International Symposium on Microarchitecture*, pages 191–201, 2000.
4. D.Sylvester and H.Kaul. Power-driven challenges in nanometer design. *IEEE Design and Test of Computers*, 18:12–22, 2001.
5. H.S.Kim, N.Vijakrishnan, M.Kandemir, and M.J.Irwin. Adapting instruction level parallelism for optimizing leakage in vliw architectures. In *ACM SIFPLAN/SIGBED Conference on Languages, Compilers, and Tools for Embedded Systems*, pages 275–283.
6. W. Liao, J. M.Basile, and L. He. Leakage power modeling and reduction with data retention. In *2002 IEEE/ACM International Conference on Computer-Aided Design*, pages 714–719, 2002.
7. M.R.Guthaus, J.S.Ringenberg, D.Ernst, T.M.Austin, T.Mudge, and R.B.Brown. Mibench: A free, commercially representative embedded benchmark suite. In *Proceedings of the IEEE International Workshop on Workload Characterization*, pages 3–14, 2001.
8. R.Nagpal and Y.N.Srikant. Compiler-assisted leakage energy optimization for clustered vliw architectures. In *6th ACM/IEEE International Conference on Embedded Software*, pages 233–241, 2006.
9. S.Dropsho, V.Kursun, D.H.Albonesi, S.Dwarkadas, and E.G.Friedman. Managing static leakage energy in micro-processor functional units. In *the 35th annual ACM/IEEE international symposium on Microarchitecture*, pages 321–332.
10. T.N.Mudge. Power: A first class design constraint for future architecture and automation. In *the 7th International Conference on High Performance Computing*, pages 215–224.
11. V. Zivojnovic, J.Martinez, C.Schlager, and H.Meyr. Dspstone: A dsp-oriented benchmarking methodology. In *Proceedings of the 1994 International Conference on Signal Processing Applications and Technology*, 1994.

Using Imprecise Computation Techniques for Power Management in Real-Time Embedded Systems

Geovani Ricardo Wiedenhoft and Antônio Augusto Fröhlich

Abstract Embedded systems present severe limitations in terms of processing and memory capabilities and are often powered by batteries, making energy an important resource to be managed. This work explores energy as a parameter for Quality of Service (QoS) of embedded systems. The goal is to guarantee the battery lifetime specified by the application and yet preserve the deadlines of essential (hard real-time) tasks. We propose equations to check at project-time if a given set of tasks are schedulable. At execution-time, a preemptive scheduler for imprecise tasks based on the EDF algorithm prevents the optional subtasks execution when ever there is the possibility of deadline loss or battery exhaustion. A prototype was developed in EPOS using power management mechanisms provided by the system.

1 Introduction

Embedded systems are computational platforms dedicated to execute an usually known set of tasks with specific objectives. Typically, these systems present severe limitations in terms of processing and memory capabilities. Some of them, due to the mobile nature of their applications, are also powered by batteries with a limited supply of energy. Considering all these limitations, it is important for the mobile embedded system to be able to manage energy consumption without compromising system's performance.

Embedded systems hardware can rely on several mechanisms to manage energy consumption. Among them, are techniques of DVS (Dynamic Voltage Scaling) and resources hibernation. Some works in the literature explore the integration of these techniques with approaches that guarantee quality of service (QoS). Most of these

---

Geovani Ricardo Wiedenhoft · Antônio Augusto Fröhlich
Laboratory for Software and Hardware Integration, Federal University of Santa Catarina, PO Box 476 – 88049-900 – Florianópolis, SC, Brazil
e-mail: grw,guto@lisha.ufsc.br

Please use the following format when citing this chapter:

Wiedenhoft, G.R. and Fröhlich, A.A., 2008, in IFIP International Federation for Information Processing, Volume 271; *Distributed Embedded Systems: Design, Middleware and Resources*; Bernd Kleinjohann, Lisa Kleinjohann, Wayne Wolf; (Boston: Springer), pp. 121–130.

approaches, however, only seek to minimize energy consumption with the main focus on traditional QoS metrics for processing, memory and communication. In a previous work [10], we argue that it is not enough just ensure traditional QoS metrics if, by doing so, the system runs out of battery and is unable to complete its computations.

We consider energy as a QoS parameter to meet the battery lifetime specified by the system developer, thus using QoS in terms of energy. In this work, the goal is not only to reduce energy consumption, but to improve the application utility in a system with limited energy charge, ensuring the battery lifetime and the deadlines of hard real-time tasks. The proposed approach expects the developer to define the period that the embedded system must be operational. By monitoring battery lifetime, the scheduler is able to select the tasks that will be executed or it can decrease QoS levels in order to reduce energy consumption and enhance system lifetime.

To achieve the proposed goal, the QoS control of applications was inspired by imprecise computation [5]. Imprecise computation divides tasks into two subtasks: one implementing a mandatory execution flow and another implementing an optional flow. The mandatory flow is the hard real-time part of the task, and it must always be executed with in its deadline. The optional flow is the *best-effort* part of the task, which is only executed if the desired timing requirements can be met. The imprecise computation scheduler does not execute the optional subtasks when there is the possibility of any mandatory subtask deadline to be lost, thus reducing the demand for system processing. Moreover, in our scheduler, we propose that the optional subtasks be prevented from executing when the energy level will not be sufficient to meet the time specified by application. This control creates more idle periods in the system, and the scheduler can use power management techniques to reduce the energy consumption of components during these idle periods.

The proposed scheduler is based on EDF (*Earliest Deadline First*) [4] scheduler, which the tasks with the lowest deadlines have the highest priorities. A prototype of this proposal was implemented in EPOS [6], a component-based embedded operating system. EPOS provides a set of mechanisms for power management, such as an infrastructure which allows applications to achieve appropriate power management [3] and a power manager with different operating modes that realize power management for application [9]. Moreover, EPOS provides a battery monitoring system, which informs the remaining energy in the platform.

2 Background

This work aims at guaranteeing that the batteries used in an embedded system can last at least the time required by the application and yet preserving the deadlines of essential tasks, i.e., the deadlines of hard real-time tasks. Our scheduler starts to decrease QoS levels in order to save energy when it detects that batteries will not last long enough to satisfy a previously defined expected system lifetime. The decreased control of application QoS levels is based on imprecise computation mechanisms [5], which divide tasks into two subtasks: a mandatory one and an optional one. The proposed scheduler is based on the EDF scheduling algorithm.

2.1 Imprecise Computation

Imprecise computation is a scheduling technique originally proposed to satisfy timing requirements of real-time tasks through decreasing levels of QoS. The control of application QoS levels done by imprecise computation worsens quality of results by not executing optional subtasks in order to guarantee that no mandatory subtask deadlines will be lost.

With the division of each task into two parts, imprecise computation unites real-time computing and *best effort* techniques for, respectively, the mandatory and optional subtasks. The mandatory subtask of imprecise tasks generates imprecise results which reflect the minimum of QoS to guarantee that these results are useful. These imprecise results have their quality enhanced when the optional subtask executes, generating the precise results.

The imprecise computation showed us favorable to use in our proposal in relation to energy. Suppose that a task consumes X energy units obligatorily. When it is divided into mandatory subtask (Y energy units) and optional subtask (Z energy units) the scheduler can save Z energy units if the optional subtask is not executed.

2.2 EDF

The EDF (*Earliest-Deadline First*) [4] algorithm is a real-time scheduling mechanism based on dynamic priorities and widely used in the literature. EDF distributes the highest priorities to the tasks with the shortest deadlines. At project-time a schedulability test evaluates the possibility of any task lose its deadline. At execution-time a preemptive scheduler selects to execute the highest priority task in *READY* state.

An exact schedulability test of the EDF algorithm is presented below. The real-time system considered contains n periodic and independent tasks, $\mathcal{T} = \{\tau_0, \tau_1, ..., \tau_{n-1}\}$. Each τ_i is characterized by three parameters, (P_i, D_i, C_i), where P_i is the period in which the task i is scheduled, D_i is the max relative deadline of conclusion in relation to instant of the task i release and C_i is the task i execution time in the worst case which included times waiting by the priorities reversal. In this test is supposed that $\forall \tau_i$, $D_i = P_i$. The utilization U_i of the task i in processing terms is represented by equation $U_i = \frac{C_i}{D_i}$. The processor's capacity is set to 1, i.e., 100%. A system with ω processors has ω capacity. Thus, in order to tasks to be schedulable in the EDF algorithm, the utilization sum of all the tasks must be less than or equal to the processors' capacity, i.e.,

$$\sum_{i=1}^{n}\left(\frac{C_i}{D_i}\right) \leq \omega \tag{1}$$

where $\omega = 1$ on a system with single-processor. If $\sum_{i=1}^{n} U_i > \omega$, the processor will be overloaded and the tasks will not be schedulable.

3 The Proposed Scheduling Strategy

Our scheduler, based on EDF, guarantees the execution of mandatory subtasks with their deadlines respectively met, independently of the system energy level. However, the optional subtasks execution is not guaranteed. The optional subtasks are executed only if the mandatory subtasks deadlines and the system's batteries lifetime desired by application are met.

The objective of this scheduler is not only save the energy consumed in the system — otherwise, the technique would simply never execute the optional subtasks — but to meet the battery lifetime specified by the application and to meet the mandatory subtasks deadlines with the execution of the maximum possible of the optional subtasks, thus optimizing the application utility.

Figure 1 presents proposed scheduler algorithm, which the subtasks are treated as tasks in terms of scheduling. π is the interval among battery charge measurements that can be specified by the application programmer and must take into consideration that each measurement consumes energy to be performed. This interval depends on the battery power state found in the last measurement.

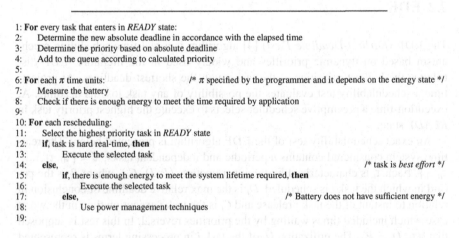

```
For every task that enters in READY state:
    Determine the new absolute deadline in accordance with the elapsed time
    Determine the priority based on absolute deadline
    Add to the queue according to calculated priority

For each π time units:        /* π specified by the programmer and it depends on the energy state */
    Measure the battery
    Check if there is enough energy to meet the time required by application

For each rescheduling:
    Select the highest priority task in READY state
    if, task is hard real-time, then
        Execute the selected task
    else,                                                          /* task is best effort */
        if, there is enough energy to meet the system lifetime required, then
            Execute the selected task
        else,                                   /* Battery does not have sufficient energy */
            Use power management techniques

```

Fig. 1 Proposed scheduler algorithm.

3.1 Schedulability Tests at Project-Time

The proposed scheduler is based on the EDF algorithm, thus it is possible to follow the same logic to calculate the tasks schedulability at project-time with a few adjustments. Suppose that the real-time system considered has n periodic and independent tasks, $\mathcal{T} = \{\tau_0, \tau_1, ..., \tau_{n-1}\}$, where $\forall \tau_i, D_i = P_i$. In the imprecise computation model, each τ_i is divided into mandatory and optional subtasks with execution times in the worst cases of μ_i and θ_i, respectively. Therefore, the total execution time of τ_i, in the worst case, is $C_i = \mu_i + \theta_i$. In order to guarantee that no mandatory subtasks deadlines will be lost, equation (2) must be respected.

$$\sum_{i=1}^{n}\left(\frac{\mu_i}{D_i}\right) + \sigma \leq \omega \tag{2}$$

Where $\omega = 1$ for a system with a single-processor and σ represents the interference in the worst cases, which includes: time spent in the operating system, context switch, scheduler algorithm. Equation (2) must be met in order for the tasks to be schedulable in relation to mandatory subtasks deadlines, otherwise, the processor is overloaded.

With the inclusion of the optional subtask execution time in equation (2), we can determine if the tasks as a whole will be executed, mandatory and optional subtasks. However, it is important to note that equation (3) is not a obligatory requirement in our algorithm and only will be relevant when equation (2) is true, otherwise, the tasks are not schedulable.

$$\sum_{i=1}^{n}\left(\frac{\mu_i + \theta_i}{D_i}\right) + \sigma \leq \omega \tag{3}$$

Mandatory and optional subtasks are schedulable in relation to their deadlines when equation (3) is respected. Otherwise, a certain fraction χ of optional subtasks is discarded. Equation (4) presents how to find the fraction χ.

$$\chi = \frac{\sum_{i=1}^{n}\left(\frac{\mu_i+\theta_i}{D_i}\right) + \sigma - \omega}{\sum_{i=1}^{n}\left(\frac{\theta_i}{D_i}\right)} \tag{4}$$

The energy-related objective can be achieved by following the same kind of logic presented thus far, but taking into account the tasks' energy consumption rate. The τ_i energy consumption in the wort case, E_i, is given by the sum of the energy consumption in the mandatory and optional subtasks worst cases times $E_{\mu i}$ e $E_{\theta i}$, respectively, ($E_i = E_{\mu i} + E_{\theta i}$). We suppose that, as with worst cases times, the worst cases energy consumptions are previously known by the application developer. These values can be obtained by energy profiling or another techniques. The maximum number of possible executions η_i of τ_i in the time required by application T_t is given by division between the time required and the execution interval of τ_i, i.e., $\eta_i = \frac{T_t}{P_i}$. T_t is given by the application developer based on battery capacity. In order to meet at least the mandatory parts of the tasks, we have equation (5) which indicates if the set of tasks will be schedulable with respect to energy.

$$\sum_{i=1}^{n}\left(\frac{E_{\mu i}\times\eta_i}{E_t}\right)+\varepsilon\leq 1 \tag{5}$$

Where E_t is the total energy of the system (battery specification), i.e., battery capacity, ε represents energy consumption in the worst case of different factors such as the energy consumed by the operating system, the context switch, the scheduler algorithm itself. The battery's capacity is set to 1, i.e., 100 %. Substituting η_i in the equation (5) we have equation (6).

$$\sum_{i=1}^{n}\left(\frac{E_{\mu i}\times T_t}{P_i\times E_t}\right)+\varepsilon\leq 1 \tag{6}$$

The tasks are schedulable in relation to energy in our algorithm if equation (6) is respected. Otherwise, the system will not meet the battery lifetime required by application for this set of tasks. The inclusion of the energy consumed by optional subtasks in equation (6) allows us to check if the tasks as a whole will be executed. As discussed previously, this is not an obligatory requirement and equation (7) only should be calculated if equation (6) is respected, i.e., mandatory subtasks met.

$$\sum_{i=1}^{n}\left(\frac{(E_{\mu i}+E_{\theta i})\times T_t}{P_i\times E_t}\right)+\varepsilon\leq 1 \tag{7}$$

All mandatory and optional parts of the tasks are executed in relation to system energy if equation (7) is respected. Otherwise, a certain fraction γ of optional subtasks will not be executed because the system would not meet the battery lifetime specified by the application. Equation (8) provides a fraction γ of optional subtasks discarded in relation to energy.

$$\gamma=\frac{\sum_{i=1}^{n}\left(\frac{(E_{\mu i}+E_{\theta i})\times T_t}{P_i\times E_t}\right)+\varepsilon-1}{\sum_{i=1}^{n}\left(\frac{E_{\theta i}\times T_t}{P_i\times E_t}\right)} \tag{8}$$

In this algorithm, the objective is to meet the two parameters in relation to time and energy, i.e., the mandatory subtasks deadlines and battery lifetime specified by the application, respectively. Thus, (9) is the full equation of our scheduler that must be true in order to tasks will be schedulable.

$$\left[\sum_{i=1}^{n}\left(\frac{\mu_i}{D_i}\right)+\sigma\leq\omega\right]\wedge\left[\sum_{i=1}^{n}\left(\frac{E_{\mu i}\times T_t}{P_i\times E_t}\right)+\varepsilon\leq 1\right] \tag{9}$$

The mandatory subtasks have their executions guaranteed in our scheduler in relation to time and energy if equation (9) is respected. The maximum fraction λ possible of optional subtasks lost in relation to time and energy can be obtained by equation (10).

$$\lambda = \max(\chi, \gamma) \tag{10}$$

3.2 Schedulability Test at Execution-Time

In order to provide QoS in terms of energy and make better use the resources with the optional subtasks execution it is necessary periodically to check at execution-time if the battery lifetime specified by the application $T_{t\kappa}$ in the instant κ can be achieved. Therefore, $T_{t\kappa}$ is recalculated in the instant κ according to the elapsed time. The total energy of the system (battery charge) $E_{t\kappa}$ also must be recalculated in the instant κ. The embedded systems platforms usually provide mechanisms to get the battery charge. Equation (11) can be recalculated with the new values in order to check if $T_{t\kappa}$ can be met in the instant κ.

$$\sum_{i=1}^{n} \left(\frac{E_{\mu i} \times T_{t\kappa}}{P_i \times E_{t\kappa}} \right) + \varepsilon \leq 1 \tag{11}$$

All mandatory subtasks are executed and optional subtasks will be scheduled if equation (11) is respected because this equation indicates there is sufficient energy to meet $T_{t\kappa}$. Otherwise, some optional subtasks will be discarded. The scheduler calls a power manager in the time that the optional subtasks would be in execution. Thus, it takes the idle time of the system in order to save energy. The optional subtasks return to be executed when it is observed that equation (11) returns to be true.

4 Implementation

A prototype was developed in order to test the proposed scheduler using EPOS (*Embedded Parallel Operating System*) [6]. EPOS is a framework of hierarchically organized components that generates application-specific runtime support systems. To do that EPOS analyzes the set of dedicated applications it must support prior to system generation time, thus configuring the system accordingly. Furthermore, through the separation of system abstractions, hardware mediators and scenario aspects, EPOS allows the development of fully platform-independent applications.

In EPOS, every system component implements a uniform power management interface [3]. This infrastructure allows applications to interact with the system to implement proper energy consumption management for embedded systems. Through the use that EPOS provides a low-overhead dynamic power manager [9]. This power manager uses re-pluggable heuristics, allowing configuration and adaptability to specific applications. The EPOS power manager has different operation modes, such as the possibility to choose if the manager will be on or off, the possibility of configuring only the desired components by the application for the power management, and if the manager will be active or passive in the power management.

EPOS also provides a battery charge monitor, which contributes to achieve the objectives of this work. The EPOS monitor is based on the battery voltage observation in order to get the battery charge, because the battery characteristic is to have its tension reduced as the use. However, there are some details to be observed, because the sampled voltage is not linearly related to battery discharge rate, the system does not have the ability to convert all provided tension in usable resource and also there is a minimum voltage that the system works. Thus, the monitor establishes a discreet relationship between the voltage and battery charge through the division of the obtained voltages in 10 time slices, which the voltages have different variations. Each slice corresponds to a nominal capacity percentage of the used battery.

The EPOS monitor does not implement a constant tracking of the real battery voltage, as each sampling consumes energy to be realized, in addition to considerably overhead for the application. In order to reduce these effects, the monitor uses a structure with information previously known which allows tracking the energy consumption in an approximate way. The information are in relation to specific characteristics of the battery and energy consumption by the system hardware components that will be monitored. The monitor verifies the battery charge through the voltage in the beginning of the execution, and during the execution updates the value with energy consumed by system peripherals.

We extended EPOS to support our scheduler with imprecise tasks and conditional executions to time and energy parameters. The tasks model in EPOS was based on monotone imprecise tasks. In this model, the monotone tasks improve the result quality at the time in execution and the worst case do not change the result. Thus, the mandatory subtasks generate results with the minimum QoS necessary to guarantee that these results are useful, and the optional subtasks realize successive refinements that results. The completion of these tasks can occur at any execution time without cause integrity problems in the results. Thus, the scheduler can decide at any instant to finalize the optional subtask execution. The application is responsible for the results integrity by different methods such as the use of control bits or the use of last data update timestamps.

The imprecise tasks implementation in EPOS was realized through the creation of two threads: one containing execution flow to handle the mandatory part and another with the execution flow to handle the optional part. The system creates these threads in a transparent manner to the programmer. This approach only expects the programmer to specify, when creating a imprecise thread, two entry points: one for the mandatory subtask and another for the optional subtask with their parameters.

The scheduler in execution always chooses the highest priority subtask in accordance with the deadlines as our algorithm is based in EDF. The optional subtasks are scheduled if there are not mandatory subtasks in *READY* state and if there is energy enough to meet battery lifetime specified by the application, i.e., optional subtasks have lower priorities than mandatory subtasks. When a mandatory subtask enters in *READY* state and its optional subtask is not yet finished the execution in the previous period, the scheduler immediately suspends this optional subtask execution. These characteristics prevent mandatory subtasks deadlines losses. The optional subtasks contexts are always restarted in a new task period.

The scheduler also updates at execution-time the $T_{\iota\kappa}$ with elapsed time and the $E_{\iota\kappa}$ using the EPOS energy monitor. Scheduler recalculates the equation (11) in periods π with these new values in order to check if the system is able to sustain the current workload without running out of battery before the required lifetime $T_{\iota\kappa}$ is achieved. π will depend on the last energy analysis. In the best case, equation (11) is respected and optional subtasks can be scheduled. Otherwise, optional subtasks are discarded and, taking advantage of the idle period created, the scheduler executes the EPOS power manager in passive mode. In addition to saving energy by not execute the optional subtasks, the power manager reduces the system energy consumption through the use of power management techniques. The optional subtasks return to execution when the scheduler identify $T_{\iota\kappa+\iota}$ can be met again in instant $\kappa+\iota$.

5 Related Work

GRACE-OS [11] is an energy-efficient operating system for mobile multimedia applications. This system uses a cross-layer adaptation technique to guarantee QoS on systems with adaptive software and hardware. It combines real-time scheduling with DVS mechanisms to dynamically manage energy consumption. It was implemented over the LINUX operating system and it only supports soft real-time tasks. GRUB-PA [8] is somehow similar to GRACE-OS. The main difference is GRUB-PA supports both soft and hard real-time tasks.

Niu [7] proposed to minimize energy consumed by soft real-time systems while guaranteeing QoS requirements. This goal is achieved by a hybrid static/dynamic scheduling algorithm that it uses DVS mechanisms and it partitions the set of tasks in mandatory and optional tasks. In this work, the QoS requirements are qualified by *(m,k)* constraints which it specifies that tasks must meet at least *m* deadlines in any *k* consecutive task releases. In a similar work, Harada [2] proposed to resolve the trade-off between QoS maximization and energy consumption minimization. It uses an allocation of processor cycles and frequency with QoS guarantees and it divides each task into mandatory and optional parts.

Other projects explore trade-off between application's QoS and energy consumption through adaptations in the applications aiming to meet the time specified by application. ODYSSEY [1] uses that idea. It monitors the energy budget and with this information it can select the correct state between energy saving and quality of application. This work also demonstrates how the applications can dynamically change their behavior ("fidelity" of the data) with the goal of saving energy.

ECOSYSTEM [12] is another operating system that supports application adaptation. This system is based in a "currency" that the applications use to allocate ("to pay") system resources (e.g., access to memory, network or disks), called *currentcy*. The system distributes *currentcies* periodically to tasks accordingly to an equation that defines the discharge rate that the system battery can assume to force the system to last for a defined period of time. This allows applications to adapt their execution based on their *currentcy* balance. This model unifies the calculation of energy on the various hardware devices and it provides a satisfactory energy allocation among the applications.

6 Conclusion

This work proposed an approach to exploit energy as a QoS parameter in order to guarantee that battery lifetime can last time desired by mobile embedded system and yet preserve the deadlines of hard real-time tasks. Our approach was inspired by imprecise tasks concepts, according to tasks can be divided into mandatory and optional parts. In this article, equations at project-time were presented with objective the of application programmer to check if a set of tasks will be schedulable in our algorithm in relation to two parameters desired, i.e., time and energy. At execution-time, our scheduler based on EDF algorithm ensures the mandatory subtasks deadlines and recalculates the equation of energy in order to check if the required battery lifetime will be met. The optional subtasks are prevented from executing, i.e, decreasing QoS levels if any required parameter will not be met. A prototype was developed in EPOS, which allowed the execution of a power manager in idle periods created by non-execution of the optional subtasks, thus reducing energy consumption by stopping or slowing down system components during these idle periods.

References

1. Flinn, J., Satyanarayanan, M.: Energy-aware adaptation for mobile applications. In: ACM SOSP '99, pp. 48–63. ACM Press, New York, NY, USA (1999)
2. Harada, F., Ushio, T., Nakamoto, Y.: Power-aware resource allocation with fair qos guarantee. In: IEEE RTCSA '06, pp. 287–293. IEEE Computer Society, Washington, DC, USA (2006)
3. Hoeller, A.S.J., Wanner, L.F., Fröhlich, A.A.: A Hierarchical Approach For Power Management on Mobile Embedded Systems. In: 5th IFIP DIPES, pp. 265–274. Braga, Portugal (2006)
4. Liu, C.L., Layland, J.W.: Scheduling algorithms for multiprogramming in a hard-real-time environment. J. ACM **20**(1), 46–61 (1973). DOI http://doi.acm.org/10.1145/321738.321743
5. Liu, J.W., Shih, W.K., Lin, K.J., Bettati, R., Chung, J.Y.: Imprecise computations. Proceedings of the IEEE **82**(1), 83–94 (1994)
6. Marcondes, H., Junior, A.S.H., Wanner, L.F., Fröhlich, A.A.: Operating Systems Portability: 8 bits and beyond. In: 11th IEEE ETFA, pp. 124–130. Prague, Czech Republic (2006)
7. Niu, L., Quan, G.: A hybrid static/dynamic dvs scheduling for real-time systems with (m, k)-guarantee. rtss **0**, 356–365 (2005)
8. Scordino, C., Lipari, G.: Using resource reservation techniques for power-aware scheduling. In: ACM EMSOFT '04, pp. 16–25. ACM Press, New York, NY, USA (2004)
9. Wiedenhoft, G.R., Hoeller, A.S.J., Fröhlich, A.A.: A Power Manager for Deeply Embedded Systems. In: 12th IEEE ETFA, pp. 748–751. Patras, Greece (2007)
10. Wiedenhoft, G.R., Hoeller, A.S.J., Fröhlich, A.A.: Quality-Of-Service: the Role of Energy. In: 9th Workshop on Real-Time Systems, pp. 107–110. Belem, Brazil (2007)
11. Yuan, W.: Grace-os: An energy-efficient mobile multimedia operating system. Ph.D. thesis, University of Illinois at Urbana-Champaign (2004)
12. Zeng, H., Ellis, C.S., Lebeck, A.R., Vahdat, A.: Ecosystem: managing energy as a first class operating system resource. In: ACM ASPLOS-X, pp. 123–132. ACM, New York, NY (2002)

A Power Model for Register-Sharing Structures

Balaji V. Iyer and Thomas M. Conte

Abstract Register files (RF) are known to consume about 20% of the power inside a processor. Embedded systems, due to area and timing constraints, generally have small register files, which can cause significant register pressure. This work explores how having a map-table or a map-vector can decrease the power dissipation in the processor. The distribution of register writes and sharing of commonly occurring values such as '0' is investigated. It is shown that systems with small register files obtain a greater power reduction than larger register files when these sharing structures are used. Finally, the proposed power model comes within 95% accuracy when compared using benchmarks on a synthesized Verilog softcore processor.

1 Introduction

Registers play a significant role to improve the instruction-level-parallelism (ILP), in modern systems [2, 5, and 11]. Large register files (RF), with the help of an optimal register allocation scheme, can greatly reduce the number of spill-code inserted in the program [1]. This can reduce the memory traffic, thus reducing the number of execution cycles necessary.

To remove false dependences in dynamically-scheduled processors, designers implement rename-map tables that map the architectural registers to physical registers [2, 3]. In statically scheduled systems, these false dependencies are resolved by using tighter register allocation schemes and/or large RF. In either case, there can be a huge amount of pressure exerted on RF [1].

Even though the idea of implementing a large RF is attractive for performance (figure-of-merit for performance is IPC), there can be setbacks in terms of energy

Balaji V. Iyer · Thomas M. Conte
Center of Efficient, Scalable and Reliable Computing, North Carolina State University, Raleigh, NC 27695
e-mail: bviyer, conte@ncsu.edu

Please use the following format when citing this chapter:

Iyer, B.V. and Conte, T.M., 2008, in IFIP International Federation for Information Processing, Volume 271; *Distributed Embedded Systems: Design, Middleware and Resources*; Bernd Kleinjohann, Lisa Kleinjohann, Wayne Wolf; (Boston: Springer), pp. 131–142.

or power dissipation, access time and chip area [12]. It is known that RF energy consumption accounts for about 10-20% of the overall energy consumption [3, 5]. For example, in the Motorola M.CORE architecture, the RF energy consumption accounts for 16% of the total processor power and 42% of the dual-path power.

Current embedded systems are required to achieve high performance, but many still must run on batteries [4, 13]. Battery technology significantly lags behind the processor's power consumption [13]. New technology processes currently allow higher integration density and larger chips, which leads to higher power consumption and heat radiation. High heat in chips can cause glitches, races and frequent errors [1].

To combat the performance degradation, researchers are exploring several hardware and software optimization techniques. Some of the software techniques include reducing value lifetimes [6, 10], content-based value storage [5], packing instructions into pairs [9], and value based register sharing [2, 11]. There are also several hardware based solutions to reduce the access time and power dissipation such as distributing the registers among clusters [10, 14] and gating certain unused registers in the RF [1].

The majority of the techniques mentioned above take advantage of value locality. The granularity of a value can be the whole word or even certain patterns in a word. These techniques exploit the fact that a large number of values written to registers are already present inside the RF. To do such value sharing between registers, some hardware addition is necessary.

The main aspect of this paper is to understand the power overhead added by these structures that aid register/value sharing. In addition, we point out when such structures are useful and help reduce the RF power dissipation. Moreover, we try to show how the patterns of register-writes can affect the power consumption of the RF. Finally, we validate our power-model using standard embedded benchmarks.

2 Related Work

Optimizing register-usage for performance improvement has been studied for the past two decades. The problems concerning power and heat dissipation in processors became a problem only in the nineties. Zyuban and Kogge in [16] study the power dissipation of an integer RF. Their models express the power consumption of a register in terms of the number of read-write ports and issue width. Similarly, Xao and Ye in [15] also provide models for finding power dissipation in RF.

Hu and Martonosi in [6] find that most read and write operations occur within a few cycles. They introduce a value aging buffer that saves recently-produced values so that the instructions requiring these values need not access them from RF. They received a power reduction of 30% with a less than 5% performance loss.

Kim and Mudge in [8] observe that only 0.1% of the cycles fully utilize a 16-bit read port of the RF. The main aim of their work was to reduce the number of read-ports, not the number of registers. They use a delay-writeback queue, an operation pre-fetch buffer and request queues. They show 22% reduction in energy per register access.

Gonzalez et al. in [5] explain ways to share partial values between registers inside a RF. They find a 50% reduction in power consumption with 1.7% IPC loss. Ayala, Veidenbaum and Lopez-Vallejo in [1] propose ways to statically find registers that are not used during certain times and turn-off these registers to reduce power. They show 46% energy reduction in the entire MiBench benchmark suite.

Seznec, Toullec and Rouchecouste in [10] propose that restricting certain function units to write and read only a subset of registers (clustering the processor) can reduce the access time by 33% and power by 50%. Jain et al. in [7] evaluate the RF for an ASIP using ARM7TDMI as a test processor. It is shown that there is a high correlation between performance improvement and energy reduction. They further prove that slight increase in number of registers will give a large amount of power reduction in ASIP (~50%).

Balakrishnan and Sohi in [2] discussed using a map-table for relieving register pressure by sharing values such as '0'. Tran et al. in [11] proposed a way to mark Reorder-buffers with one bit to indicate if the instruction's result from the ALU is a zero. [11] also discusses using a map-table as a possibility. These two papers are quoted extensively for value sharing inside the RF. In this work, we find the power contributions of these two types of structures for different configurations and percentage of zeros-writes in RF.

3 Experimental Frameworks

In order to view the register-value patterns, we picked four machines with different register-file sizes: ARM (thumb), OpenRISC, Simplescalar (PISA), and IA64. Table 1 below shows the register configuration of these four machines. The benchmark-set consists of 10 benchmarks from the EEMBC workload [20]. Table 2 explains these benchmarks. EEMBC is considered one of the most representative benchmarks in the industry today. Secondly, we modeled different RF configurations along with the appropriate sharing structures using Verilog. The original RF was extracted from the Verilog model of the OpenRISC 1000 processor [17]. The RF contains 2 read ports and 1 write port. These models were synthesized (0.18 μm IIT/OSU-standard-cell library) using Synopsys Design Analyzer and simulated using the Cadence NC-Verilog simulator to generate the VCD waveform files.

Table 1 Register file sizes of different architectures

Processor/Architecture	Number of Registers
ARM (thumb mode)	16
OpenRISC 1000 Processor	32
Simplescalar 2.0 Simulator (PISA) (using hard float)	64
IA-64 (using software floating point)	128
IA-64 (using hardware floating point)	256

Table 2 EEMBC Benchmarks Description

Benchmarks	Description
aifir01	FIR Filter
conven00	Convolutional encoder
Dither	Floyd-Steinberg error diffusion Dithering Algorithm
Ospf	Open-shortest path first/Dijkistra's Algorithm
Puwmod	Pulse Width Modulation Algorithm
rotate01	Image Rotation Algorithm
Routelookup	IP Datagram forwarding Algorithm
rspeed01	Road Speed Calculation
ttsprk01	Tooth-to-Spark tests in automobiles
viterb00	Viterbi Decoder

The synthesized register files along with the sharing structures are placed-and-routed using Cadence Design Encounter. The parasitic information is extracted during this process. Power analysis was done by Synopsys Primepower software using the VCD files, parasitic information and the synthesized gate-level verilog model. RF Inputs are discussed in section 5. Primepower is considered one of the most accurate power measurement tools, second only to SPICE [19].

4 Preliminary Analysis

To benefit from register sharing it is necessary to see if there is a great deal of duplicate values and constant values written into the registers. It was found by experimentation that '0' is the most frequent value written in the register-file. Table 3 shows the percentage of zero-writes and duplicate-writes (dupl. writes) in the ten benchmarks used in this work. Zero-writes are not necessarily a subset of duplicate writes, since in the life-time of a program, certain values can be re-written several times but not duplicated in the RF.

Table 3 Percentage of Zero-Writes and Duplicate-Writes for Different Architectures.

	ARM (Thumb Mode)		OpenRISC 1000		Simplescalar 2.0		IA-64 (Soft Float)		IA-64 (Hard Float)	
Benchmark	Zero-Write	Dupl. Write	Zero-Write	Dupl. Write	Zero-Write	Dupl. Write	Zero-Write	Dupl. Write	Zero-Write	Dupl. Write
aifirf01	24%	43%	13%	46%	20%	67%	1%	5%	1%	5%
conven00	15%	48%	30%	49%	25%	48%	1%	7%	1%	7%
dither	8%	14%	8%	21%	10%	15%	2%	10%	2%	10%
puwmod	3%	25%	6%	39%	3%	30%	1%	9%	1%	10%
rotate	3%	17%	3%	23%	3%	17%	1%	10%	1%	11%
routelookup	5%	40%	7%	53%	5%	44%	1%	5%	1%	5%
rspeed01	4%	20%	21%	45%	3%	23%	1%	7%	1%	7%
ttsprk01	5%	28%	25%	53%	3%	39%	1%	8%	1%	8%
viterbi	11%	31%	12%	40%	7%	42%	1%	6%	1%	6%
ospf	6%	35%	19%	41%	3%	32%	1%	5%	1%	5%

There are a large number of duplicate and zero-writes occurring inside a RF. The distribution of these writes also varies across benchmarks. In some benchmarks such as dither, the zero-writes occur in a pattern, but in benchmarks such as routelookup, they are very bursty. In the remaining benchmarks they are more or less random.

5 Register Sharing Techniques

Power dissipation of the RF is a popular research area. Many register optimization techniques can greatly help in improving the performance of the program. Most register-sharing techniques typically encompass using either a map-table [2] or a map-vector [11]. Figure 1 explains the top-level block diagram of these two structures.

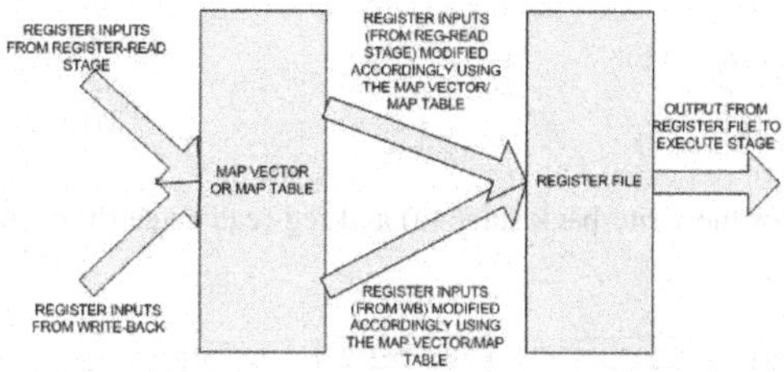

Fig. 1 Top-level block diagram of the map-table or the map-vector.

A register map-table is used to map certain architectural registers to physical registers that hold the certain values. Since there is a significant amount of '0' written into the RF, we choose one architectural register (r0) that is permanently grounded to zero. Any register whose value is zero is mapped to r0. The primary advantage of this scheme is that we do not access the RF for zero-writes, thus saving power.

A Second approach is to use a map-vector to indicate which registers hold the zero value. Each register is assigned a bit in the vector to indicate if its result is zero. If the corresponding bit is set, then the register-file is not accessed. In our experiments, map-vectors generally consume about 30-40% less power than a map-table. As soon as we reach the write-back stage, we know the register value along with the result to be written. If the value written is zero then a certain bit is set in a map-table and the RF is not accessed. Otherwise the value is forwarded to the RF and written to the appropriate register. Figure 2 present flow-charts for the steps in these stages. These structures were designed such that the processor's clock-cycle remains unaffected. The base processor's clock-period remains unaffected by using these structures.

To accurately portray register writes, 1-million register writes and 2-million register reads were generated. In each run we increased the number of zeros by a set percentage. Throughout the paper, the number of zeros in the stream is given in terms of percentage. It is worth mentioning that we only read registers that have already been written (with the exception of the stack pointer and the return value

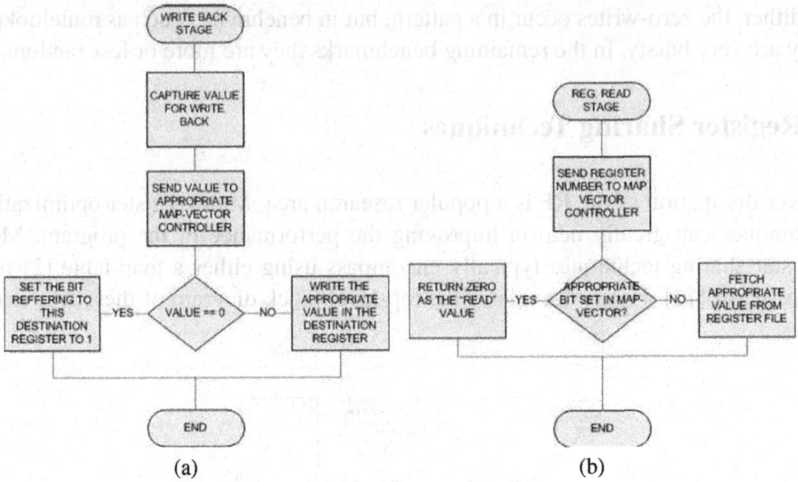

Fig. 2 Flow-diagram for the write-back stage (a) and reg-read stage (b) of the processor that uses a map-vector.

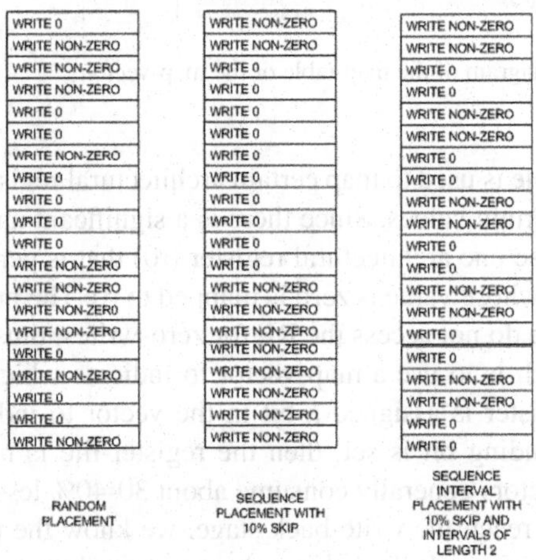

Fig. 3 Example of Different placement of zero-writes in our experiments (50% zero-writes) for 20 register-writes

register[1]). Figure 3 explains different test-input schemes. In Figure 3, the number of writes was reduced to 20 for the ease of explanation.

In addition, we also created sequences of zeros writes into the RF. These sequences of writes are placed in different regions. For example the sequence 40-10 implies that the first 10% of the register writes are non-zero values. Next 40% of the writes are zeros. Then, the remaining 50% of the values are non-zero writes.

[1] Registers r1 and r9 are designated as stack pointer and return register as described in [17].

We take this model further and break this zero sequence into intervals to see their effects. For example, 40-40-10 implies that the first 40% of the writes are non-zeros, and then in the next 60%, the 40% zeros (bold) are divided into intervals of 10%. In the next section we explain the results of these distributions.

6 Results

To see the impact of the RF size on power dissipation a 32-bit RF of size 16, 32, 64, 128 and 256 registers is modeled. The percentage of zero-writes (distributed randomly) is varied from 0-100% in 5% intervals. Figure 4-8 show our findings.

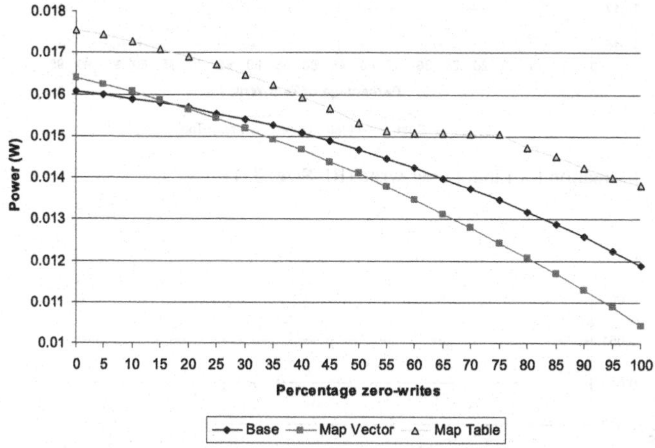

Fig. 4 Power dissipation (PD) for random reg-write for (RF size: 16)

In all cases, using a RF with a map-table consumed more power than using just the RF without any value sharing (the "base" case). The map-vector gives a power advantage when we have 20% and 45% of zeros for the RF size of 16 and 32, respectively. The map vector fails to provide a power-reduction for the 128 and 256-size RF. This is because the internal power of the cell dominates significantly for larger RF. For 64, the break-even point is after 95%.

In this work, leakage power is not a major factor. Static power, however, is a problem in the memory hierarchy [18]. Inside the processor, the dynamic power is a major contributor (~90-95%). In addition, the static power is not activity-based. The only way to reduce static power is through turning-off certain units, which is beyond the scope of this work [18].

Next the impact of writing zeros into RF in burst sequences placed at different parts of the trace is examined. Specifically, we wanted to see if scheduling a chunk of zero-writes in the beginning, middle or end would be most beneficial. Zero-writes were placed at 10%, 40% and 80% of the trace to see their impact. The chunk-size was modeled from 10-80% (whenever applicable). Table 4 shows our findings.

Positive values in tables 4 and 5 indicate a power reduction, while negative values indicate a power increase. Since the map-table failed to provide any power reduction for the overall system, we do not show its results for the rest of the paper.

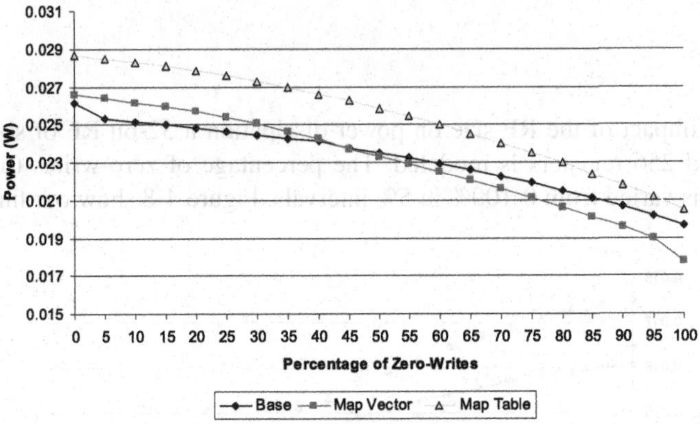

Fig. 5 Power dissipation for random reg-write (RF Size: 32)

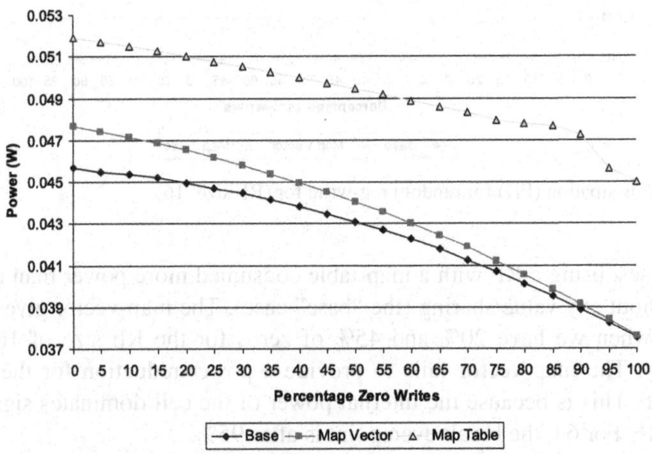

Fig. 6 Power-dissipation for random reg-write (RF size: 64)

It can be seen that for smaller register files, there is a power reduction even when zero-writes are not significant. As the register-file size increases, there must be a significant burst of zeros to get a power reduction. To understand why, we converted the register file into an appropriate SPICE model using the Synopsis Virtuoso toolset ("icfb") to see the transistor layout. We noticed that on large register files, the map-vectors created a significant amount of latches, which consumed a non-negligible amount of power. In addition, the wire-lengths between these map-vectors and the register-file interface were also huge. This increase in length caused an increase in wire-capacitance (verified using design encounter's parasitic values, and the capacitance using SPICE), which increased the dynamic power.

Now, we extend our previous results further and divide these sequences into burst interval chains. Typically in a program, the compiler will have an easier time to distribute 5-2% zero-write chains as supposed to a one single 10% chain. The values of intervals where chosen as 2%, 5%, and 10% respectively. These values are chosen because they are common divisors of 10, 40 and 80, thus making a fair comparison. Table 5 displays the results of this experiment. The trends noticed in this experiment are similar to the ones given in Table 4.

According to Table 4, small register-files greatly benefited with such structures when there were significant number of bursts. For small bursts, the map-vector contributed negatively to the power dissipation. One odd trend in Table 4 and 5 is that for the same set of sequences, a RF of size 64 did slightly worse than 128. Registers were chosen to write and read based on a random number generator. For a 128 RF, the probability of picking the same register to be written twice is significantly less than that of a 64 RF. Thus, there was more switching inside the RF of 64 than that of 128, thus we find a 0.3-0.5% difference. This phenomenon did not affect the 256 RF.

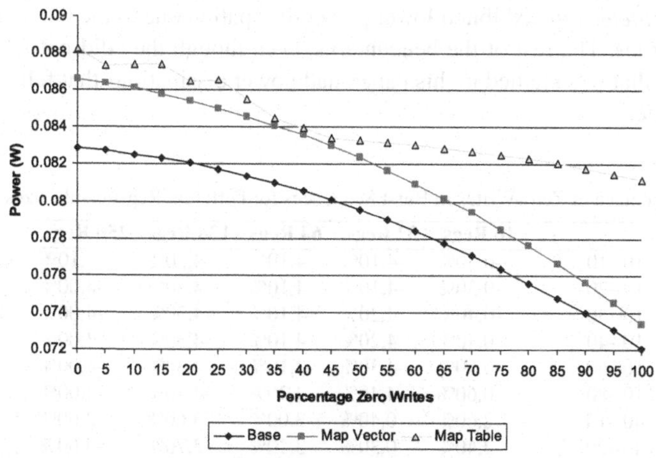

Fig. 7 Power Dissipation for random reg-write (RF size: 128)

The next step is to validate our power-model. For this work, we use the Open-RISC 1000 (OR32) processor. This processor is considered a valid representation of modern embedded systems [17]. The ten benchmarks mentioned in section 3 were executed on a Verilog-core of OR32 and the power values of each processor unit are captured separately. For this work, we only present the power-savings of the register-file. Table 6 displays our results. It can be seen that the power savings depicted using our synthetic benchmarks matched very closely to the values obtained using representative benchmarks. For example, the benchmark *conven00* had 30% zero-writes, and exhibited a 1.44% power reduction. Value obtained from the syn-

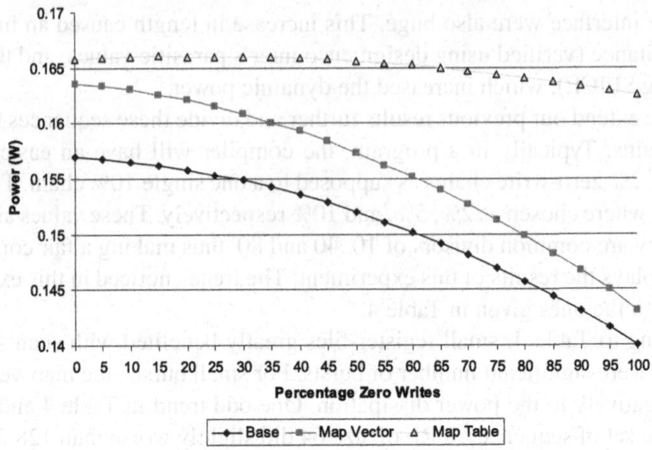

Fig. 8 Power Dissipation for random reg-write (RF size: 256)

thetic benchmarks in Figure 5 show a 1.47% reduction in power. The difference is mainly due to pipeline stalls and the differences in values that are written into the register. Similarly, *dither*, even though had approximately the same number of zero-writes as *routelookup*, exhibited lower power dissipation due to the bursty nature of the zero-writes. The rest of the benchmarks, even though they did not fall into the granularity that was studied in this paper, had power dissipations that fell within the correct range.

Table 4 Percentage of Zero-Writes in Burst Sequences for Different Register-file sizes

	16 Regs.	32 Regs.	64 Regs	128 Regs	256 Regs.
10--10	-0,30%	-4,10%	-4,10%	-4,30%	-4,10%
10--20	-0,30%	-4,10%	-4,10%	-4,30%	-4,00%
10--30	-0,40%	-4,20%	-4,10%	-4,30%	-4,00%
10--40	-0,40%	-4,20%	-4,10%	-4,30%	-4,00%
10--60	-0,50%	-4,30%	-4,10%	-4,30%	-4,00%
10--80	-0,60%	-4,40%	-4,20%	-4,30%	-4,00%
40--10	2,60%	0,40%	-3,00%	-3,60%	-3,60%
40--20	2,40%	0,30%	-3,10%	-3,70%	-3,60%
40--30	2,00%	0,30%	-3,20%	-3,80%	-3,60%
40--40	1,80%	0,40%	-3,40%	-3,80%	-3,70%
40--50	1,60%	0,50%	-3,40%	-3,90%	-3,70%
80--10	7,40%	6,90%	-1,60%	-2,70%	-3,00%
80--20	6,50%	7,40%	-1,80%	-2,90%	-3,10%

Table 5 Percentage of Zero-Writes in Sequence-intervals for Different Register-file sizes

	16 Regs.	32 Regs.	64 Regs	128 Regs	256 Regs.
10--10--2	-25,30%	0,40%	-2,70%	-1,70%	-5%
10--10--5	-25,40%	0,40%	-2,80%	-1,70%	-5%
10--10--10	-25,40%	0,40%	-2,80%	-1,70%	-5,00%
10--40--2	-25,30%	0,40%	-2,70%	-1,70%	-5,10%
10--40--5	-25,30%	0,40%	-2,80%	-1,70%	-5,00%
10--40--10	-25,30%	0,40%	-2,70%	-1,70%	-5%
10--80--2	-25,40%	0,40%	-2,70%	-1,70%	-5,00%
10--80--5	-25,30%	0,40%	-2,70%	-1,70%	-5,00%
10--80--10	-25,40%	0,40%	-2,80%	-1,70%	-5,00%
40--10--2	4,00%	2,30%	-1,90%	-1,10%	-3,60%
40--10--5	3,80%	2,10%	-2,10%	-1,30%	-3,50%
40--10--10	3,80%	2,10%	-2,20%	-1,40%	-3,60%
40--40--2	3,10%	1,70%	-2,20%	-1,30%	-4,90%
40--40--5	3,00%	1,50%	-2,40%	-1,50%	-4,80%
40--40--10	3,00%	1,50%	-2,40%	-1,50%	-4,60%
80--10--2	10,10%	2,70%	-2,00%	-1,00%	-1,70%
80--10--5	9,90%	2,50%	-2,10%	-1,30%	-1,70%
80--10--10	9,00%	2,70%	-2,10%	-1,30%	-2,10%

Table 6 Power Reduction using Map-vector on EEMBC Benchmarks

	Percent Zero Writes	Power Savings
aifirf01	13%	-1,06%
conven00	30%	1,44%
dither	8%	-0,78%
puwmod	6%	-1,33%
rotate	3%	-1,33%
routelookup	7%	-1,33%
rspeed01	21%	0,28%
ttsprk01	25%	0,74%
viterbi	12%	-0,95%
ospf	19%	0,23%

7 Conclusion

This study reveals several power dissipation patterns of the RF. First, adding a map-vector can cause a power reduction only when there is a significant amount of zero-writes present in the workload. Similarly, scheduling multiple zero-writes together, regardless of the destination registers, can give some power reduction for a small RF. Some power-reduction can also be achieved if it is able to divide the register write into intervals rather than just placing them at random. Finally, the power difference obtained when using such structures is at least 95% accurate when verified using real benchmarks.

These techniques can be extended to a physical or an architectural register file. The impact of zero-writes on power dissipation can be useful in several ways. For example, a compiler can use this information and schedule instructions that potentially have a zero-write together and form chunks. In addition, the processor can gate a map-vector when the compiler or a profiler can predict and communicate that the number of zero-writes in the system is low. Another option is to run a similar workload in a simulator to predict the amount of zero-writes and have the compiler schedule specialized instructions that enables or disables the register sharing structure based on the workload.

References

1. J. L. Ayala, A. Veidenbaum, M. Lopez-Vallejo, "Power-Aware Compilation for Register file energy reduction," *International Journal of Parallel Programming,* Vol. 31, No. 6, 2003
2. S. Balakrishnan, G. S. Sohi, "Exploiting Value Locality in Physical Register Files," *Intl. Symposium on Microarchitecture,* 2003
3. R. Balasubramonian, S. Dwarkadas, D. H. Albonesi, "Reducing the Complexity of the Register File in Dynamic Superscalar Processors," *Intl. Symposium on Microarchitecture, 2001*
4. A. Bechini, T. M. Conte, C. A. Prete, "Opportunities and Challenges in Embedded Systems," *Proc. of the Intl. Symposium on Microarchitecture*, August 2004.
5. R. Gonzalez, et al., "A Content Aware Integer Register File Organization," *ISCA*, 2004
6. Z. Hu, M. Martonosi, "Reducing Register File Power Consumption by Exploiting Value Lifetime Characteristics," *Workshop on Complexity Effective Design, 2000*
7. M. K. Jain, et al., "Evaluating Register File Size in ASIP Design," *Proc. of 9th Intl. Symposium on Hardware-Software Codesign,* 2001
8. N. S. Kim, T. Mudge, "The Microarchitecture of a Low Power Register File," *ISLPED,* 2003
9. M. T, Lee, et al., "Power Analysis and Minimization Techniques for Embedded DSP Software," *IEEE Trans. on VLSI Systems, Vol.* 5, No. 1, 1997
10. A. Seznec, E. Toullec, O. Rochecouste, "Register Write Specialization Register Read Specialization: A Path to Complexity-Effective Wide-Issue Superscalar Processors," *International Symposium on Microarchitecture,* 2002
11. L. Tran, et al., "Dynamically Reducing Pressure on the Physical Register File through Simple Register Sharing," *Intl. Symposium on Performance Analysis of Systems and Software,* 2004
12. M. Pericas, et al., "An Optimized Front-end Physical Register File with Banking and Writeback Filtering," *Workshop on Power-Aware Computer Systems,* 2004
13. L. Wehmeyer, et al., "Analysis of the Influence of Register File size on energy consumption, code-size and execution time," *IEEE Transactions on Computer-Aided Design of Integrated Circuits and Systems,* Vol. 20, No. 11, November 2001
14. J. Zalamea, et al., "Hierarchical Clustered Register File Organization for VLIW Processors," *Proc. of the Intl. Parallel and Distributed Processing Symposium, 2003*
15. X. Zhao, Y. Ye, "Structure Configuration of Low-power register file using energy model," *Proc. of the IEEE Asia-Pacific Conference on Application-Specific Integrated Circuits,* 2002
16. V. Zyuban, P. Kogge, "The Energy Complexity of Register Files," *Proc. of ISLPED,* 1998.
17. "OpenRISC Architecture Manual," http://www.opencores.org, 2003
18. N. S. Kim et al., "Leakage current: Moore's law meets static power," IEEE Computer, Vol. 26, Issue 12, 2003
19. R. Goering, "Synopsys launches more powerful power-analysis tool," EE-times, 2000
20. "Embedded Benchmark Consortium", http://www.eembc.org/

Design and Implementation of a FTT-CAN Communication Infra-Structure for the RT-femtoJava Processor

Rita Kalile Almeida Andrade, Thomás Alimena Del Grande, Tiago Bücker, and Carlos Eduardo Pereira

Abstract The paper describes the development of a flexible time-triggered (FTT) communication infrastructure for a customizable Real-time Java processor called RT-FemtoJava. The proposed infrastructure allows a holistic scheduling of both messages and tasks in the platform. It permits a high level of abstraction for implementing distributed and communicating tasks. Two different results are presented: (i) the incorporation of a FTT-CAN communication and a holistic scheduler for the RT-FemtoJava processor and (ii) the design and implementation of the FTT-communication profile on top of a wireless protocol. The developed infrastructure allows the deployment of real-time distributed embedded systems that can balance performance and resource constraints.

1 Introduction

When dealing with Distributed Embedded Real-Time Systems (DERTS), having a reliable and deterministic communication system is mandatory, especially when it involves critical operations, such as in flight-control or process control systems. Additional to this need for a deterministic temporal behavior, the requirement for flexible operation is becoming increasingly important in modern industrial systems. The FTT-CAN protocol [1] is an approach that aims to meet both deterministic vs flexible behavior requirements by supporting both time-triggered (TT) and event-triggered (ET) communication schemes.

Rita Kalile Almeida Andrade
Federal University of Rio Grande do Sul - UFRGS - Informatics Institute

Thoms Alimena Del Grande, Tiago Bcker
Federal University of Rio Grande do Sul - UFRGS - Electrical Engineering Department

Carlos Eduardo Pereira
Federal University of Rio Grande do Sul - UFRGS - Informatics Institute and Electrical Enginnering Department

Please use the following format when citing this chapter:

Andrade, R.K.A., et al., 2008, in IFIP International Federation for Information Processing, Volume 271; *Distributed Embedded Systems: Design, Middleware and Resources*; Bernd Kleinjohann, Lisa Kleinjohann, Wayne Wolf; (Boston: Springer), pp. 143–150.

In this work, an FTT interface for the RT-FemtoJava processor [8] is presented. The RT-FemtoJava is a custommizable processor that interprets Java bytecodes, allowing a high level of abstraction when it comes to writing the software and is suitable for real-time applications for having a real-time clock and an API designed for such utilization. Tasks executed on the RT-FemtoJava processor are scheduled by a holistic scheduler which schedules messages and tasks according to system timing requirements.

The remainder of this paper is organized as follows. A brief overview of the FTT-CAN is presented in Section 2. Section 3 describes related works dealing with the use of FTT-CANs extensions. Section 4 introduces the RT-FemtoJava processor. Section 5 presents the implementation of the FTT-CAN protocol for the RT-FemtoJava and a wireless solution for the same platform in Section 6. Section 7 proposes a holistic scheduler. Concluding, the final remarks are presented in Section 8.

2 Flexible Time Triggered on CAN (FTT-CAN) - briefly review

As already mentioned, FTT-CAN combines time- and event-triggered communication with temporal isolation. An elementary cycle separates the communication in two phases: one for time-triggered messages and another one to event-triggered messages. The scheduling of time-triggered messages is performed at runtime by a master node.

Additionally, the FTT-CAN uses the collision avoidance that is intrinsic of the CAN protocol, reducing the communication overhead. The protocol uses a master-multi-slave transmission control, meaning that the same master message can trigger simultaneously the transmission of the messages in different nodes [1]. CANs arbitration control is also used to control the event-triggered traffic, eliminating the need for pooling messages. Slaves try to transmit pending event-triggered messages immediately after the starting of the appropriate phase. Interested readers should refer [1] for details on FTT-CAN.

3 Related Works

Recent proposals address extensions to FTT protocol to improve some drawbacks. The approach presented in [2] introduces an extension to the FTT-CAN that improves the bit stuffing pessimism and eliminates priority inversion situation and introduces an offset method to enforce correct message order. Additionally, to reduce the jitter, a time slot for TT tasks was proposed in order to reduce the interference of the ET messages within the TT phase. The extension was implemented over an embedded Real-Time Linux.

In [4] a framework was built to support design of task and message dispatching that uses a centralized approach through a holistic scheduler. This work specifies necessary tasks and messages parameters and a mechanism to synchronize the scheduling of them. This mechanism was validated by the SimHol simulator.

In [3] a computational model based on RMI and RTSJ definition was presented. That work assembles a convergence layer that manages the underlying resources involved in a master-slave communication through a new API. It is based on the Flexible Time-Triggered communication paradigm adapted to the unicast environment provided by RT-RMI. The cost of sending and processing a trigger signal is evaluated using a mono-processor environment. Both master and slaves reside in the same virtual machine, in order to minimizes the network effects on the application. For that work uses the jTime [3] virtual machine.

This work differs from the presented approaches above, in the sense that it proposes a holistic scheduling systems that follows the RTSJ standard and the FTT-CAN paradigm. From developers point of view, calls to remote methods do not differ from calls to local objects. Event-triggered messages are scheduled according to the actual runtime situation (i.e. messages priority and ready tasks's priorities) without disturbing time-triggered messages. The proposed mechanism runs over the configurable Java platform called RT-FemtoJava platform.

4 RT-FemtoJava

RT-FemtoJava is a configurable platform that implements a stack machine processor with different organization (e.g. multicycle, pipeline, VLIW) which natively executes Java bytecodes and provides a set of APIs to implement the embedded systems software. The RTFemtoJava processor is configured through the SASHIMI environment [6], which takes as input Java bytecoded. Additionally, it optimizes the binary code to assure the predictability of applications software. Details on this optimization process can be found in [7].

The embedded systems software is written using an API based on the Real-Time Specification for Java (RTSJ) which was developed to express time and other constraints of the embedded real-time applications. This specification introduces the concept of schedulable objects, which are instances of classes that implement the Schedulable interface, such as the RealtimeThread. It also specifies a set of classes to store parameters that represent a particular resource demand from one or more schedulable objects. For example, the ReleaseParameters class (superclass from AperiodicParameters and PeriodicParameters) includes several useful parameters for the specification of real-time requirements. Moreover, it supports the expression of the following elements: time values (absolute and relative time), timers, periodic and aperiodic tasks, asynchronous events and their handlers, and different scheduling policies.

The next section a proposal to integrate the RTSJ-based API with the communication API trough a holistic scheduler that follows the FTT-CAN protocol will be presented.

5 FTT-CAN Integration

In order to allow a RT-FemtoJava processor to communicate over a FTT-CAN network, a FTT-CAN module was written in VHDL language. Advantages of this solution from a software implementation are the lower jitter and lower processor utilization. The main disadvantage is, clearly, higher die area.

It utilizes a CAN module that implements the native CAN protocol, that involves data framing, bit synchronization, bit stuffing, CRC checking, bus arbitration and so on. Taking advantage of that, the FTT-CAN module is built on top of the CAN module, by means of finite state machines that manage the timing constraints imposed by the FTT-CAN protocol.

Before synthesizing the project, one needs to specify if the node in question is a possible master or not. Bus masters are responsible for generating the Trigger-Message. They are also responsible for scheduling the TT messages. For this purpose, it was used a dual-port RAM memory, allowing a future development of an admission control system either by the RT-FemtoJava or a separate entity. In the current version, the master node reads parameters -like period and phase - from this memory, and schedules the messages with the granularity of one Elementary Cycle, that means, the smaller period of a synchronous message is the period of the Elementary Cycle.

By the start of the Trigger Message, the nodes set a global counter to 0 (zero), so that all FTT-CAN nodes in the network are synchronized. This process avoids priority inversion in the synchronous window because the transmission of the message with the highest priority will not be delayed by any means, while in a software implementation the transmission could be delayed by another thread or process running in the processor. Bit-stuff pessimism in the synchronous window is also avoided with the creation of time-slots that are longer than the longest message (considering all possible bit stuffing).

The interface between the RT-FemtoJava and the FTT-CAN module is obtained via memory-mapped registers. In the current configuration, the processor writes in specific registers the message identifiers that it wishes to produce to or consume from the bus. After that, the processor can write data in transmission registers that will have identifiers previously configured and read data from reception registers. The processor is responsible for polling a status register to know if determined messages have arrived or have been transmitted successfully.

6 A wireless approach for FTT

Additional to the us of a FTT-CAN approach, a wireless FTT interface was also implemented on the top of IEEE 802.15.4 standard, taking advantage of the superframe structure, shown in figure 1. The superframe is bounded by the transmission of periodic beacon frames, followed by a Contention Access Period (CAP) and an optional contention free-period (CFP), used by low latency applications. A simple equivalence between the elementary cycle of FTT and this superframe structure gives an interesting solution to develop a FTT wireless system.

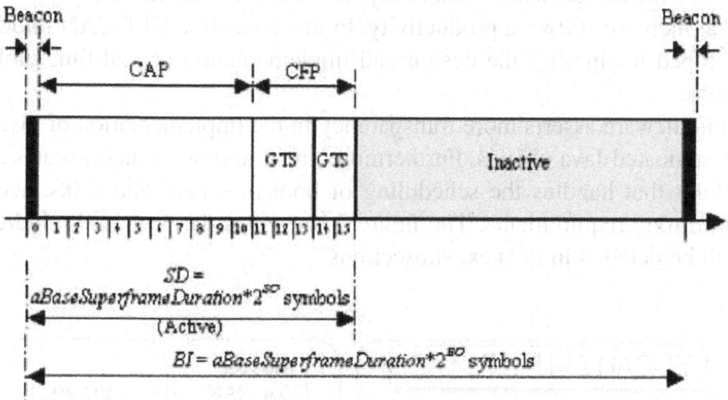

Fig. 1 Exemple of Superframe Structure.

The FTT communication over the IEEE 802.15.4 standard was also written in VHDL language and connected to the RT-FemtoJava. The master node, defined before synthesizing the project, broadcast the beacon frames at periodic intervals according to the generics sets in the top of the entity. Like in the FTT-CAN module, the scheduled of TT messages are supported by a dual-port RAM memory. In this case, however, the memory must also contain the address of nodes able to transmit. If any TT message is sent in the current elementary cycle, the master node sends the correct CFP parameters to allocate a guaranteed time slot where only the scheduled node can transmit.

Slave synchronization is done in every beacon frame receipt, when a counter starts and produces the 15 time slots of the active superframe structure. In the CAP region, when a node wants to transmit, the transceiver is set to energy detection mode and returns an interrupt signalling whether the channel is busy or not. This mechanism allows the traffic of asynchronous messages. How said in the last paragraph, TT traffic are in the CFP region, where only the scheduled node can transmit. Traffic isolation is promoted by the beacon frame subfield final CAP slot.

The interface between RT-FemtoJava and FTT module is the same defined in the previous section. A little difference is related to the producer/consumer model implemented, where slave nodes use a point-to-point communication with master to produce its message and this one broadcasts it. Therefore, the master must consume all network messages.

7 The FTT-CAN Middleware

Software is increasingly becoming the major cost factor for embedded devices. Nowadays, with the growing complexity of DERTS, it is necessary to use techniques that increase software productivity. In this context, a FTT-CAN middleware was developed to simplify the design and implementation of real-time embedded applications.

This middleware asserts more transparency in the implementation of distributed and communicated Java objects. Furthermore, the middleware incorporates a holistic scheduler that handles the scheduling of both messages and tasks, according to system timing requirements. The figure 2 illustrates the proposed middleware - which will be detailed in the next subsections.

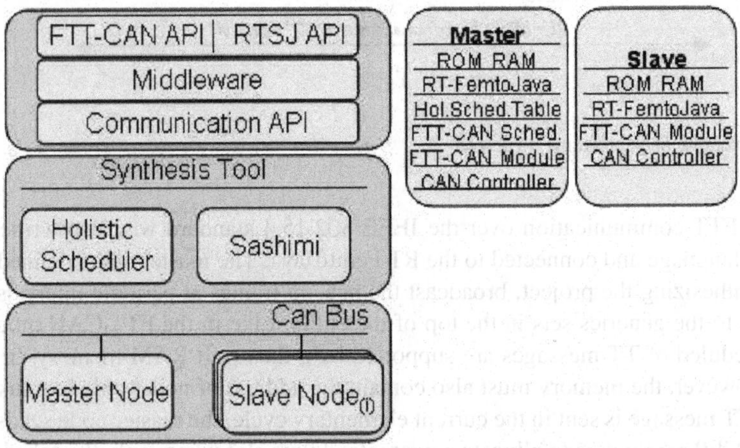

Fig. 2 Design flow of the Platform.

7.1 The Framework

This framework is composed of a middleware and APIs who allows to abstract inherent details about the distribution and the communication protocol. Standalone tasks must follow the RTSJ-based API, mentioned at Section 4. Communicating tasks must be specified using primitives of the FTT-CAN API and their temporal parameters using the RTSJ-based API.

The middleware identifies temporal tasks parameters and their messages and organize them to be used by the FTT-CAN Scheduler, that composes the FTT-CAN Module. The messages are separated in asynchronous or event-triggered (ET) and synchronous or time-triggered (TT) which are based at priority and periodicity, respectively. Messages parameters are marshalled and unmarshalled by the middleware, making the distribution transparent to programmers.

Communication facilities are provided through the APICOM for the RT-FemtoJava processor, which adds an interface between the application layer and the communication system detailed in Section 5 and 6. The communication system was proposed to provide synchronous and asynchronous message exchange among objects running at different RT-FemtoJava processors into the same chip and/or running at different nodes connected through a communication network. The API allows applications to establish a communication channel through the network, which is used to send and receive messages. The service allows the assignment of different priorities and periods to messages and runs in a multithread environment. From the application point-of-view, the system is able to open and close connections, in a client-server mode, or run in publisher-subscriber mode.

7.2 The Holistic Scheduler

According to the communication paradigm, every communicating task uses messages to exchange data with other tasks. However, at a first moment, the ET tasks are not considered by holistic scheduling process, but they are equally supported by the platform development. Although predictability is a requirement for both ET and TT phases, our focus here is on the response time of the TT phase because it requires a high degree of responsiveness (since TT are usually time critical with hard real-time requirements).

The FTT-CAN Scheduler in the Master Node uses a table to make the global synchronization to join the dispatching of tasks and messages exchanges. This table is built by the holistic scheduler. The holistic scheduler creates a graph which contains the order of dependences among communicating tasks. From this graph the scheduler is made by selecting tasks (node-centric) or messages (netcentric) and adapting its dependences, which are known by through the graph, according to system timing requirements. This scheduler follows the approach specified in [4].

8 Final Remarks

This paper presents an ongoing work that proposes a holistic scheduler component, which will integrate an RTSJ-based API and a communication API. The selected communication protocol is the FTT-CAN. This choice was made mainly due to the characteristics of the FTT-CAN protocol, which can provide features such admission control and flexibility. Additionally, was implemented a wireless approach. Both modules, FTT-CAN and wireless, are integrated to RTFemtoJava processor and synthesized in a Virtex-II Pro Xilinx [5] FPGA.

A holistic scheduler was implemented, as well as the parameters describing communication characteristics of task. Currently the system is being validated through some case studies in order to ensure that the proposed scheduler meet all specified application requirements. In future work, we intend to complete the middleware integration to the platform and obtain results about jitter and latency.

References

1. L. Almeida, J. Fonseca, and P. Fonseca. The FTT-CAN Protocol: Why and How. *IEEE Transactions on Industrial Electronics*, 49(6), December 2002.
2. F.H. Athaide, C.E. Pereira, and V.F. Silva. A new approach for time-triggered phase in the FTT-CAN protocol a case study in an automotive system. In *Proc. of RTSS*, 2006.
3. P. Basanta-Val, L. Almeida, and M. Garca-Valls. Towards a synchronous scheduling service on top of a unicast distributed real-time Java. In *Proc. of Real Time and Embedded Technology and Applications Symposium*, 2007.
4. M. J. Calha. A holistic approach towards flexible distributed systems. Technical report, Universidade de Aveiro Departamento de Electrnica e Telecomunicaes, 2006.
5. http://www.xilinx.com.
6. S. Ito, L. Carro, and R.P. Jacobi. Making Java work for micro-controller applications. *IEEE Design & Test of Computers*, 18(5):100–110, 2001.
7. M. A. Wehrmeister, C. E. Pereira, and L. B. Becker. Optimizing the generation of object-oriented real-time embedded applications based on the real-time specification for Java. In *Proc. of DATE06*, pages 806–811, Munich, Germany, 2006.
8. M.A. Wehrmeister, L.B. Becker, and C.E. Pereira. Optimizing real-time embedded systems development using a RTSJ-based API. *Lecture Notes in Computer Science*, 3292:292, 2004.

Communication Paradigms for High-Integrity Distributed Systems with Hard Real-Time Requirements

Santiago Urueña, Juan Zamorano, José A. Pulido, and Juan A. de la Puente

Abstract The development and maintenance of high-integrity software is very expensive, and a specialized development process is required due to its distinctive characteristics. Namely, safety-critical systems usually execute over a distributed embedded platform with few hardware resources which must provide real-time communication and fault-tolerance. This work discusses the adequate communication paradigms for high-integrity distributed applications with hard real-time requirements, and proposes a restricted middleware based on the current schedulability theory which can be certified and capable to obtain the required predictability and timeliness of this kind of systems.

1 Introduction

On-board embedded computers play a crucial role in spacecrafts, where they perform both platform control functions, such as guidance and navigation control or telemetry and tele-command management, and payload specific functions, such as instrument control and data acquisition. One distinctive characteristic of on-board computer systems is that hardware resources are scarce, due to the need to use radiation-hardware chips and limitations in weight and power consumption, and these resources are distributed due to the physical distance between the instruments and to replicate mission-critical components. Another key aspect of these systems is the presence of high-integrity and hard real-time requirements, which raises the need for a strict verification and validation (V&V) process both at the system and software levels [1]. This new step in the development process is called *certification*. It is a very expensive process which will shape the complete development tools and methods of the system.

Santiago Urueña · Juan Zamorano · José A. Pulido · Juan A. de la Puente
Technical University of Madrid (UPM), Dept. of Telematic Systems Engineering (DIT), Spain.
e-mail: {suruena, jzamorano, pulido, jpuente}@dit.upm.es

Please use the following format when citing this chapter:

Urueña, S., et al., 2008, in IFIP International Federation for Information Processing, Volume 271; *Distributed Embedded Systems: Design, Middleware and Resources*; Bernd Kleinjohann, Lisa Kleinjohann, Wayne Wolf; (Boston: Springer), pp. 151–160.

It is worth noting that inside a high-integrity system not all the software has the same criticality: while some applications have a direct implication in the safety of the system, a fault in other parts of the code will result only in minor effects [2]. Therefore, not all the software is certified to the highest *criticality level* to save costs. *Ravenscar* is a computational model designed for high-integrity, hard real-time, embedded systems [3]. It is a profile that specifies the set of operations that the real-time operating system (RTOS) has to provide, and also the set of forbidden operations that would made the system unpredictable. On the one hand, Ravenscar compliant real-time kernels have to provide less functionality than other RTOSs, and therefore they are be smaller and easier to certify. On the other hand, applications developed under the Ravenscar restrictions are suitable to temporal analysis.[1]

Due to the specific characteristics of this kind of systems a general purpose middleware cannot be used to develop high-integrity code. The objective of this paper is to describe the design principles used in a safety-critical middleware for the European Space Agency (ESA), discussing the most adequate communication paradigms and the requirements of a high-integrity middleware. In the end, the main goal is to be able to analyze statically the schedulability of its hard real-time deadlines. This paper is organized as follows. Section 2 describes the contributions and related work, while Section 3 sets the computational model. Section 4 defines a set of restrictions for building safety-critical distributed systems, including the implementation requirements and an analysis of the adequate communication paradigms. Finally, Section 5 summarizes the main conclusions of this work.

2 Contributions and related work

This paper builds upon current advances in scheduling theory for distributed hard real-time systems. Tindell and Clark [4] extended the response time analysis techniques used for event-triggered single processors to distributed systems, introducing the concept of holistic schedulability. Later, Palencia and González Harbour [5] improved the technique to reduce the pessimism of transactions.

The main objective of this work was the development of a Ravenscar-compliant middleware for next-generation space-crafts. Specifically, the main contributions of this paper are:

1. Specification of the distribution requirements of the aero-space industry;
2. Modelization and response time analysis of the specific distributed system;
3. Restrictions needed for a safety-critical middleware, and adequate communication paradigms.

Some of the restrictions specific to the Ada programming language were published previously by the authors [6], but this paper extends that work and makes the requirements language independent.

[1] Actually *Ravenscar* is a village in England, where experts from industry and academy in high-integrity and hard real-time systems met to define the profile.

Kopetz elaborated the Time-Triggered Architecture (TTA) [7] to provide hard real-time communication for safety-critical distributed systems. However, a time-triggered middleware presents similar scalability problems for development and maintenance than cyclic executives. In contrast, a Ravenscar-compliant middleware supports time-triggered and event-triggered programming. Some past publications about the specific topic of Ravenscar-compliant distributed systems exists [8], but only discussing the research challenges.

3 Computational model

3.1 Industrial requirements

The following list of requirements has been extracted from the needs expressed by different companies from the aero-space industry. Namely, they represent the middleware requirements found during the development of different projects for the European Space Agency (ESA), including self-maintained long-term satellites, mission-critical unmanned space vehicles, and satellite fleets:

- **Predictability**: End-to-end transfers in bounded time for messages with hard real-time deadlines.
- **Fault tolerance**: Replication of network links and/or routers for resilience to hardware failures.
- **Diagnostic information**: The application should be able to know the status of a node and communication links.
- **Multicast communication**: One-to-many communication, even if the network does not support broadcasting operations.
- **Message segmentation**: The partitioning of messages greater than the maximum transfer unit should be done by the middleware.
- **Message forwarding**: Transparent communication between nodes not directly connected.

Some of these requirements complicate the implementation of the middleware and the static analysis of the whole system. However, it should be noticed that not all these requirements are needed in every application nor in every criticality level. In fact, the system integrator should be able to disable the unwanted functionality at design time to ease the certification of the system and to reduce the performance penalty. Therefore, the middleware must be tailorable at compilation time to be adapted to specific application needs.

3.2 Restrictions for the RTOS

As said above, the certification entailed by every safety-integrity system shapes its development process, thus a strict set of restrictions is needed when developing high-integrity software. These are the main restrictions dictated by the Ada 2005 Ravenscar Profile [9, § D.13.1] for the RTOS:

- A static number of threads and shared resources
- No thread termination (and no abortion)
- No dynamic memory at the kernel level
- Only a single thread can wait on a given condition variable

In addition, the threads are scheduled according to Fixed Priority Preemptive Scheduling (FPPS), using the Immediate Ceiling Priority Protocol (ICPP) for shared resources [10]. Thanks to these restrictions the implementation of the kernel is small enough to be certified, while offering a sufficient set of services that allow the *schedulability analysis* of the application. Another derived advantage for embedded systems is that Ravenscar implementations require very low resources and have a high performance. In addition, the ICPP assures that deadlocks cannot ever occur, a highly desirable property specially for safety-critical systems.

4 A restricted middleware for high-integrity systems

4.1 Holistic schedulability analysis

Current mono-processor response-time analysis can evaluate a static number of *periodic* or *sporadic tasks* (i.e. threads), each having a worst-case execution time (WCET), and synchronize by using a static number of shared resources. The response-time analysis method has been also extended for distributed systems [4]. The holistic schedulability analysis assumes that each sender thread can send a fixed set of messages, and no thread can receive more than one message. In addition, each message must have a bounded size, and a fixed destination thread.

A *transaction* Γ_i, composed of a set of tasks $\tau_{i,j}$ with precedence relations, is another important concept for the response time analysis of distributed systems. The objective is to analyze the end-to-end response time of each transaction to assess the schedulability of the system. And although each task of the system has a unique priority, due to their precedence relations every task of a transaction (except the first one) is activated by the preceding task of the transaction, even if the second one has a higher priority. As a side note, the deadline of a task inside a transaction is usually longer than its period because the transaction can start another activation even if the last one is still running.

For example (see figure 1), the transaction Γ_1 is composed of task $\tau_{1,1}$ (which runs over the node N_1), message $m_{1,1}$ (transmitted via the network A), and task $\tau_{1,2}$

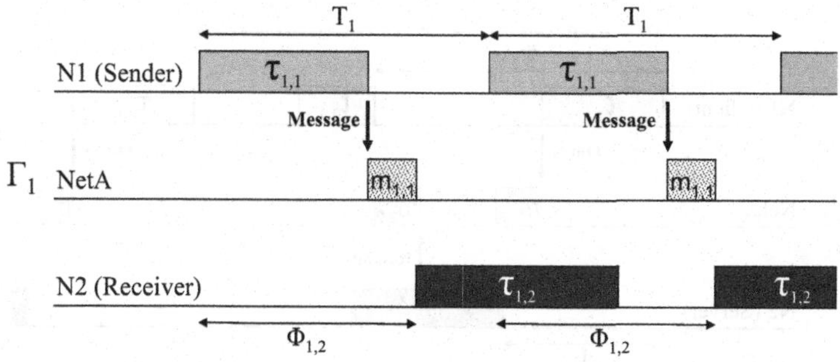

Fig. 1 Example of a distributed transaction.

(executing inside N_2). The transaction has a period T_1 (i.e. the number of times the transaction is activated per second), and $\tau_{1,2}$ has the offset $\Phi_{1,2}$ since the start of transaction. Thus the network can be modeled as a CPU (but messages cannot be preempted), and each message is like a task, with a fixed priority, a period, and a worst-case transmission time. The original holistic schedulability method had been improved with more exact response time analysis [5]. Later, the system model was extended with the analysis of multiple events [11], a message can activate more than one task, or also a task can be activated by multiple messages.

Although the computational model can be seen as too restrictive, it is rich enough to provide the common services needed in a safety-critical system. However, current response time analysis techniques require a *single activation point* for each task (either an event for sporadic tasks or a timer for periodic ones). But in some communication paradigms including Remote Procedure Call (RPC) and Remote Method Invocation (RMI), the client thread sends a message to the server, and blocks until the other thread sends another message with the response (two activation points). A general method should be developed to analyze more than one activation point.

4.2 *Modelization of synchronous calls*

In this paper, each thread is modeled by $n+1$ tasks inside a transaction, where n is the number of activation points of the thread. As can be seen in figure 2, although the transaction Γ_2 is composed by two *threads*, it is modelled as three *tasks*:

1. the sender thread sends a query to the server, and then performs a blocking receive operation (task $\tau_{2,1}$).
2. the server thread processes the petition and then sends-back the response (task $\tau_{2,2}$).
3. finally, the message wakes-up the client thread and reads the answer (task $\tau_{2,3}$).

Although a RPC or RMI can be modeled using this technique, the analysis is not completely accurate because multiple activations of a transaction can be executing at

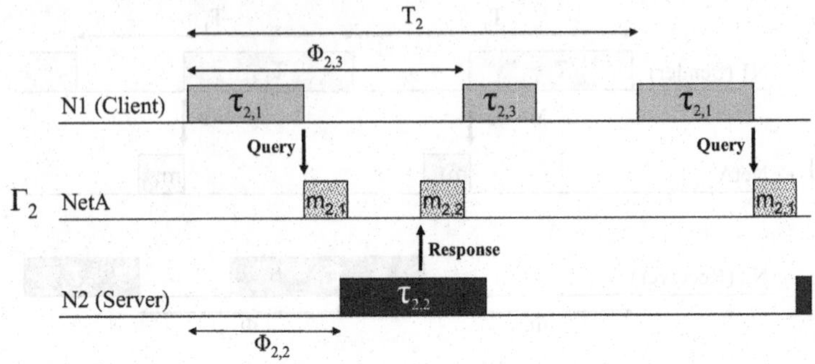

Fig. 2 Model of a Remote Procedure Call.

the same time unlike an RPC (the client thread cannot start another activation until the last one is complete). Blocking operations are required not only for RPC-like operations, but also for message segmentation, and one-to-many communication in a point-to-point topology or for networking technologies with no broadcast support. It is worth noting that not all transactions are distributed. For example, using this technique it is possible to model blocking system calls, like a read operation from a file where the thread is blocked until the information is read from the hard disk. However, all the tasks of the same thread share the same priority, thus the response time analysis methods must be extended to cope with non-unique priorities.

4.3 Implementation requirements

Multiple design choices were studied when developing the middleware for this specific ESA project. It is desirable that a task invoking a remote operation does not delegate the message generation (including data marshalling, message partitioning, composition of message headers, and even message queueing) to another task to avoid priority inversion. *Priority inversion* is an undesired effect typically found when a task cannot execute until a lower-priority task exits from a shared resource. Total priority inversion is in general not possible but it can (and must) be bounded. From the point of view of the middleware, if the message generation is done by a specific task of the communications stack then a high-priority task will be preempted by this task even if the message is sent by another task with the lowest priority of the node. Therefore, it is encouraged that the middleware code for message generation is executed directly by the sender task, i.e. with its priority.

For the transfer of the message, there are typically two possible implementations:

1. **middleware thread**: the sender task puts its message into a buffer, which will be sent by a sporadic thread of the middleware.
2. **self service**: the sender task calls the device driver directly.

The advantage of the first implementation is that the sender task can be completely asynchronous. In contrast, the self-service model should have to wait until the message is completely transferred to know the status of the sent operation. In the other hand, the self-service implementation has a lower priority inversion.

Therefore, if the remote operation is asynchronous, the call to the middleware can be fully non-blocking. However, if the operation is synchronous (e.g. a RPC) the call will be blocking, and in addition the middleware must set a timer to detect a communication problem, e.g. the message was lost or the receiver node is not responding. Otherwise, the sender thread will be blocked forever. It is worth noting that message acknowledgement and retransmissions are not usually done by software in a safety-critical distributed system because guaranteed delivery is provided by the hardware communication bus.

Communication networks also introduce some priority inversion: The network is normally non-preemptable, so if a low-priority message is being transferred then another message with a higher priority cannot be sent until that frame is completely transmitted. For that reason, the maximum size of a message must be bounded. Of course, in the first implementation, the middleware thread will sent the output-messages by priority.

At the destination node, the receiver thread should then process each call with the priority specified in the message. The above guideline about message generation is also applicable at the receiver side of the middleware: it is desirable that the composition and unmarshalling of the message are performed directly by the receiver task. It should be noticed that each partition can still have an independent run-time system. No clock synchronization is needed because the communication is message oriented [12, p. 1.27], but of course a mechanism to obtain a certain degree of common time is desirable in a real-time system.

In summary the implementation must document the architecture of the middleware, specifying if any step is delegated by another task in the caller or called node. Also, the metrics of the maximum blocking time of the biggest critical section should also be documented, otherwise a complete response time analysis of the whole system would be not possible.

4.4 Restrictions for the middleware

In addition to the restrictions for the RTOS explained in section 3.2, another set of constraints is needed for safety-critical middlewares. As said above, the schedulability theory assumes a static computational model, where the number of connections and messages does not change at all during the mission. That is, there is a *static number of nodes*, where *no dynamic connections* are allowed, and where all the nodes perform a *coordinated initialization* to start the application at the same time (in a real-time system it is not acceptable to enqueue a request until the server node is active).

Nodes are not allowed to stop its execution, as enforced by the RTOS restriction about no thread termination. And if the connections are not dynamic, there is a static number of messages, and each one has a fixed origin and destination, as well as a fixed priority. Finally, the computational model also assumes *bounded size messages* to be able to compute the maximum transfer time. This does not mean that each message has a fixed size but a maximum size limit.

Another implicit restriction is that *no concurrent remote calls* are allowed. Therefore, while in a general-purpose middleware usually a thread pool serves all requests—including calls to the same remote operation at the same time—in this restricted middleware there is a unique thread per remote operation that receives and processes each message. It is worth noting that an interesting property derived from this restriction is that distributed deadlocks are not possible in this restricted middleware, thus reducing the costs of the certification of the whole system [13].

In addition to the above restrictions which always must be enforced, there is also another set of **optional restrictions** which is not deemed essential for all safety-critical middlewares, but some kinds of distributed systems can benefit from it [6]. The key goal of these restrictions is to simplify the implementation of the middleware, thus facilitating its certification, and to ease the response time analysis of the system, reducing the main sources of pessimism and unpredictability. However, some of these restrictions have no impact in the implementation of the middleware, and even are difficult to detect violations statically.

The first optional restriction is to allow *asynchronous calls* only, i.e. to forbid all blocking remote operations (like a remote procedure call). A related restriction is "*no segmentation*", so only messages up to the MTU are allowed. This avoids a blocking send operation until all the parts of the message are sent. For the same reasons, "*no multicast*" is also needed if the hardware does not support the broadcasting of messages, however this restriction is always required to avoid the analysis of multi-event systems.

Finally, it can be useful to enforce the *no complex remote types* rule, i.e. a parameter of a remote operation cannot be an unconstrained or recursive type (e.g. linked list). With those types the exact size of the message cannot be computed until run-time, including its maximum size. So thanks to this restriction the maximum size of every message can be computed statically and thus the worst-case transfer time, and in addition the middleware does not need to handle the serialization of complex data [14].

4.5 Adequate Communication Paradigms

The communication paradigms supported in this Ravenscar-compliant middleware includes *message passing*, *remote procedure calls* (RPC), and *real-time publish/subscribe* (P/S). These paradigms can be implemented with little code, and they are supported by current response time analysis techniques to asses the schedulability of the system. But, due to its blocking nature, the RPC paradigm requires more code and timers than the the message passing or the P/S paradigm, and therefore it can be more difficult to certify.

However, although the Remote Method Invocation (RMI) can also be analyzed using similar techniques, in general it is difficult to ensure some restrictions in this communication paradigm. For example, although the number of distributed objects can be static, it is possible to send a remote reference to another node and therefore a new connection would be created at run-time, clearly violating the restriction about no dynamic connections. It is worth noting that OOP is not usually employed in safety-critical software due to its highly dynamic nature.

The Distributed Shared Memory (DSM) paradigm also presents some problems for safety-critical middlewares. The main advantage of DSM is that the programmer does not have to write explicitly the data transfer because at run-time the middleware transparently handles this, also easing the port of existing applications to distributed platforms. But this transparency is difficult to modelize and thus to perform the schedulability analysis of the application.

In summary, the message passing paradigm is well understood, and simple to learn, codify and analyze, and therefore it is very adequate for the development of high-integrity systems. The P/S paradigm, needed to fully meet the industrial requirements because it allows multicast communications, is also adequate for a safety-critical middleware because it can also be certified, although the response time analysis of multi-event systems can be more difficult to perform. The RPC paradigm can also successfully be used in a safety-critical middleware, although its blocking nature makes harder the certification at the highest-criticality levels.

However, as said above the RMI and DSM paradigms are the less adequate of the studied communication paradigms. Although *shared memory* can be used for inter-partition communication inside a node (e.g. among different criticality levels), DSM is not recommended for hard real-time communication in a safety-critical distributed system.

5 Conclusions and future work

All safety-critical systems must be certified prior deployment, and thus adequate development methods and tools must be used for this type of high-integrity software (like the Ravenscar profile). This heavily affects the middleware, which usually have to support hard real-time communication over a resource-constrained embedded platform.

This paper has described the design of a Ravenscar-compliant safety-critical middleware with hard real-time deadlines for future projects of the European Space Agency (ESA). After analysing the industrial requirements and the current schedulability theory for distributed systems, a set of restrictions and implementation and documentation requirements was proposed to allow certification of the middleware and to perform the response time analysis of distributed applications.

Finally, it was discussed the most adequate communication paradigms for this kind of systems. Simple paradigms like message passing or publish/subscribe are expressive-enough and can be implemented and analyzed more easily than remote procedure calls, distributed shared objects, or distributed shared memory.

Acknowledgements This work has been funded in part by the Spanish Ministry of Science and Technology (MCYT), project TIC2005-08665-C03-01 (THREAD), by the IST Programme of the European Commission under project IST-004033 (ASSERT), and by the Council for Education of the Community of Madrid and the European Social Fund.

References

1. ECSS. *ECSS-Q-80B Space Product Assurance — Software Product Assurance*, 2003. Available from ESA.
2. RTCA Inc. *Software Considerations in Airborne Systems and Equipment Certification — RTCA/DO-178B*, 2002.
3. ISO/IEC. *TR 24718:2005 — Guide for the use of the Ada Ravenscar Profile in high integrity systems*, 2005. Based on the University of York Technical Report YCS-2003-348 (2003).
4. Ken Tindell and John Clark. Holistic schedulability analysis for distributed hard real-time systems. *Microprocessing and Microprogramming*, 40(2–3):117–134, April 1994. Euromicro Journal (Special Issue on Parallel Embedded Real-Time Systems).
5. Juan Carlos Palencia Gutiérrez and Michael González Harbour. Exploiting precedence relations in the schedulability analysis of distributed real-time systems. In *RTSS 1999: Proceedings of the 20th IEEE Real-Time Systems Symposium*, pages 328–339, December 1999.
6. Santiago Urueña and Juan Zamorano. Building high-integrity distributed systems with Ravenscar restrictions. volume XXVII, pages 29–36, August 2007. Proceedings of the 13th International Real-Time Ada Workshop (IRTAW 2007).
7. Hermann Kopetz and Günther Bauer. The time-triggered architecture. *Proceedings of the IEEE*, 91(1):112–126, January 2003.
8. Neil Audsley and Andy Wellings. Issues with using Ravenscar and the Ada distributed systems annex for high-integrity systems. In *IRTAW '00: Proceedings of the 10th international workshop on Real-time Ada workshop*, pages 33–39, New York, NY, USA, 2001. ACM Press.
9. ISO SC22/WG9. *Ada 2005 Annotated Reference Manual. ISO/IEC 8652:1995(E) with Technical Corrigendum 1 and Amendment 1*, 2006. Available on `http://www.adaic.com/standards/ada05.html`.
10. Lui Sha, Ragunathan Rajkumar, and John P. Lehoczky. Priority inheritance protocols: An approach to real-time synchronization. *IEEE Tr. on Computers*, 39(9), 1990.
11. J. Javier Gutiérrez, J. Carlos Palencia, and Michael González Harbour. Schedulability analysis of distributed hard real-time systems with multiple- event synchronization. In *Proc. 12th Euromicro Conference on Real-Time Systems*, pages 15–24. IEEE CS Press, June 2000.
12. Juan Carlos Palencia Gutiérrez. *Análisis de planificabilidad de Sistemas Distribuidos de Tiempo Real basados en prioridades fijas*. PhD thesis, Universidad de Cantabria, 1999. Supervisor: Michael González Harbour.
13. César Sánchez, Henny B. Sipma, Zohar Manna, Venkita Subramonian, and Christopher Gill. On efficient distributed deadlock avoidance for real-time and embedded systems. In *Proceedings of the 20th International Parallel and Distributed Processing Symposium, 2006. IPDPS 2006*. IEEE Computer Society, April 2006.
14. Daniel Tejera, Alejandro Alonso, and Miguel Ángel de Miguel. Predictable serialization in Java. In *IEEE International Symposium on Object-Oriented Real-Time Distributed Computing (ISORC'07)*, May 2007.

TinyOS Extensions for a Wireless Sensor Network Node Based on a Dynamically Reconfigurable Processor

Enkhbold Ochirsuren, Heiko Hinkelmann, Leandro Soares Indrusiak, and Manfred Glesner

Abstract Wireless sensor networks (WSNs) present design issues and challenges in both hardware and software platform development. This paper presents the implementation of a hardware-dependent component library that extends TinyOS in order to create an abstraction layer on top of a dynamically reconfigurable hardware architecture. Such hardware architecture is based on a SPARC-compliant processor and it is the core component of a generic sensor node platform targeted for future smart sensor networks. Considered as an application programming interface (API), the components of the implemented library allow the application developer to fully exploit the functionality of the dynamically reconfigurable function unit (RFU). Besides the RFU, the library also provides an interface to other standard system peripherals such as a timer, sensor, and radio transceiver. A simple TinyOS application, which includes gathering data from an attached sensor and wirelessly communicating to other sensor nodes has been demonstrated on the prototype nodes. In addition, a software visualization tool has been developed and integrated to a commercial logic simulator in order to facilitate software debugging during the cycle-accurate simulation of the hardware architecture model, described in the VHDL.

1 Introduction

As being a networked embedded system, WSNs present design issues and challenges in both hardware and software platform development. Generally, the hardware architecture of a wireless sensor node comprises of three components: processor, communication interface and sensors. The previous survey of the state-of-the-art sensor node platforms has shown that the main processing units of currently existing generic sensor node platforms are mostly based on the low-power, 8/16-bit

---

Enkhbold Ochirsuren · Heiko Hinkelmann · Leandro Soares Indrusiak · Manfred Glesner
Institute of Microelectronic Systems - Darmstadt University of Technology, Karlstrasse 15, 64283 Darmstadt, Germany. e-mail: boldoo, hinkelmann, indrusiak, glesner@mes.tu-darmstadt.de

---

Please use the following format when citing this chapter:

Ochirsuren, E., et al., 2008, in IFIP International Federation for Information Processing, Volume 271; *Distributed Embedded Systems: Design, Middleware and Resources*; Bernd Kleinjohann, Lisa Kleinjohann, Wayne Wolf; (Boston: Springer), pp. 161–170.

microcontrollers [7]. For the high-performance sensor nodes, the 16/32-bit RISC processor cores are utilized. All these processor-based platforms can provide flexibility so that they can be used for a wide variety of WSN applications. But they can suffer from low performance and low energy efficiency. This is often dealt by using ASICs. Even though ASIC-based, special-purpose sensor nodes can be utilized for some extremely low-power applications, they are not flexible and has limited functionality making it difficult to incorporate new applications. An alternative approach would be to integrate a hardware accelerator in the processing core of a sensor node. This would give us flexibility as well the meet the energy and performance requirements. Such hardware accelerators are often intended to execute specific computation-intensive tasks or tasks with real-time requirements, such as secure high-speed communication protocols, which are inefficient on general-purpose processors.

A new generic sensor node architecture for future smart sensor node platforms has been proposed in [9]. It includes a coarse-grained, domain-specific RFU in a SPARC-compliant processor core to achieve high energy efficiency. Dynamic reconfiguration technique that changes the hardware functionality quickly during run-time is used to reconfigure the RFU.

This paper presents an alternative operating system and its programmability support for a WSN node based on such a dynamically reconfigurable processor. The abstraction of the target sensor node architecture is implemented on top of the TinyOS operating system [8].

The remaining paper is structured as follows. Section 2 gives an overview on the integration of reconfigurable hardware into the generic sensor node architecture and the TinyOS operating system. Section 3 describes the new target architecture for a generic sensor node platform. Section 4 presents TinyOS extensions for the target architecture. The TinyOS portability is evaluated in Section 5, and the paper ends with a conclusion and an outlook on future work.

2 Related work

Although, the processing units of currently existing generic sensor nodes are mostly based on either microcontroller or microprocessor, there have been a few efforts to integrate reconfigurable hardware into a sensor node architecture to increase performance and lifetime of a sensor node.

A conceptual sensor node architecture that includes reconfigurable hardware has been proposed in PicoNode [13]. In this architecture reconfigurable modules have been used in both processing and communication components to provide ultra-low power operation. Modular construction idea of a versatile sensor node for WSNs has been described in [12]. Here, a FPGA coupled with a microprocessor comprises the processing unit of the sensor node and this FPGA is reconfigured to deal with complex signal processing tasks, hence decreasing the load on the microprocessor.

In order to effectively manage limited hardware capabilities and to support concurrent operations, an operating system is often needed for a sensor node. Many WSN applications have been developed on top of TinyOS, an open-source runtime environment designed for sensor network nodes. It is specialized for use on extremely resource constrained embedded systems and employs an event-driven execution model. This execution model allows the underlying hardware to operate relatively longer without battery re-charge by putting it into sleep mode when there no event occurs. Also, component based modular design enables the minimal code size and allows rapid application development by wiring only necessary components. A TinyOS program consists of a scheduler and components that are written in a nesC [6] programming language, which is an extension to the C language.

3 The new target architecture of the generic sensor node platform

The target sensor node architecture that has been used within this work is depicted in Fig. 1. It consists of a processing unit that is based on a RISC processor with a RFU; configuration, instruction and data memories; on-chip peripherals such as an interrupt controller, timer, and UART, generic sensor and transceiver interfaces; a simple bus and its arbiter module.

3.1 The dynamically reconfigurable processor

The processing unit of the architecture consists of a 32-bit LEON2 processor [5], which is the single threaded, SPARC-compliant RISC processor. The RFU is directly added into the processors instruction pipeline so that it can process the predefined computational-intensive tasks with minimumal processor intervention. For efficiency reason, the original processor architecture has been slightly modified. Its

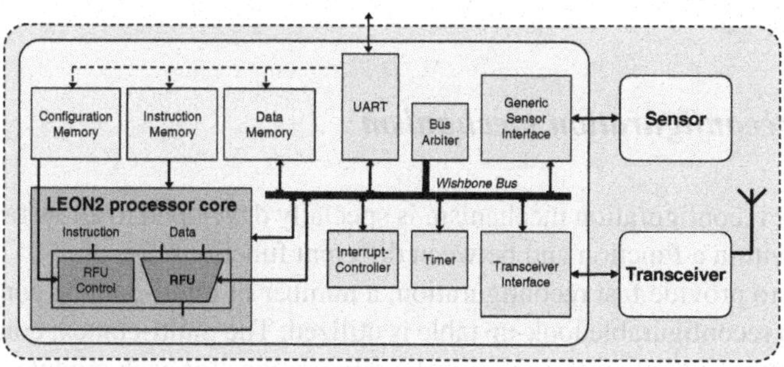

Fig. 1 The architecture of the generic sensor node platform.

caches and unnecessary peripherals were removed and the AMBA bus was replaced by a simpler wishbone bus.

The current implementation of the RFU supports following three functions:

- coding and decoding of the Cyclic Redundancy Check (CRC) with code lengths up to 32 bit
- coding and decoding of Bose-Chaudhuri-Hocquenghem (BCH) codes with code length up to 255 bit and with error correction capabilities of up to 16 errors
- encryption and decryption of the Advanced Encryption Standard (AES) with a data block size of 128 bit and key lengths of 128, 192 and 256 bit

A brief description of the overall RFU control, data path and the configuration mechanism is given in the next subsections.

3.2 The RFU control and data path

The RFU is controlled by three special instructions, which perform single- and multi-cycle operations on the RFU and reconfiguration: single-cycle execution (ESR), multi-cycle execution (EMR), and reconfiguration (CRT). These special instructions have been added to the original SPARC V8 instruction set. The EMR and CRT instructions are executed independently by the RFU, by allowing the processor to execute instructions in parallel with the RFU.

The RFU's data path includes specifically tailored modules for error correction and encryption algorithms, such as a multiply accumulate module (MAC), an inversion module, registers, a local memory and a memory access unit as well as flexible interconnections. The MAC module is based on Galois Field (GF) multiplier and GF adder cells. The inversion module performs GF division operation that is required by the AES algorithm. In order to increase local storage capabilities the registers and the memory modules have been implemented. The memory module can be configured either as look-up table for logic operations or a FIFO buffer with parameterized width and depth. The memory access unit supports block data computation and packet processing by reading or writing data from/to memory consecutively, starting from the given start address.

3.3 The reconfiguration mechanism

A two-layer reconfiguration mechanism is specially developed to allow rapid reconfiguration within a function and between different functions.

In order to provide fast reconfiguration, a number of multi-context configuration tables and a reconfigurable look-up table is utilized. The multi-context configuration tables are responsible for storing several configurations for each module of the data path. A desired configuration can then be selected with a special tag within one cycle. Tag generation is done by the reconfigurable look-up table, which also specifies the sequence of tags for multi-cycle operations and allows jumps and loops. Hence, the RFU can autonomously execute very long computations that comprise of multiple cycles. This tag-driven reconfiguration belongs to the first layer reconfiguration.

Loading of configuration data from an external configuration memory to these tables becomes the second layer reconfiguration. For this purpose, the compressed control information, which is called a reconfiguration profile, is composed and stored in the configuration memory along with complete configuration data. The profile exactly specifies how many entries need to be loaded to each table. In addition, a task manager module monitors reconfiguration process by verifying the current configuration in the tables and can skip unnecessary configuration overhead. As a result, the reconfiguration latency achieved is one cycle to reconfigure within a function, and less than hundred cycles to completely reconfigure an another function.

4 The TinyOS extensions for the target architecture

Even though TinyOS supports several existing sensor node platforms, none of them uses a SPARC-compliant processor as a processing unit. Thus, it requires the preliminary work of porting TinyOS to the target hardware architecture. The whole porting process will be briefly described in the next subsections according to the completion order.

4.1 Platform definitions

In order to define and locate platform specific files, a new subdirectory, called "leon2mote", with associated files has been created in the TinyOS directory tree. These files include: "leon.h", "leon2_hardware.h" and "hardware.h". The "leon.h" file includes details about the LEON2 processor, whereas the "leon2_hardware.h" and "hardware.h" files contain macros for pin assignment, functions for supporting atomic statements and other specific hardware definitions for the sensor node.

4.2 Hardware presentation layers

The TinyOS hardware presentation layers (HPLs) are the lowest level components that directly interact with the underlying hardware. They access the hardware in the usual way, either by memory or by port mapped input/output (I/O). In the reverse direction, the hardware can request services by signalling an interrupt. Using this communication scheme, the HPLs abstract the details of the hardware and provide a more usable interface for the upper layer components.

Even though each HPL component will be as unique as the underlying hardware, all of them will have a similar general structure. Each HPL component should have:

- commands for initialization, starting and stopping of the hardware that are necessary for effective power management policy
- "get" and "set" commands for the registers that control the operation of the corresponding hardware
- commands with descriptive names for the most frequently used operations
- commands for enabling and disabling interrupts triggered by the hardware
- interrupt handlers for the interrupts that are triggered by the hardware

According to the target architecture description, HPLs for the hardware initialization, LEDs, timer, sensor and radio interfaces, and the RFU have been implemented. With exception of the RFU, the rest for the underlying hardware module are accessed by memory mapped I/O addresses. The timer, sensor and radio interfaces respond to the overlaying HPLs by generating interrupts that are defined in the LEON2 interrupt assignment scheme. Table 1 shows all HPLs and the system components that have been developed within this work.

Table 1 The developed TinyOS components.

Component type	Component name	Description
Hardware specific HPLs	HPLInitM.nc	HPL for the hardware initialization
	HPLTimer.nc	HPL for the timer unit of the LEON2 processor
	HPLLeds.nc	HPL for the LEDs attached to the prototype board
	HPLRfmRx.nc	HPL for the radio interface (receiver mode)
	HPLRfmTx.nc	HPL for the radio interface (transmitter mode)
	HPLPhotoM.nc	HPL for the sensor interface
	HPLRFU_CRC.nc	HPL for the RFU (CRC checksum calculation)
	HPLRFU_AES.nc	HPL for the RFU (AES block (en)-decryption)
System components	LeonTimerM.nc	A system timer component
	LeonSenseToInt.nc	Gathers sensor sample and displays to the LEDs
	LeonIntToRfmM.nc	Sends data to the radio interface
	LeonRfmToIntM.nc	Receives data from the radio interface
	AESM.nc	An AES encryption and decryption component

In case of the RFU, the implementation of associated HPLs is different than others. For each function (cf. Sect. 3.1) that is provided by the RFU, a number of task specific subfunctions are assigned. Each task is associated with one specific function of the RFU with fixed parameters, like 8-bit CRC checksum calculation of a 32-bit data block. Generally, tasks are executed in the RFU in following steps:

- allocate a new task and reconfigure the RFU for that task (CRT instruction)
- load the required parameters for the task (mainly ESR instruction)
- execute the task and return a result (ESR and/or EMR instructions)

Hence, each of these steps is defined as a subfunction and further these subfunctions are used in creating a task specific HPL for the RFU.

Two distinct HPLs have been implemented for the RFU: "HPLRFU_CRC.nc" and "HPLRFU_AES.nc". The former HPL sets up the RFU for 8-bit CRC checksum calculation on 32-bit data block, starts the calculation in the RFU and returns a resulting checksum. The latter HPL reconfigures the RFU for the AES encryption and decryption algorithm with 128-bit key, initiates the algorithm in the RFU and returns a cipher or decrypted data, each having 128-bit block size.

All subfunction definitions are packed in an external library. As stated in Sect. 3.2, the RFU introduces three new instructions for reconfiguration and execution purpose. In order to make these new instructions available to the standard cross-compiler for the LEON2 processor, compiler's source code is modified by including the mnemonics of these new instructions.

4.3 System components

A TinyOS system component provides a concrete system service to the overlying application components. It can be used by any application without modifications.

The typical system service in TinyOS is a system timer that can function as multiple timers, each of which can be managed independently. For this purpose the first timer of the LEON2 timer unit has been chosen. An implementation of the system timer component, "LeonTimerM.nc", has been derived from the original TinyOS timer component "TimerM.nc". The main reason of such a distinct timer component is regarding to the operational mode of the LEON2 processors timer unit. The timer unit decrements its counter value on each timer tick and generates a timer interrupt when the counter value underflows. Therefore, the only difference between them is a modification that reflects such behaviour to the "Timer" interface implementation.

A new block cipher component, "AESM.nc", that performs the AES encryption and decryption has been implemented. The component considers an optimized software implementation of the AES algorithm on 32-bit platforms proposed in [1]. The applied strategy is to restructure the standard algorithm by introducing a transposed version of the state matrix. Due to the transposed state matrix considerable amount of computation is saved by eliminating the rotation operations both from MixColumns and Inverse MixColumns, resulting a performance gain. Moverover, it employs only the nonlinear byte substitution tables (Sbox and Inverse Sbox) as look-up tables to keep the required memory as less as possible.

The list of the developed system components is given in Table 1.

5 The validation and evaluation of TinyOS porting

In order to validate the TinyOS porting and demonstrate a typical sensor node operation, the following TinyOS application was developed. One node periodically gathers samples from a light sensor, displays light intensity on the LEDs and sends the samples wirelessly to other nodes. Other nodes listen to the radio interface until data is received. When the transmitted data is received, they display it on the LEDs and wait for next reception. We have not used any networking mechanism so there is neither addressing nor routing algorithms included. Hence, our applications are not directly similar to the standard "SenseToRfm" and "RfmToLeds" applications.

The validation test that checks TinyOS port is done in the ModelSim logic simulator by simulating a VHDL model of the sensor node architecture programmed with TinyOS application code. In order to track software execution on VHDL model, an additional monitoring tool has been developed and integrated to ModelSim (cf. Fig. 2). During VHDL simulations, it informs component interactions of the currently executing TinyOS application with exact timing information. Besides that it shows the current state of the LEON2 processor core, which includes control/state register contents (%psr, %tbr, %wim), register file contents (%g0-%g7, %l0-%l7, %i0-%i7), and state of all the pipeline stages.

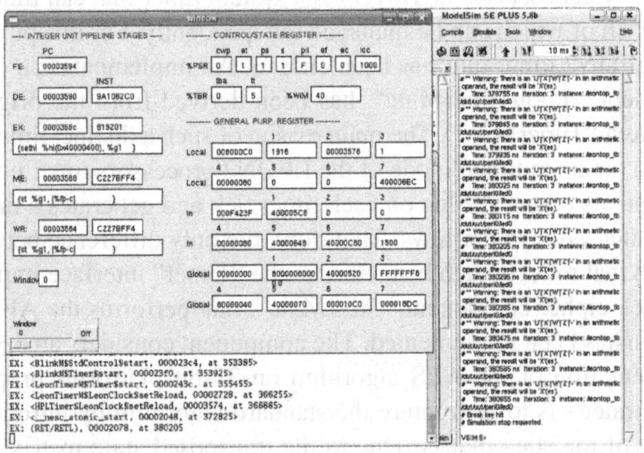

Fig. 2 The GUI of the monitoring tool added to ModelSim.

The benefit of the RFU is proved by the execution time analysis on the example applications. In order to show the impact of the RFU on computing a CRC checksum and encrypting a cipher by the AES algorithm, a couple of example applications are developed for each case: one uses a software (nesC) component and other one uses RFU. It can be obviously seen that the execution of CRC and AES functions in RFU is much faster than if they are executed in software (cf. Table 2). The speed-up factor of up to 93 and 71 can be reached compared to the software implementations.

For demonstration of example applications, prototypes that consist of an FPGA board and an additional board have been used. In the FPGA board the complete sen-

Table 2 Execution time comparison.

Function name	Version	Execution, cycles
CRC	RFU	11
	software (nesC)	1029
AES (encryption)	RFU	238
	software (nesC)	17093

sor node design, including processor, RFU, memories, peripherals, interfaces and bus, is implemented. On the additional board the Xemics DP1203 radio transceiver, a planar antenna and ten LEDs, and extension pins are mounted.

The portability of TinyOS has been evaluated by code size and concurrency potential.

A TinyOS application code size should be as little as possible to fit in resource constraint hardware. Compared to the compiled applications for the Mica mote, code size of our test applications are quite large (cf. Table 3). The reason is that the code includes additional 9Kbytes of code that includes processor boot sequence (1.5KB), trap table (4KB), trap handling routines (2KB), and processor specific constants (1KB). While the amount of required instruction and data memory seems to be large, it is still in the range that most sensor nodes have [2].

Table 3 Code size comparison.

Application name	Mica mote, bytes		LEON2+RFU, bytes	
	ROM	RAM	ROM	RAM
Blink	1652	48	14416	1780
Sense	3602	83	15408	1780
RfmToLeds	7538	280	17072	1804
SenseToRfm	9970	372	17728	1796

The main metric for the concurrency potential is context switching speed. The most expensive switching is related to the hardware interrupt handling. On an average it takes around 75 clock cycles to signal the respective event after a hardware interrupt is triggered.

6 Conclusion and future work

This paper presents the first port of the TinyOS operating system (version 1.x) to a new generic wireless sensor node platform that is based on the customized LEON2 RISC processor with the integrated dynamically reconfigurable function unit (RFU). The most common TinyOS components that can be contained in every application have been implemented and tested by using both the commercial hardware simulator and FPGA-based prototype nodes. The analyses from compilations show that the amount of required memories is still within the range that the most existing generic sensor node platforms have. From the simulations, it was shown that the RFU significantly speeds up error checking and data (en)-decryption processes.

In order to test the TinyOS porting and track software execution during simulation, an additional monitoring tool has been developed and integrated to the commercial hardware simulator, ModelSim. The monitoring tool facilitates software debugging on cycle-accurate simulation of any LEON2 processor based system-on-chip (SoC) design.

The further work is directed to improve the current extension and add network simulation. Hence, some work will be done towards to support the Active Messaging (AM) protocol stack [3], which is basic communication protocol for the TinyOS applications. Currently, the TinyOS based sensor network models are only simulated in TOSSIM [10], a TinyOS simulator with networking support. Therefore, there is a necessity to implement the TOSSIM components for the target platform and added to the TOSSIM library. The TOSSIM components can later be used in other existing frameworks for modelling wireless systems, such as Viptos [4] and SENSIM [11].

References

1. G. Bertoni, L. Breveglieri, P. Fragneto, M. Macchetti, S. Marchesin, Efficient software implementation of AES on 32-bit platforms, CHES '02: Revised Papers from the 4th International Workshop on Cryptographic Hardware and Embedded Systems, 2003, pp. 159–171.
2. J. Beutel, Metrics for sensor network platforms, REALWSN'06: Proceedings of the ACM Workshop on Real-World Wireless Sensor Networks, 2006, pp. 26–30.
3. P. Buonadonna, J. Hill, D. Culler, Active message communication for tiny networked sensors, Submitted to IEEE INFOCOM 2001, 2001.
4. E. Cheong, E. A. Lee, Y. Zhao, Viptos: A graphical development and simulation environment for TinyOS-based wireless sensor networks, SenSys '05: Proceedings of the 3rd International Conference on Embedded Networked Sensor Systems, 2005, pp. 302–302.
5. J. Gaisler, LEON2 processor users manual, version 1.0.21 XST edition, Available at Gaisler Research. http://www.gaisler.com. Nov. 2003.
6. D. Gay, P. Levis, R. von Behren, M. Welsh, E. Brewer, D. Culler, The nesC language: A holistic approach to networked embedded systems, PLDI '03: Proceedings of the ACM SIGPLAN 2003 Conference on Programming Language Design and Implementation, 2003, pp. 1–11.
7. J. Hill, M. Horton, R. Kling, L. Krishnamurthy, The platforms enabling wireless sensor networks, Commun. ACM, Vol. 47 (2004) No. 6, pp. 41–46.
8. J. Hill, R. Szewczyk, A. Woo, S. Hollar, D. Culler, K. Pister, System architecture directions for networked sensors, SIGPLAN Not., Vol. 35 (2000), No. 11, pp. 93–104.
9. H. Hinkelmann, P. Zipf, M. Glesner, A domain-specific dynamically reconfigurable hardware platform for wireless sensor networks, ICFPT '07: International Conference on Field-Programmable Technology, 2007, pp. 313–316.
10. P. Levis et al., TOSSIM: Accurate and scalable simulation of entire TinyOS applications, Proceedings of the First ACM Conference on Embedded Networked Sensor Systems (SenSys 2003), 2003.
11. C. Mallanda, A. Suri, V. Kunchakarra, S. S. Iyengar, A. Durresi, Simulating wireless sensor networks with OMNET++, Submitted to IEEE Computers 2005, 2005.
12. J. Portilla, A. de Castro, E. de la Torre, A modular architecture for nodes in wireless sensor networks, Journal of Universal Computer Science, Vol. 12 (2006), pp. 328–339.
13. J. M. Rabaey, M. J. Ammer, J. L. da Silva, D. Patel, S. Roundy, PicoRadio supports ad hoc ultra-low power wireless networking, Computer, Vol. 33 (2000) No. 7, pp. 42–48

Scheduling Dependent Distributable Real-Time Threads in Dynamic Networked Embedded Systems

Sherif Fahmy, Binoy Ravindran, and E. D. Jensen

Abstract We consider scheduling distributable real-time threads with dependencies (e.g, due to synchronization) in partially synchronous systems in the presence of node failure. We present a distributed real-time scheduling algorithm called DQBUA. The algorithm uses quorum systems to coordinate nodes' activities when constructing a global schedule. DBQUA detects and resolves distributed deadlock in a timely manner and allows threads to access resources in order of their potential utility to the system. Our main contribution is handling resource dependencies using a distributed scheduling algorithm.

1 Introduction

Some emerging networked embedded systems are dynamic in the sense that they operate in environments with uncertain properties (e.g., [1]). These uncertainties include transient and sustained resource overloads (due to context-dependent activity execution times), arbitrary activity arrivals and completions, and arbitrary node failures and message losses. Reasoning about *end-to-end* timeliness is a difficult and unsolved problem in such systems. Another distinguishing feature of such systems is their relatively long activity execution time scales (e.g., milliseconds to minutes), which permits more time-costly real-time resource management.

Maintaining end-to-end properties (e.g., timeliness, connectivity) of a control or information flow requires a model of the flow's locus in space and time that can be reasoned about. Such a model facilitates reasoning about the contention for resources that occur along the flow's locus and resolving those contentions to seek optimal system-wide end-to-end timeliness. The *distributable thread* programming

Sherif Fahmy · Binoy Ravindran
ECE Dept., Virginia Tech, Blacksburg, VA 24061, USA, e-mail: {fahmy, binoy}@vt.edu

E. D. Jensen
The MITRE Corporation, Bedford, MA 01730, USA, e-mail: jensen@mitre.org

Please use the following format when citing this chapter:

Fahmy, S., Ravindran, B. and Jensen, E.D., 2008, in IFIP International Federation for Information Processing, Volume 271; *Distributed Embedded Systems: Design, Middleware and Resources*; Bernd Kleinjohann, Lisa Kleinjohann, Wayne Wolf; (Boston: Springer), pp. 171–180.

abstraction which first appeared in the Alpha OS [3], and later in the Real-Time CORBA 1.2 standard, directly provides such a model as their first-class programming and scheduling abstraction. A distributable thread is a single thread of execution with a globally unique identity that transparently extends and retracts through local and remote objects. We focus on distributable threads as our programming abstraction, and hereafter, refer to them as *threads*, except as necessary for clarity.

Contributions. In this paper, we consider the problem of scheduling dependent threads in the presence of the previously mentioned uncertainties. Past efforts on thread scheduling (e.g., see [6] and references therein) can be broadly categorized into two classes: *independent node scheduling* and *collaborative scheduling*. In the independent scheduling approach, threads are scheduled at nodes using propagated thread scheduling parameters and without any interaction with other nodes. Thread faults are managed by *integrity protocols* that run concurrent to thread execution. Integrity protocols employ failure detectors (or FDs), and use them to detect thread failures. In the collaborative scheduling approach, nodes explicitly cooperate to construct system-wide thread schedules, detecting node failures using FDs while doing so. We design a collaborative thread scheduling algorithm, DQBUA, that can handle dependencies. To the best of our knowledge, this is the first collaborative scheduling algorithm to consider dependencies. We compare DQBUA to RTG-DS [8], a dependent thread scheduling algorithm that uses gossip ro improve the reliability of the communication layer and to find the next head node of a thread. RTG-DS falls under the independent category of thread scheduling algorithms.

2 Models and Objective

Distributable Thread Abstraction. Distributable threads execute in local and remote objects by location-independent invocations and returns. The portion of a thread executing an object operation is called a *thread segment*. Thus, a thread can be viewed as being composed of a concatenation of thread segments. A thread can also be viewed as being composed of a sequence of *sections*, where a section is a maximal length sequence of contiguous thread segments on a node.

We assume that execution time estimates of sections of a thread are known when it arrives into the system. The sequence of remote invocations and returns made by a thread can typically be estimated by analyzing the thread code. The total number of sections of a thread is thus assumed to be known a-priori. The application is thus comprised of a set of threads, denoted $\mathbf{T} = \{T_1, T_2, \ldots\}$ and the set of sections of a thread T_i is denoted as $[S_1^i, S_2^i, \ldots, S_k^i]$. See [7] for more details.

Timeliness Model. A thread's time constraint is expressed using a Time/Utility Function (TUF) [9]. A TUF decouples the urgency of a thread from its importance. This is useful since the urgency of a thread may be orthogonal to its importance. A thread T_i's TUF is denoted as $U_i(t)$. A classical deadline is unit-valued—i.e., $U_i(t) = \{0, 1\}$, since importance is not considered. Downward step TUFs generalize classical deadlines where $U_i(t) = \{0, \{m\}\}$. We focus on downward step TUFs, and denote the maximum, constant utility of a TUF $U_i(t)$, simply as U_i. Each TUF has an initial time I_i, which is the earliest time for which the TUF is defined, and a termination time X_i, which, for a downward step TUF, is its discontinuity point. $U_i(t) > 0, \forall t \in [I_i, X_i]$ and $U_i(t) = 0, \forall t \notin [I_i, X_i], \forall i$.

System Model. We consider a networked embedded system to consist of a set of client nodes $\Pi^c = \{1, 2, \cdots, N\}$ and a set of server nodes $\Pi = \{1, 2, \cdots, n\}$ (*server* and *client* are logical designations given to nodes to describe the algorithm's behavior). Bi-directional logical communication channels are assumed to exist between every client-server and client-client pair. We also assume that these basic communication channels may lose messages with probability p, and communication delay is described by some probability distribution. On top of this basic communication channel, we consider a reliable communication protocol that delivers a message to its destination in probabilistically bounded time provided that the sender and receiver both remain correct, using the standard technique of sequence numbers and retransmissions. We assume that each node is equipped with two processors (a processor that executes thread sections on the node and a scheduling co-processor as in [3]), have access to GPS clocks that provides each node with a UTC time-source with nanosecond accuracy (e.g., [11]) and are equipped with appropriately tuned QoS failure detectors (FDs) [2] (see [7] for further details).

Exceptions and Abort Model. Each section of a thread has an associated exception handler. We consider a termination model for thread failures including time-constraint violations and node failures. If either of these events occur, exception handlers are triggered to restore the system to a safe state. The exception handlers we consider have time constraints expressed as relative deadlines. See [7] for details.

Failure Model. Nodes are subject to crash failures. When a process crashes, it loses its state memory — i.e., there is no persistent storage. If a crashed client node recovers at a later time, we consider it a new node since it has already lost all of its former execution context. A client node is *correct* if it does not crash; it is *faulty* if it is not correct. In the case of a server crash, it may either recover or be replaced by a new server assuming the same server name (using DNS or DHT — e.g, [5] — technology). We model both cases as server recovery. Since crashes are associated with memory loss, recovered servers start from their initial state. A server is *correct* if it does not fail; it is *faulty* if it is not correct. DQBUA tolerates up to $N-1$ client failures and up to $f^s_{max} \leq n/3$ server failures (see [6]). The actual number of failures is denoted as $f^s \leq f^s_{max}$ for servers and $f \leq f_{max}$ where $f_{max} \leq N-1$ for clients.

Resource Model. Threads can access serially reusable non-CPU resources located at their nodes during their execution. We consider the single resource model — i.e., a thread cannot have more than one outstanding request at any given instance of time. Resources are shared under mutual exclusion constrains and a thread explicitly releases all granted resources before termination. Threads are assumed to access their resources in arbitrary order — i.e., which resources are needed by which threads is not known a priori. Consequently we employ deadlock detection and resolution methods instead of prevention and avoidance techniques.

Resource request/release pairs are assumed to be confined within one node, however it is possible for a thread to lock a resource on a node and then make a remote invocation to another node carrying the lock with it. Such a lock is released when the thread's head returns back to the node on which the resource was acquired.

Scheduling Objectives. Our primary objective is to design a thread scheduling algorithm to maximize the total utility accrued by all threads as much as possible in the presence of dependencies. Further, the algorithm must provide assurances on the satisfaction of thread termination times in the presence of (up to f_{max}) crash failures. Moreover, the algorithm must bound the time threads remain in a deadlock.

3 Algorithm Rationale

In [6], we develop QBUA, a scheduling algorithm for real-time threads in partially synchronous systems. Here, we extend QBUA to handle resource dependencies and precedence constraints, we call the resulting algorithm DQBUA. As in [4], precedence constraints can be programmed as resource dependencies and are handled the same way. When a node detects a distributed scheduling event (the failure of a node, the arrival of a new thread or a resource request) it contacts a quorum system requesting permission to run an instance of DQBUA. Once permission is granted, it broadcasts a message to all other nodes requesting their scheduling information. When the requesting node receives this information, it computes a system-wide schedule, which we call a System Wide Executable Thread Set (or SWETS), and multicasts any updates to nodes whose schedule has been affected.

The purpose of the quorum system is to arbitrate among nodes that detect a distributed scheduling event concurrently. This arbitration reduces thrashing by minimizing the number of instances of DQBUA that are started to handle the same or concurrent scheduling events. Due to space limitations, we do not reproduce the details of the quorum arbitration algorithm, see [6] for details.

While computing a system-wide schedule, threads are ordered in non-increasing order of their global Potential Utility Density (PUD) (which we define as the ratio of a thread's utility to its remaining execution time), the threads are then considered for scheduling in that order. Favoring high global PUD threads allows us to select threads for scheduling that result in the most increase in system utility for the least effort. This heuristic attempts to maximize total accrued utility [4].

DBQUA handles both distributed and local deadlock using a deadlock detection and resolution protocol that ensures that deadlocks are resolved in a timely manner and that the loss in accrued system utility is minimized when deadlocks are resolved.

4 Algorithm Description

Once the arbitration phase of the algorithm is complete and a node has been granted permission to run an instance of DQBUA, that node sends a message to all other nodes requesting their scheduling information. The node then waits for $2T$ time units to receive replies and then invokes Algorithm 3 to construct a system wide schedule using the collected information. Algorithm 3 performs two basic functions, first, it computes a system wide order on threads by computing their global PUD. It then attempts to insert the remaining sections of each thread, in non-increasing order of global PUD, into the schedule. After the insertion of each thread, the schedule is checked for feasibility. If it is not feasible, then the thread is removed from SWETS (after scheduling the appropriate exception handlers if necessary).

We define the global PUD of a thread as the ratio of the utility of the thread to the total remaining executing time of its sections (see [7] for details). Therefore, global PUD is a measure of the "return on investment" of that thread, [4] shows that considering threads in non-decreasing order of PUD maximizes accrued utility.

In the absence of dependencies, the global PUD of a thread represents the utility that would be accrued if a thread where to execute immediately. However, in the presence of dependencies, the utility of a thread can only be accrued if all threads it depends on are scheduled first. Thus, when a section requests a resource, we compute its dependency chain by following the chain of resource requests and ownership. Since a resource request is a distributed scheduling event, the node that gets permission to run an instance of DQBUA (after arbitration by the quorum system) will be sent all the information necessary for it to compute the dependency chain.

Once the dependency chain has been computed, we compute the PUD of the current thread by using a least effort heuristic —i.e., while examining the threads in the dependency chain to compute PUD, if it is faster to abort them than to continue execution, then the threads are aborted and vice versa. Thus we compute the PUD of a thread if it is executed as soon as possible. A similar heuristic is used in [4]. Note that this heuristic minimizes the amount of time a high utility thread waits for a resource, at the expense of having to possibly re-execute threads that have been aborted (see [4] for details).

Algorithm 1: computePUD

Input: T_i, $Dep(i,k), j$; //j: where request occured
$Ut \leftarrow 0$; $Time \leftarrow 0$; $Seen \leftarrow \emptyset$;
for *each* $Dep(i,k)$ **do**
  for *each* $S \in Dep(i,k)$ **do**
    if $S.ID \notin Seen$ **then**
      $Seen \leftarrow Seen \cup S.ID$;
      //Γ_1: sections S till last visit to j
      $S.Rem \leftarrow \Sigma_{k \in \Gamma_1} RE_k^{S.ID}$;
      //Γ_2: all downstream sections
      $S.Abort \leftarrow \Sigma_{k \in \Gamma_2} S_k^h.ex$;
      if $S.Abort > S.Rem$ **then**
        $Time \leftarrow Time + S.Rem$;
        $Ut \leftarrow Ut + U_T(t_{curr} + S.Rem)$
      else $Time \leftarrow Time + S.Abort$;
$Time \leftarrow Time + GE_i$; $Ut \leftarrow Ut + U_i(t_{curr} + GE_i)$;
$T_i.PUD = Util/Time$; return $T_i.PUD$;

Algorithm 2: isFeasible

Input: σ_i; //Schedule for each node
for $1 \le i \le N$ **do**
  $pos_i \leftarrow 1$;
Until ($pos_i = \text{length}(\sigma_i)$, $1 \le i \le N$) **do**
  for $1 \le i \le N$ **do**
    $S_i \leftarrow \text{getElement}(\sigma_i, pos_i)$;
    $pre \leftarrow \text{getElement}(\sigma_i, pos_i - 1)$;
    if $pos_i = 1$ **then** $pre.Fin \leftarrow 0$;
    if $i = 1$ **then** $S_{i-1}.Fin \leftarrow S_i.Arr$; $T \leftarrow 0$;
    $Start \leftarrow \max(pre.Fin, S_{i-1}.Fin + T)$;
    if $Start \neq \infty$ **then**
      $S_i.Fin \leftarrow S_i.ex + Start$;
      if $S_i.Fin > S_i.tt$ **then**
        return *false*;
      $pos_i \leftarrow pos_i + 1$;
return *true*;

We now turn our attention to the method used to check schedule feasibility. For a schedule to be feasible, all the sections it contains should complete their execution before their assigned termination time. Since we are considering threads with end-to-end termination times, the termination time of each section needs to be derived from its thread's end-to-end termination time. This derivation should ensure that if all the section termination times are met, then the end-to-end termination time of the thread will also be met. For the last section in a thread, we derive its termination time as the termination time of the entire thread. The termination time of other sections is the latest start time of the section's successor minus the communication delay.

Similarly, we drive the termination times of exception handlers as the sum of their start time and their execution time. However, we perform the decomposition backwards starting with the termination time of the last handler which is computed as the termination time of that handler's section plus the execution time of the handler. The termination time of other handlers is the latest termination time of the handler's successor plus the communication delay plus the handler's execution time. This ensures that handler termination times are arranged in LIFO order. See [7] for more details. Using these derived termination times, we can check a schedule's feasibility.

Algorithm 3: ConstructSchedule

input: Γ; //Set of threads in the system
input: σ_j^p, $H_j \leftarrow$ nil; //σ_j^p: Previous schedule of node j, H_j: set of handlers scheduled
for *each* $T_i \in \Gamma$ **do**
    if *for some section* $S_j^i \in T_i$, $t_{curr} + S_j^i.ex > S_j^i.tt$ **then** $T_i.PUD \leftarrow 0$;
    else
        Compute $Dep(i,j)$, resolving deadlock if necessary;
        $T_i.PUD \leftarrow$ ComputePUD$(T_i, Dep(i,j))$;
for *each task* $el \in \sigma_j^p$ **do**
    if *el is an exception handler for section* S_j^i **then** Insert$(el,\ H_j,\ el.tt)$;
$\sigma_j \leftarrow H_j$;
$\sigma_{temp} \leftarrow$ sortByPUD(Γ);
for *each* $T_i \in \sigma_{temp}$ **do**
    $T_i.stop \leftarrow false$;
    if *do not receive* σ_j *from node hosting* $S_j^i \in T_i$ **then** $T_i.stop \leftarrow true$;
    if $T_i.PUD > 0$ *and* $T_i.stop \neq true$ **then** insertByEDF$(T_i, Dep(i,j))$;
for *each* $j \in N$ **do**
    if $\sigma_j \neq \sigma_j^p$ **then** Mark node j as being affected;

Algorithm 2 shows how this is done in DQBUA. If the estimated completion time, $S_i.Fin$, of a section is greater than its derived termination, $S_i.tt$, then the schedule is not feasible (lines 13-14). We compute $S_i.Fin$ as the sum of the start time of a section and its execution time. However, it is important to note that, except for current and previous head nodes, these sections haven't arrived in the system when Algorithm 2 is invoked. Therefore we need to estimate the start time of these sections when computing their estimated completion time.

We estimate the start time of a section to be the maximum of the estimated completion time of the section preceding it in the local queue (line 10) and the arrival time of the section on a node (which we estimate as the sum of the completion time of the section's predecessor and the communication delay, $S_{i-1}.Fin + T$). We assume that each section's estimated completion time, $S_i.Fin$, is set to infinity before algorithm Algorithm 2 is run.

We use this relatively expensive method for checking the feasibility of schedules since alternative methods can be misleading. The expedient method, used in some previous work, of using a section's latest start time (computed as its predecessor's latest termination time plus a communication delay, $S_{i-1}.tt + T$) as an estimate for its start time means that the section will have no slack. Thus, the section cannot tolerate any interference by other sections. This leads to pessimistic results with some threads being rejected from an underloaded system. Algorithm 2 handles this by computing a better estimate of section start times, albeit at a higher cost.

In Algorithm 3, each node, j, sends the node running DQBUA its current local schedule σ_j^p. Using these schedules, the set of threads in the system, Γ, is derived. In lines 3-8, DQBUA computes the global PUD of each thread in Γ. If a section belonging to a thread cannot meet its termination time if it were scheduled immediately, the thread is assigned a PUD of zero since it cannot possibly accrue any utility to the system (line 4). Otherwise, we compute the dependency chain for the thread's sections and call Algorithm 1 to compute its global PUD (lines 6-7). In line 6, we check for cycles to detect any deadlock that may exist. If a cycle is found, it is broken by aborting the thread with the least PUD by executing its exception handler.

Algorithm 4: insertByEDF

input: σ_j^p, σ_j;
$\sigma_j^{tmp} \leftarrow \sigma_j$; // make a copy of the schedule
for *each remaining section, S_j^i, belonging to T_i* **do**
    if $S_j^i \notin \sigma_j^{tmp}$ **then**
        Insert($S_j^i, \sigma_j^{tmp}, S_j^i.tt$); $TT_{cur} \leftarrow S_j^i.tt$;
        if $S_j^h \notin \sigma_j^p$ **then** Insert($S_j^h, \sigma_j^{tmp}, S_j^h.tt$);
        for $\forall S_n^k \in Dep(i,j)$ **do**
            if $S_n^k \in \sigma_n^{tmp}$ **then**
                if *S_n^k is an abortion handler* **then** Remove all sections belonging to S_n^k's thread;
                $TT \leftarrow$ lookUp(S_n^k, σ_n^{tmp});
                if $TT < TT_{cur}$ **then** $TT_{cur} \leftarrow TT$; Continue;
                else
                    Remove($S_n^k, \sigma_n^{tmp}, TT$); Insert($S_n^k, \sigma_n^{tmp}, TT_{cur}$); $\delta \leftarrow TT - TT_{cur}$;
                    for *all predecessors, S_l^x, of S_n^k* **do**
                        //If S_n^k is an abortion handler, S_l^xs are also abortion handlers.
                        //Otherwise, S_l^xs are normal sections
                        $TT \leftarrow$ lookUp(S_l^x, σ_l^{tmp}); $\gamma \leftarrow \delta$;
                        if $S_n^k.tt - TT < \delta$ **then** $\gamma \leftarrow \delta - (S_n^k.tt - TT)$;
                        Remove($S_l^x, \sigma_l^{tmp}, TT$); Insert($S_l^x, \sigma_l^{tmp}, TT - \gamma$);
            else
                $TT_{cur} \leftarrow \min(TT_{cur}, S_n^k.tt)$; Insert($S_n^k, \sigma_n^{tmp}, TT_{cur}$);
                if *S_n^k is not an abortion handler* ***and*** $S_n^h \notin \sigma_n^p$ **then** Insert($S_n^h, \sigma_n^{tmp}, S_n^h.tt$);
if *isFeasible(σ_j^{tmp}'s)=true* **then** $\sigma_j \leftarrow \sigma_j^{tmp}$ for all j;
return σ_j for all j;

It is necessary to ensure that the exception handlers of any thread that has been accepted into the system can meet their termination time to ensure that the system is restored to a safe state if the thread fails. This is done by inserting the handlers of sections that were part of each node's previous schedule into that node's current schedule (lines 8-9). Since these handlers were part of σ_j^p, and DQBUA maintains the feasibility of a schedule as an algorithm invariant, these handlers will meet their termination times. In line 11, we sort the threads in non-increasing order of PUD and consider them for scheduling in that order (lines 12-15). In line 14 we mark as failed any thread that has a section hosted on a node that does not participate in the algorithm. If a thread can contribute non-zero utility to the system and has not been rejected from the system, then we insert its sections, and their dependencies, into the scheduling queue of the nodes responsible for them in non-decreasing order of termination time by calling Algorithm 4 (lines 15).

When Algorithm 4 is invoked, a copy is made of the current schedule so that any changes that result in an infeasible schedule can be undone (line 2). For each of the sections of the current thread, if the section does not already belong to the current schedule (because it was part of the dependency chain of a previous thread), the section and its handler are tentatively inserted into the schedule (lines 5-6).

We then consider the dependencies of that section (lines 7-20). Although sections are considered for scheduling in non-increasing order of global PUD, they are inserted into the schedule in non-decreasing termination time order. Thus during underloads, when no threads are rejected, the resulting schedule is a deadline ordered list. So during underloads, DQBUA defaults to Earliest Deadline First (EDF) scheduling, which is an optimal realtime scheduling algorithm [10] that accrues 100% utility during underloads. Note that if a section, S_n^k, in the dependency chain, $Dep(i, j)$, needs to be aborted in order to reduce the blocking time of a thread, then all the sections belonging to S_n^k's thread need to be aborted as well (line 9).

To ensure that the order of the dependencies is maintained, if the termination time of a section is greater than the termination time of a section that depends on it, its termination time is moved up to the termination time of the section that depends on it (line 13). In addition, all its predecessors have their termination time adjusted to reflect this new value (lines 14-19). Finally, the feasibility of the tentative schedule is checked (line 23) and the changes are made permanent if the schedule is feasible.

5 Algorithm Properties

We establish several properties of DQBUA. Due to space limitations, some of the properties and all of the proofs are omitted here, and can be found in [7]. Below, T is the communication delay, Γ is the set of threads in the system and k is the maximum number of sections in a thread.

Theorem 1 *A distributed scheduling event is handled at most $O(|\Gamma|^2 k^3 \log(|\Gamma|k) + T)$ time units after it occurs, with high, computable, probability, P_{hand}.*

Theorem 2 *If all nodes are underloaded, no nodes fail (i.e. $f = 0$) and each thread can be delayed $O(|\Gamma|^2 k^3 \log(|\Gamma|k) + T)$ time units once and still be schedulable, DQBUA meets all the thread termination times yielding optimal total utility with high, computable, probability, P_{alg}.*

Theorem 3 *If $N - f$ nodes do not crash, are underloaded, and all incoming threads can be delayed $O(|\Gamma|^2 k^3 \log(|\Gamma|k) + T)$ and still be schedulable, then DQBUA meets the termination time of all threads in its eligible execution thread set, Γ, with high computable probability, P_{alg}.*

Theorem 4 *A deadlock is resolved in at most* $O(|\Gamma|^2 k^3 \log(|\Gamma|k) + T)$ *time units by terminating the thread that can contribute the least amount of utility to the system.*

Theorem 5 *Resource contention is resolved in order of thread PUD.*

Theorem 6 *DQBUA limits thrashing by reducing the number of instances of DQBUA spawned by concurrent distributed scheduling events.*

6 Experimental Results

We performed a series of simulation experiments on ns-2 to compare the performance of DQBUA to RTG-DS in terms of Accrued Utility Ratio (AUR) and Deadline Satisfaction Ratio (DSR). We define AUR as the ratio of the accrued utility (the sum of U_i for all completed threads) to the utility available (the sum of U_i for all available jobs) and DSR as the ratio of the number of threads that meet their termination time to the total number of threads. We considered threads with three segments. Each thread starts at its origin node with its first segment. The second segment is a result of a remote invocation to some node in the system, and the third segment occurs when the thread returns to its origin node to complete its execution.

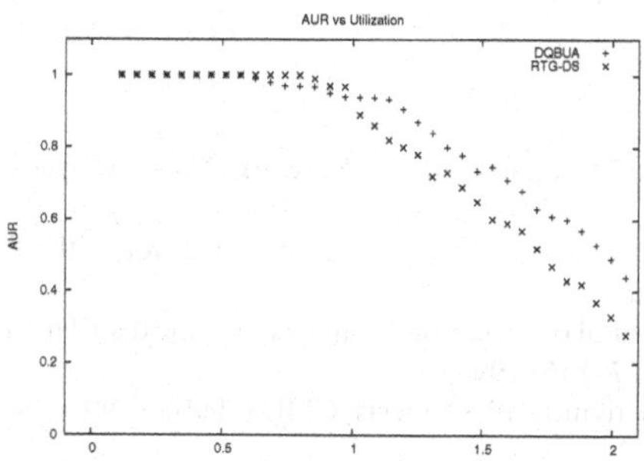

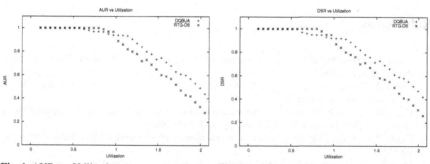

Fig. 1 AUR vs. Utilization

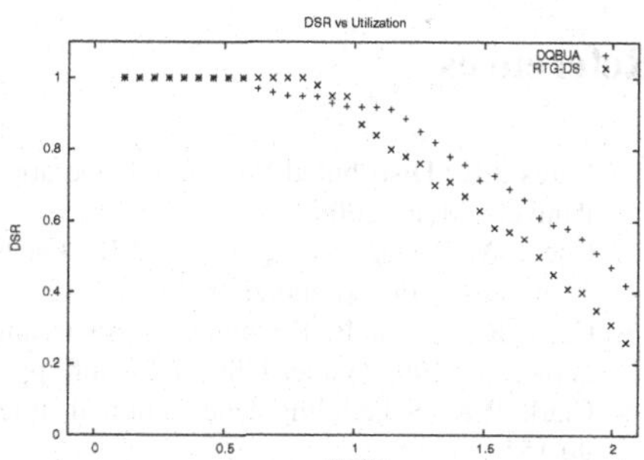

Fig. 2 DSR vs. Utilization

The periods of the threads are fixed, and we vary their execution times to obtain a range of utilization from 0 to 200%. For fair comparison, all algorithms were simulated using a synchronous system model, where communication delay varied according to an exponential distribution with mean and standard deviation 0.02 seconds and an upper bound of 0.5 seconds. Our system consisted of fifty client nodes and five servers. System utilization is considered the *maximum* utilization experienced by any node. We assume that there are two, different, resources on each node. A section randomly chooses which resource, if any, it wishes to acquire and the time spent holding a resource is a uniformly distributed random number that represents a proportion of that section's remaining execution time. See [7] for more details.

As can be seen in Figures 1 and 2, the performance of DQBUA is better than that of DTG-DS during overloads. This occurs because DQBUA performs collaborative scheduling thus maximizing, as much as possible, **system-wide** accrued utility. RTG-DS does not perform collaborative scheduling and therefore performs worse during overloads. However, during underloads, RTG-DS outperforms DQBUA as the utilization of the system approaches one, since DQBUA has higher overhead.

7 Conclusion and Future Work

We presented an algorithm, DQBUA, for scheduling dependent distributable threads in a partially synchronous system. We showed that it accrues optimal utility during underloads and attempts to maximize the accrued utility during overloads. We experimentally compared DQBUA to another scheduling algorithm for dependent threads, RTG-DS, and showed that DQBUA outperforms RTG-DS during overloads. However, during underloads, RTG-DS has better performance since it has lower overhead. Future work includes considering more dynamic networks such as mobile ad hoc networks and finding more sophisticated methods for breaking a wait-for graph when distributed deadlock is detected.

References

1. Cares, J.R.: Distributed Networked Operations: The Foundations of Network Centric Warfare. iUniverse, Inc. (2006)
2. Chen, W., Toueg, S., Aguilera, M.K.: On the quality of service of failure detectors. IEEE Transactions on Computers **51**(1), 13–32 (2002)
3. Clark, R., Jensen, E., Reynolds, F.: An architectural overview of the alpha real-time distributed kernel. In: 1993 Winter USENIX Conf., pp. 127–146 (1993)
4. Clark, R.K.: Scheduling dependent real-time activities. Ph.D. thesis, CMU (1990). CMU-CS-90-155
5. Druschel, P., Rowstron, A.: PAST: A large-scale, persistent peer-to-peer storage utility. In: HOTOS '01, pp. 75–80 (2001)
6. Fahmy, S.F., Ravindran, B., Jensen, E.D.: Fast scheduling of distributable real-time threads with assured end-to-end timeliness. Tech. rep., Virginia Tech, ECE Dept. (2007). Available at: `http://www.real-time.ece.vt.edu/RST_TR.pdf`
7. Fahmy, S.F., Ravindran, B., Jensen, E.D.: Scheduling dependent distributable real-time threads in dynamic networked embedded systems (2007). Available at: `http://filebox.vt.edu/users/fahmy/TR-DIPES.pdf`
8. Han, K., Ravindran, B., Jensen, E.D.: Exploiting slack for scheduling dependent, distributable real-time threads in mobile ad hoc networks. In: RTNS 2007, pp. 225–234 (2007)
9. Jensen, E., Locke, C., Tokuda, H.: A time driven scheduling model for real-time operating systems (1985). IEEE RTSS, pages 112–122, 1985.
10. Liu, C.L., Layland, J.W.: Scheduling algorithms for multiprogramming in a hard-real-time environment. Journal of the ACM **20**(1), 46–61 (1973)
11. Sterzbach, B.: GPS-based clock synchronization in a mobile, distributed real-time system. Real-Time Syst. **12**(1), 63–75 (1997)

An Efficient Time Annotation Technique in Abstract RTOS Simulations for Multiprocessor Task Migration

Henning Zabel and Wolfgang Müller

Abstract Complex control oriented embedded systems with hard real-time constraints require real-time operation system (RTOS) for predictable timing behavior. To support the evaluation of different scheduling strategies and task priorities, we use an abstract RTOS model based on SystemC. In this article, we present an annotation method for time estimation that supports flexible simulation and validation of real-time-constraints for task migration between different target processors without loss of simulation performance and less memory overhead.

1 Introduction

Complex control oriented embedded systems with hard real-time constraints require real-time operation system (RTOS) for predictable timing behavior [1]. Different scheduling strategies are applied and evaluated to guarantee deadlines for a given task set. If accurate execution times for tasks are known, a schedulability analysis can validate if the selected trategy leads to feasible schedules for a given task set.

Interrupts complicate the predictability of deadlines as they do not rely on the RTOS scheduling decisions. Accurate timing analysis in consideration of interrupts are currently executed by means of instruction set simulators (ISS), which implement a complete model of the target processor including I/Os, interrupts, pipelines and memories. The use of ISS requires the embedded software to be fully implemented and is therefore only applicable in late development phases. Schedulability tests and response time analysis helps to evaluate different scheduling strategies and task priorities in early design phases. For this, timing information for execution times of atomic blocks of a task has to be available. Those timing information can be achieved by worst case execution time analysis (WCET) or empirical studies.

Henning Zabel · Wolfgang Müller
University Paderborn, e-mail: henning, wolfgang@c-lab.de

Please use the following format when citing this chapter:

Zabel, H. and Müller, W., 2008, in IFIP International Federation for Information Processing, Volume 271; *Distributed Embedded Systems: Design, Middleware and Resources*; Bernd Kleinjohann, Lisa Kleinjohann, Wayne Wolf; (Boston: Springer), pp. 181–190.

In combination with an abstract RTOS model library, SystemC allows functional simulations of task scheduling with timing. This approach has proven to be adequate for early HW/SW co-design decisions and delivers good approximations for timing analysis with small errors compared to complex instruction set simulations and gives a simulation speedup up to 1000x [2].

In our approach, we simulate a given task set based on our abstract SystemC RTOS model. For schedulability and interrupt analysis, tasks are divided into atomic blocks and each block is annotated by its execution time on a specific target processor. To validate real-time constraints for task migration in multi processor environments, the annotated execution times have to be flexibly adapted to the target processor for each migration. For analysis of the execution time and implementation of the annotation it has some advantages to annotate the start and not the end of an atomic block, which is explained later. Thus, the execution time of an atomic block is simulated at the beginning of the next atomic block. Typically, a block can have different predecessors and thus the previous simulated block must be identified to simulate the correct execution time. This can be realized by:
(i) hard-coded switch-statements, which are very efficient but do not support task migration and flexible adaptation and
(ii) a look-up table, where the column index identifies the previous atomic block and the row the actual atomic block. These tables are of quadratic size in the number of atomic blocks.
Our approach uses processor-specific look-up tables to store execution times. For each target processor one look-up table, which is of linear size in the number of atomic blocks, is generated. Task migration can be simply performed by the exchange of tables. We compare our approach with the two above mentioned solutions for time annotation. Our evaluation shows, that our approach compares to the fast simulation of alternative solutions but due to the linear table size our tables support more complex applications and are easily applicable to different processor platforms.

The paper is structured as follows. Section 2 gives an overview about existing RTOS models. In Section 3 we present our main approach, which is evaluated in Section 4. The article closes with a conclusion in Section 5.

2 Related Work

Today, the functional analysis of embedded SW is mostly executed on an Instruction Set Simulator (ISS). ISS simulations can give accurate timing analysis for a specific target processor if the software code is already available. However, such simulations are considerably slow and thus can have only limited use for early design stages. Early design steps typically apply a static Worst case Execution Time (WCET) analysis [3]. WCET analysis takes the static program in higher-level programming language or machine code and typically extracts graph representations, e.g., control and/or data flow graphs, for worst case runtime estimation computation.

For this approach we use a representation similar to T-Graphs [7] as input. Currently available professional WCET tools for static analysis like aiT (AbsInt) and SymTA/S (SymtaVision) support static WCET execution and response time analysis. Advanced processor behavior like pipelining, caching, and branch prediction are considered. ISS based simulation is usually very accurate since it executes the real SW on a virtual platform. However, it also comes with a very slow execution (i.e., 0,5-500MHz) so that no detailed evaluations and analysis like the evaluation of different scheduling strategies can be efficiently performed. Due to this drawback several research groups have developed abstract canonical RTOS models implemented in SpecC and SystemC give simulation speeds 500-1000 faster than the comparable ISS execution [2, 5, 4, 6]. Whereas those models lacked precision in the beginning, most recent reports indicate an accurate simulation and a well coverage of task and interrupt scheduling behavior with a fast simulation speed at the same time.

Gerstlauer et al. present a methodology based on SpecC/C in [2] for transaction level based refinement. They introduce a canonical abstract RTOS model for scheduling analysis of tasks which covers basic operations for process state transitions, context switching, and semaphores. Tasks are annotated by additional control statements. Synchronization between the scheduler and tasks and between tasks is realized by events. Their approach covers task and interrupt scheduling.

Huss and Klaus present a similar RTOS model in SystemC [5]. They introduce a scheduler class with basic RTOS functions where individual schedulers can be inherited from. Their model covers task scheduling but lacks interrupt management.

Posadas et al. [6] considers tasks divided into different basic blocks. A separate time manager monitors interrupts and segment execution times where non-predictable and predictable (i.e., timer and timeouts) are distinguished. The simulation is based on a implementation of the POSIX API in SystemC. They report an 8% worst case deviation with respect to ISS. This work estimates execution times during simulation by replacing C++ operators, which comes at costs of longer simulation times.

We have developed a canonical SystemC library based on the concepts of [2] for simulation at PV-T (programmers view with timing) transaction level which also overcomes the drawback of non-preemptive tasks for accurate interrupt management including nested and prioritized interrupts. In contrast to other works, our approach comes with separated management for tasks and interrupts to support the analysis of different interrupt and task scheduling strategies.

All those approaches are based on the insertion of timing estimation information of the target platform. Timing information, which defines the consumed CPU time of a particular SW block, is typically directly inserted into the SW code by back annotation. In this article, we present an approach to include timing information into SystemC by means of a table. Thus, we can easily exchange the timing information without the need of recompilation of the complete model. We introduce an approach with lookup tables of size 2*n where n is the number of annotated atomic blocks. Our experimental results demonstrate that our lookup tables are a flexible approach and have no impact on the simulation time.

3 Automated Runtime Estimation

RTOS analysis focuses on the time points when a specific basic block is executed. This supports tracing of simulation results with respect to their execution time. Especially for timing analysis in combination with interrupts, this is of great help. For analysis of execution times, the code is separated into atomic blocks and annotated by its execution time. By means of our SystemC RTOS model we can simulate tasks and allocate them to different virtual CPUs to analyze their timing behavior. To define these blocks the designer marks individual locations in the source code. The automated runtime estimation is then performed in two phases: (1) the execution time from one mark to the next mark is evaluated by disassembling the firmware for target processor and (2) the source code is back-annotated by extending marks with time labels of the estimated times. This code can be compiled for simulation on common PC which allows a runtime estimation of the software with high performance. We present an annotation technique based on a small sized table with for fast simulation. The possibility to exchange those tables during runtime supports the efficient simulation of task migration.

3.1 Code Estimation

For dividing the source code of functions into atomic blocks, the designer marks specific points in the source code by, e.g., special C-macros like *Mark_CC*(). To keep changes to the source code as small as possible we use assembler labels to mark specific points in the source. Therefore C-macros are mapped to assembler labels for cost estimation. Labels are used to mark entry points followed by some lines of code.

```
short rc = 0;
if (a > b)
{
  rc = b;
  if (a > 0)
  {
    rc = -b;
    MARK_CC(A);
  }
  MARK_CC(B);
}
MARK_CC(end)
```

```
short rc = 0;
if (a > b)
{
  MARK_CC(B);
  rc = b;
  if (a > 0)
  {
    MARK_CC(A);
    rc = -b;
  }
}
MARK_CC(end);
```

Fig. 1 Different Annotations: end of an if-statements is marked with a label (left) and beginning of each if-statement is marked with a label (right)

There are two possibilities to mark blocks by labels, like depicted Figure 1:

(1) the end of a block is marked. Because the marks are replaced by back annotations later on, this location refers to the annotation of a atomic block after its execution.

(2)the beginning of each branch of a conditional control flow is marked. Therefore the end of a block is implicit defined at the start of the next one. Here the previous mark has to be considered to annotate an execution time.

In the first approach, it is most likely that the optimization made by the compiler will remove label "A", because the entry-point of "A" and "B" are the same. This eliminates the separation between the two if-statements so that the mark becomes useless for timing estimation. As the second approach does not have this problem, we apply marking at the beginning of branches.

To give an example, we evaluate the cost estimation for the Atmel AT90CAN128 RISC processor. The CPU uses a 2 stage pipeline with no cache. The above mentioned marks have to be added into each function of the program. If the source code is not available, the estimation tool can also follow calls to subroutines. However, subroutines must have no loops. When the function has conditional branches with different exertion times, the estimated costs can be inaccurate. For estimation the labels of marks are mapped to assembler labels like shown in Figure 2 by the example of the Euclidean algorithm.

```
short euklid (short a,short b)
{
  MARK_CC(euklid_start);
  while (b != 0){
    MARK_CC(euklid_loop);
    short h = mod (a,b);
    a = b;
    b = h;
  }
  MARK_CC(euklid_end);
  return a;
}
```

```
000000e2 <euklid>:
  e2: cf 93          push r28
  e4: df 93          push r29
  e6: 9c 01          movw r18, r24
  e8: eb 01          movw r28, r22

000000ea <euklid_start>:
  ea: 67 2b          or r22, r23
  ec: 11 f4          brne .+4         ; 0xf2
  ee: 09 c0          rjmp
.+18       ; 0x102
  f0: ec 01          movw r28, r24

000000f2 <euklid_loop>:
  f2: be 01          movw r22, r28
  f4: c9 01          movw r24, r18
  f6: 0e 94 51 00    call 0xa2 <mod>
  fa: 9e 01          movw r18, r28
  fc: 00 97          sbiw r24, 0x00 ; 0
  fe: c1 f7          brne .-16        ; 0xf0
 100: 9e 01          movw r18, r28

00000102 <euklid_end>:
 102: c9 01          movw r24, r18
 104: df 91          pop r29
 106: cf 91          pop r28
 108: 08 95          ret
```

Fig. 2 Euclidean algorithm in C and the corresponding assembler for the Atmel AT90CAN128 processor

The compiler links these labels to unique addresses in program memory space. Thereafter, an estimation tool can generate a time graph $G = (V,E)$ from those addresses. Each address defines a node $N \in V$ in the graph and an edge $e \in E$ denotes the costs, i.e., estimated execution times. For the Euclidean example nodes are N_0="euklid", N_1="euklid_start" (start), N_2="euklid_loop" (loop), N_3="euklid_end" (end) and N_4="ret" where the latter is given by the return-instruction. We can now compute the cost $C_{i,j}$ from node N_i to N_j by disassembling the firmware and evaluating all possible execution paths through the control flow by depth-first search (DFS). The DFS assigns values for each pair of $N_i, N_j \in \{1,..,\#N\}$ and to the return-instruction. The DFS terminates when a label in $N \setminus \{N_j\}$ is reached. The case $i = j$ is important for loop estimation. If at least one direct path from N_i to N_j is detected an edge is added to the graph with the estimated worst case execution time. For the above example, this estimation leads to a graph like it is shown in Figure 3.

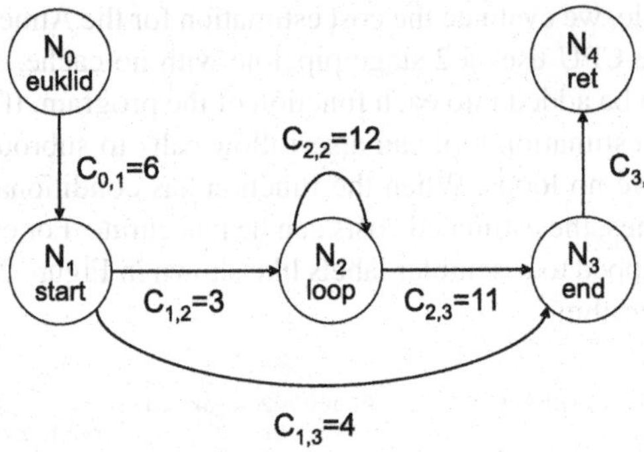

Fig. 3 Annotation Graph: Nodes are identified by annotated marks and edges denote costs given in numbers of CPU cycles.

When there is more than one path between two nodes in the assembler, costs can be an interval and the annotation is only an upper bound.

3.2 Back-annotation

For simulation the marks in the source code are replaced by function calls to simulate the execution time of the previous block. The time consumption is simulated by means of the SystemC. For annotating node N_i all edges leading to N_i must be onsidered. The fastest and most obvious way doing this, is to implement the graph by a C++ **switch-statement**, which store the successor-predecessor relationships of nodes by their index. Alternatively, a **look-up table** of size $(\#N)^2$ can be used to store the cost of $e_{i,j}$. Our approach uses a table presentation with a direct access through the node index and a reduced table size of $2 \cdot \#N$. The key idea in our table representation is to assign relative input costs C_i^{IN} and static output costs of C_i^{OUT} to each node N_i like depicted in Figure 4.

When leaving mark N_i a variable *_cc_cost* is initialized with output cost C_i^{OUT} and when reaching mark N_j the relative cost C_j^{IN} is added to *_cc_cost* and consumed by a function call. Additionally, it has to be ensured, that $C_i^{OUT} + C_j^{IN}$ is exactly the cost $C_{i,j}$ of the edge from N_i to N_j. Figure 4 gives a possible solu-

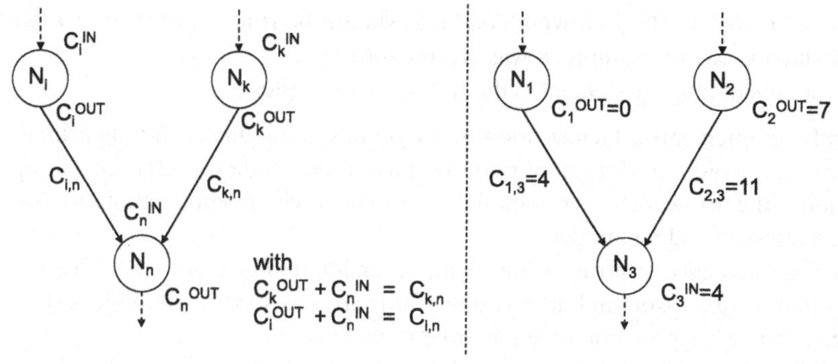

Fig. 4 general graph with divided input and output costs (left), timing graph for the Euclidean algorithm example with nodes N_1-N_3

tion for N_1-N_3 of the Euclidean example. The equations $C_i^{OUT} + C_j^{IN} = C_{i,j}$ forms a system of linear equations and can be solved by the Gauss algorithm as follows. Let $A \in M(\#E, 2*\#N, \mathcal{N})$ be a matrix (#N number of nodes and #E number of edges in the time graph) and $b \in \mathcal{N}^{\#E}$ a vector with $\forall e_l = (N_i, N_j) \in E, l \in \{1..\#E\} : A_{l,2*i+1} = 1, A_{l,2*j} = 1, b_l =$ cost from N_i to N_j. Then solving $Ax = b$ with $x = (C_1^{IN}, C_1^{OUT}, .., C_{\#N}^{IN}, C_{\#N}^{OUT}) \in \mathcal{N}^{\#N}$ delivers the wanted values for the in- and out-cost, if and only if $Ax = b$ is solvable. Since we only need one solution it is not important if this solution is unique or not. If the linear equations are unsolvable, this annotation technique is not applicable at the moment.

The result x is finally stored in an integer-array with exactly $2 \cdot \#N$ elements. The relative incoming cost C_i^{IN} of N_i is stored at index $2 \cdot i$ and the static outgoing cost is stored at index $2 \cdot i + 1$. Therefore the table look-up can be implemented easily without complex access function to retrieve the corresponding costs for node N_i.

4 Evaluation

We evaluated our approach by four examples for the Atmel AT90CAN128 processor. The examples are at first simulated with the AVR-Studio 4.12 from ATMEL to get reference values t_{ref} for the execution times in CPU cycles. Thereafter, we analyzed the binaries with our execution time estimation tool and annotated the source code as mentioned above with a table with the solutions of our linear equations, namely "table 2N" next. We finally compared simulation speed of "table 2N" with hard-coded switch-statements and the table with $(\#N)^2$ entries and direct access, i.e., "table N^2".

Our estimation tool generates header files for each annotation, which redefines the previous introduced marks. Thus, the annotation can be performed without changing the original source code. The annotated code is compiled on a standard PC (with Core2 Duo 6600) and simulated to achieve the required cycles t_{sim} and the simulation speed. The following condition should be true: $|t_{ref} - t_{sim}| < \varepsilon$ with a very small ε. In our example, ε was always zero.

Our benchmarks implemented the following examples:

primf implements a factorization of 4 byte unsigned integer into its primal factors. To avoid the addition of optimized assembler code for 32bit integer operation to the firmware by avr-compiler, we use our own implementations to evaluate the quotient and remainder.

sort implements an array sorting with recursion and nested loops. The array is sorted by quick-sort and then a copy of this array is sorted by bubble sort. In the end these arrays are compared in order to validate both results.

chk implements a small checksum check with bit-wise operations. The checksum is combined by an evaluation of a linear function.

fib implements the computation of a Fibonacci number as a final example for recursion.

All functions are invoked once for cost estimation and 10^6 times during simulation. Figure 5 shows the simulation results with not optimized code and Figure 6 with optimized code. The optimization corresponds to the compilation of the firmware, for simulation the embedded software is always compiled with optimization.

	Cycles	Switch	Array N^2	Array $2N$
primf	310421(*)	33.5us 2692	32.17us 3608	34.4us 2916
sort	288130	19.78us 3243	20.01us 3259	22.4us 2991
chk	30007	12.54us 1898	14.77us 2220	12.5us 2068
fib	233815	30.56us 1474	27.56us 1598	32.3us 1566

(*) 308111 for Array 2*N*, since some edges are estimated via two pathes

Fig. 5 Evaluation results for non-optimized firmware (-O0)

	Cycles	Switch	Array N^2	Array $2N$
primf	76682	33.46us 2676	31.45us 3452	32.6us 2740
sort	97888	21.11us 3243	19.42us 3259	22.5us 2991
chk	12655	12.43us 1896	14.78us 2168	12.2us 2060
fib	119373	30.55us 1474	31.54us 1598	32.2us 1566

Fig. 6 Evaluation results for optimized firmware (-O2)

The tables show the estimated cycles, measured execution times and the code size of the simulation. The estimated cycles are almost the same for all solution and match the reference values from the AVR-Studio. Only for *primf* the value for the array 2*N* differs by about 0.7%. The execution times for the simulation remain similar for the different annotations. This demonstrates that our approach can be applied without loss of performance. The smaller object size for Array 2*N* (compared to Array N^2) are due to the smaller table size with our approach. This is mainly due to the smaller data sections, which includes the tables. The advantage of the table approach is that the implementation of the marks for simulation is independent from the generation of the lookup-tables, means the accessed data. When using switch statements, as mentioned above, implementation and annotation is one part. Additionally, the table can be replaced during runtime to simulate a task migration without the loose of performance.

We also measured the execution speed of the AVR-Studio with 220 thousand instructions per second. Our backannotated simulation was executed with around $1-10 \cdot 10^9$ instructions per second, which finally is a speed-up of more than 4000x. Here, simulation times for optimized and unoptimized code were almost the same, because during simulation only the cost for the edges changes, but not the simulated code (except some constant optimization made by the compiler). Because the optimized code for the AT90CAN128 is considerably smaller than the unoptimized one, that leads to significant differences in performance during an instruction set simulation.

5 Conclusion

In this article, we present a method for time estimation and back-annotation based on an abstract RTOS in SystemC. It supports the flexible simulation and validation of real-time-constraints for task migration between different target processors without loss of simulation performance and less memory overhead.

For our approach we use prepared source code as input, which contains marks at the beginning of each branch. For timing estimation the marks are mapped to assembler and we evaluate a timing graph, where the edges denote the cost from one mark to another. We separate the cost of each edge as static output and relative input cost for each node (mark) by solving a system of linear equations. The solution is stored as an array of size $2 \cdot n$, where n is the number of nodes (marks). Then, the back-annotation can be efficiently implemented by table lookups, since the table-indices are static at compile time.

We demonstrated our approach by four examples for the Atmel AT90CA128 processor. At first, our back-annotated simulations deliver the same cycle counts like simulations with the AVR-Studio. At second, this annotation approach achieves similar simulation performance in comparison to hard-coded switch statements and uncompressed tables, but needs less space and allows easy simulation of task migration by replacing the tables.

Acknowledgments

The work described herein is partly funded by the DFG through the Sonderforschungsbereich 614, the German Ministry for Education and Research (BMBF) through the ITEA2 project TIMMO (01IS07002), and by the EU through COCONUT (FP7-ICT-3217069).

References

1. Giorgio C. Buttazzo and Giorgio Buttanzo. *Hard Real-Time Computing Systems: Predictable Scheduling Algorithms and Applications.* Kluwer Academic Publishers, Norwell, MA, USA, 1997.
2. A. Gerstlauer, H. Yu, and D. Gajski. Rtos modeling for system level design. In *Proceedings of Design, Automation and Test in Europe, March 2003.*, 2003.
3. Kopetz H. *Real-Time Systems. Design Principles for Distributed Embedded Applications.* Springer Verlag, Dordrecht, Netherlands, 1997.
4. M. AbdElSalam Hassan, Keishi Sakanushi, Yoshinori Takeuchi, and Masaharu Imai. Rtk-spec tron: A simulation model of an itron based rtos kernel in systemc. In *DATE '05: Proceedings of the conference on Design, Automation and Test in Europe*, pages 554–559, Washington, DC, USA, 2005. IEEE Computer Society.
5. Sorin A. Huss and Stephan Klaus. Assessment of real-time operating systems characteristics in embedded systems design b systemc models of rtos services. In *DVCon 07: Design and Verification Conference and Exhibitation*, San Jose, CA, 2007.
6. Hector Posadas, Jesús Ádamez, Pablo Sánchez, Eugenio Villar, and Francisco Blasco. Posix modeling in systemc. In *ASP-DAC '06: Proceedings of the 2006 conference on Asia South Pacific design automation*, pages 485–490, New York, NY, USA, 2006. ACM Press.
7. Peter P. Puschner and Anton V. Schedl. Computing maximum task execution times - a graph-based approach. *Real-Time Systems*, 13(1):67–91, 1997.

Handling QoS Dependencies in Distributed Cooperative Real-Time Systems

Luís Nogueira and Luís Miguel Pinho

Abstract Due to the growing complexity and adaptability requirements of real-time embedded systems, which often exhibit unrestricted inter-dependencies among supported services and user-imposed quality constraints, it is increasingly difficult to optimise the level of service of a dynamic task set within an useful and bounded time. This is even more difficult when intending to benefit from the full potential of an open distributed cooperating environment, where service characteristics are not known beforehand. This paper proposes an iterative refinement approach for a service's QoS configuration taking into account services' inter-dependencies and quality constraints, and trading off the achieved solution's quality for the cost of computation. Extensive simulations demonstrate that the proposed anytime algorithm is able to quickly find a good initial solution and effectively optimises the rate at which the quality of the current solution improves as the algorithm is given more time to run. The added benefits of the proposed approach clearly surpass its reduced overhead.

1 Introduction

Most of today's embedded systems are required to work in highly dynamic environments, where the characteristics of the computational load cannot always be predicted in advance and resource needs are usually data dependent and vary over time as tasks enter and leave the system [1]. Nevertheless, response to events still have to be provided within precise timing constraints in order to guarantee a desired level of performance.

One promising solution is to support cooperation among nodes of a distributed system. A careful partitioning of the workload between a device and their remote

---

Luís Nogueira · Luís Miguel Pinho
IPP-Hurray Research Group, Polytechnic Institute of Porto
e-mail: luis, lpinho@dei.isep.ipp.pt

Please use the following format when citing this chapter:

Nogueira, L. and Pinho, L.M., 2008, in IFIP International Federation for Information Processing, Volume 271; *Distributed Embedded Systems: Design, Middleware and Resources*; Bernd Kleinjohann, Lisa Kleinjohann, Wayne Wolf; (Boston: Springer), pp. 191–200.

neighbours has been proved to achieve power and performance gains [2, 4]. Nevertheless, supporting the maximisation of each user's quality of service (QoS) requirements in such a distributed service execution is a key issue [7]. This need imposes a complexity that may prevent the possibility of computing an optimal QoS configuration within an useful and bounded time. It is therefore beneficial to build systems that can trade off the needed computation time for the quality of the achieved solution. In [9], an iterative refinement QoS optimisation that maximises the provided QoS of a set of independent tasks was proposed. The configuration process can be interrupted at any time and still provide a solution and a measure of its quality.

However, the problem is even more complex when tasks exhibit QoS dependency relations among them. Such dependency relations specify that a task offers a certain level of QoS under the condition that some specified QoS will be offered by the environment or by other tasks. In this case, the negotiation process has to ensure that a source task provides a QoS which is acceptable to all consumer tasks and lies within the QoS range supported by the source task. This paper proposes an anytime local QoS optimisation, assuming that services share resources and their execution behaviour and input/output qualities are interdependent, i.e., a constraint on one quality or resource parameter can constrain other system's parameters. To guarantee that a valid solution is available at any time, QoS dependencies are tracked and the performed changes are propagated to all the affected attributes at each iteration of the algorithm. To the best of our knowledge no other works propose an anytime approach for a distributed QoS configuration of resource intensive services in open real-time embedded services with the ability to handle tasks' inter-dependencies and maximise the satisfaction of each user's quality preferences.

2 System model

With tasks joining and leaving the system at any time both resource demands and availability can fluctuate rapidly and unpredictably. This may affect the ability to individually execute services with specific user-imposed QoS constraints and drive devices to group themselves in a coalition for a cooperative service execution [7].

A real-time service $S_i = \{w_{i1}, w_{i2}, \ldots, w_{in}\}$ is a collection of one or more work units w_{ij} that can be executed at varying levels of QoS to achieve an efficient resource usage that constantly adapts to the embedded devices' specific constraints, nature of executing tasks and dynamically changing system conditions. Each work unit $w_{ij} = \tau_{i1}, \tau_{i2}, \ldots, \tau_{in}$ is a set of one or more tasks τ_{ij} that must be executed in the same node due to local dependencies. Dependencies are modelled as a directed graph G_{ij}, with each graph node representing a task and the edges representing the data flow between the tasks. Correct decisions on service partitioning are made at run time when sufficient information about the workload and communication requirements become available [12].

Given the heterogeneity of services to be executed, users' preferences, underlying operating systems, networks, devices, and the dynamics of their resource usages,

QoS specification becomes an important issue in the context of a distributed QoS-aware cooperative service execution framework. Nodes must either have a common understanding of how QoS should be specified, or be able to map their individual specifications into a common one. A sufficiently expressive scheme for defining the QoS dimensions subject to negotiation, their attributes and the quality constraints in terms of possible values for each attribute, as well as inter-dependency relations between some of those QoS parameters was proposed in [7] and can be expressed in several QoS description languages [3]. This scheme is used to specify in the service's description, known at admission time, how a task's output quality depends on the quality of its inputs and on the amount of resources it uses to produce the output. These inter-dependency relations among the QoS parameters of a particular service S_i can be present (i) among two or more QoS attributes of a single task τ_i; (ii) among two or more tasks within a work unit w_{ij}; or (iii) among two or more work units that may be executed in the same or in different nodes.

Based on a domain's QoS characterisation, users provide a single specification of their own range of QoS preferences Q_i for a complete service S_i, without having to understand the individual work units that make up the service. Preferences are defined in a qualitative way, imposing a relative decreasing order of importance on QoS dimensions, their attributes, and acceptable values. Given the spectrum of the user's acceptable QoS levels, each node formulates the best instantaneous service level agreement (SLA) it can offer. The local QoS optimisation recomputes the set of QoS levels for the new set of tasks, as it tries to find a feasible set of service configurations that maximises users' satisfaction with the provided service as well as minimises the impact on the current QoS of the previously accepted tasks. At each iteration, the search of a better solution is guided by a heuristic evaluation function that optimises the rate at which the quality of the current solution improves overtime. The time to find a feasible service solution is dynamically imposed as a result of emerging environmental conditions [10]. A SLA also includes a stability period Δ_t, guaranteeing that during a specific time interval the promised QoS will be assured by the node's local QoS optimisation. Δ_t is dynamically determined in response to fluctuations in the tasks' traffic flow, relating observations of past and present system's conditions and extending users' influence also to the services' adaptation during execution [8].

With several independently developed applications with different timing requirements coexisting in the same node, it is important to guarantee a predictable performance under specified load and failure conditions, and ensure a graceful degradation when those conditions are violated. This is strictly related to the capacity of controlling the incoming workload, preventing abrupt and unpredictable degradations and achieving isolation among services, providing service guarantees to critical applications [10, 11].

3 Optimising the QoS of a inter-dependent task set

The formation of a cooperative coalition should enable the selection of individual nodes that, based on their own resources and availability, will constitute the group that maximises the user's QoS requirements Q_i associated with service S_i, expressed in decreasing preference order. Each $Q^i_{kj} = \{Q^i_{kj}[0], \ldots, Q^i_{kj}[n]\}$ is a finite set of n quality choices for the jth attribute of the kth QoS dimension associated with a work unit w_{ij} of the new service S_i.

This paper extends the anytime local[1] QoS optimisation introduced in [9] by allowing tasks to exhibit unrestricted inter-dependencies among them, only know at admission time. Service negotiation is based on a iteratively refinement of each node's local QoS level, maximising the provided QoS for the new service and minimising the quality degradation of previously accepted tasks. The proposed approach ensures that a source task provides a QoS which is acceptable to all consumer tasks and lies within the QoS range supported by the source task. Based on the new service's data flow graph G_i and on its set of inter-dependency relations $Deps_i$, Algorithm 1 tracks QoS dependencies and propagates the performed changes in one attribute to all local affected attributes at each iteration. If, by following the chain of dependencies, the algorithm finds a task that is already in its list of resolved dependencies, a deadlock is detected and the service proposal formulation is aborted.

In order to be useful in practice, an anytime approach must try to quickly find a sufficiently good initial proposal and gradually improve it if time permits, conducting the search for a better feasible solution in a way that maximises the expected improvement in the solution's quality. Algorithm 1 starts by keeping the QoS levels of previously guaranteed tasks and by selecting the lowest requested QoS level for the new tasks in w_{ij} that complies with any eventual QoS dependency with currently executing tasks. Note that this is the service configuration with the highest probability of being feasible without degrading the current level of service of previously accepted tasks.

The algorithm iteratively work on the problem of finding a feasible set of service configurations and produces results that improve in quality over time. At each iteration, the search of a better feasible solution is guided by the maximisation of the users' expected satisfaction with the provided service. When w_{ij} can be accommodated without degrading the previously accepted tasks' QoS, the configuration that maximises the increase in the obtained reward of the new service is incrementally selected. On the other hand, when QoS degradation is needed to accommodate w_{ij}, the algorithm incrementally selects the configuration that minimises the decrease in the obtained reward for all services.

Rewards are determined by considering the proximity of a service proposal with respect to the weighted user's QoS preferences expressed in decreasing order (Equation 1). The *penalty* parameter can be fine tuned and its value should increase with the distance to the user's preferred value for a particular quality attribute.

---

[1] Dependencies among tasks running on different nodes will be handled in future work

Algorithm 1 Service proposal formulation

Let τ^p be the set of previously accepted tasks
Let τ^e be the set of tasks whose stability period Δ_t has expired
Let $\tau^* = \tau^p \cup w_{ij}$ be the new set of tasks

Step 1: Improve the QoS level of each task $\tau_a \in w_{ij}$
Select $Q_{kj}[n]$, the lowest requested level of service for all k QoS dimensions, considering the dependencies with the previously accepted tasks τ^p, for all newly arrived tasks τ_a in w_{ij}
Keep the current QoS level of previously accepted tasks τ^p
while the new set of local tasks τ^* *is* feasible **do**
  for each task $\tau_a \in w_{ij}$ **do**
    for each attribute without dependencies with τ^p receiving service at $Q_{kj}[m] > Q_{kj}[0]$ **do**
      Upgrade attribute j to the next possible value $m-1$
      Follow dependencies of attribute j in w_{ij} and change values accordingly
      Determine the utility increase of this upgrade
    end for
  end for
  Find task τ_{max} whose reward increase is maximum and perform upgrade
end while

Step 2: Find the local minimal service degradation in τ^* to accommodate each $\tau_a \in w_{ij}$
while the new set of local tasks τ^* *is not* feasible **do**
  for each task $\tau_i \in \tau^e \cup w_{ij}$ receiving service at $Q_{kj}[m] > Q_{kj}[n]$ **do**
    for all QoS attributes **do**
      Degrade attribute j to the previous possible value $m+1$
      Follow dependencies of attribute j in all local tasks τ^* and change values accordingly
      Determine the utility decrease of this downgrade
    end for
  end for
  Find task τ_{min} whose reward decrease is minimum and perform downgrade
end while
return new local QoS optimisation

$$reward(S_i) = 1 - \sum_{j=0}^{\forall Q_{jk} < Q_{best_j}} w_j * penalty_j \tag{1}$$

By combining the rewards of all services' configurations, a measure of a node's global satisfaction with the proposed QoS for the new task set can be obtained (Equation 2).

$$R = \frac{\sum_{i=1}^{n} reward(S_i)}{n} \tag{2}$$

Note that unless all services are executed at their highest requested QoS level, there is a difference between the current node's local reward $R_{current}$ and the maximum theoretical local reward R_{max}. This difference can be caused by either resource limitations, which is unavoidable, or poor load balancing. The later can be improved by using the nodes' local rewards to select the nodes that are going to constitute the new cooperative coalition [7]. Selecting the node with a higher local reward for similar service proposals, not only maximises a particular user's satisfaction with the provided service, but also maximises the global system's utility, since a higher local reward clearly indicates that the node's previous set of tasks had to suffer less QoS degradation in order to accommodate the new tasks.

Algorithm 1 always improves or maintains the current solution's quality as it has more time to run. This is done by keeping the best feasible solution so far, if the result of each iteration is not always proposing a feasible service configuration for the new task set. However, each intermediate configuration, even if not feasible, is used to calculate the next solution, minimising the search effort. Instead of a binary notion of the solution's correctness, the algorithm returns a proposal and a measure of its quality. Equation 3 considers the reward achieved by the new arriving service rs_i, the impact on the provided QoS of previous existing tasks rs_p and the value of the previous generated feasible configuration Q'_{conf}. Initially, Q'_{conf} is set to zero and its value is only updated if the achieved solution is feasible.

$$Q_{conf} = \left(rs_i * \frac{\sum_{i=0}^{n} rs_p}{n} \right)^{(1-Q'_{conf})} \tag{3}$$

The algorithm can be interrupted at any time as a consequence of the dynamic nature of the environment [10], or finishes when it finds a feasible configuration whose quality cannot be further improved, or when it finds that even if all the node's tasks would be served at the lowest requested QoS level it is not possible to accommodate the new requesting tasks in w_{ij}. In this later case, the service request is rejected and the previously accepted tasks continue to be served at their current QoS levels.

4 Behaviour and Evaluation

Since we are primarily interested in dynamic open real-time scenarios a special attention was devoted to introduce a high variability in the characteristics of the conducted simulations. The number of simultaneous nodes in the network varied from 10 to 50 with resources' capacities being randomly partitioned among all the nodes. As a result of this non-equal partition, some nodes could have amounts of some resources which are significantly different from the average, generating a heterogeneous environment.

An application that captures, compresses and transmits frames of real-time data to end users using a diversity of users' QoS preferences and inter-dependency relations among tasks was used as a scenario. The application was composed by a source unit to collect the data, a compression unit to gather and compress the data that may come from multiple sources, a transmission unit to transmit the data over the network, a decompression unit to convert the data into the user's specified format, and an user unit to display the data in the user's end device.

At randomly generated times, one or more users generated new service requests at randomly selected nodes expressed the spectrum of acceptable QoS levels in a qualitative way, ranging from a randomly generated desired QoS level to the randomly generated maximum tolerable service degradation. The relative decreasing order of importance imposed in dimensions, attributes and values was also randomly generated. The QoS domain used to generate the requests was composed by 4 quality dimensions, each with 5 attributes and 10 possible values for each attribute. Promised stability periods were determined by taking into consideration the observed variations in the tasks' traffic flow and correspondent resource usage, adapting the system to the observed environmental changes [8].

Since the proposed algorithm clear splits the formulation of a new service proposal in two different scenarios according to resource availability, the evaluation of its behaviour was based on those two scenarios. In the first one, the average amount of resources per node was greater than the average amount of resources necessary to execute a new service, while in the second one, average service requirements were greater than the average amount of available resources per node, demanding QoS degradation of previously accepted services. The reported results were observed from multiple and independent simulation runs, with initial conditions and parameters, but different seeds for the random values used to drive the simulations, obtaining independent and identically distributed variables, with a reasonably good statistical performance [5]. The random values were generated by the Mersenne Twister algorithm [6].

The first study evaluated the algorithm's behaviour when approaching its optimal solution. Anytime algorithms correlate the output's quality with time in a performance profile [14], a function that maps the time given to an anytime algorithm (and in some cases also input quality) to the quality of the algorithm's produced solution. The performance profile of the proposed anytime algorithm was estimated by normalising the results of the conducted simulations with respect to the algorithm's completion time [13], which is the minimal time when the expected quality is maximal, rather than measuring the algorithm's absolute execution time on every run of the simulation.

When there are enough resources to improve the initial feasible solution without degrading the current QoS of the previous tasks (Figure 1 (a)), the solution's quality Q_{conf} is incrementally improved by increasing the new service's reward. Consequently, the node's local reward that is affected by the initial proposed solution of serving the new arrived service with the minimal requested QoS level, also increases as the algorithm approaches its final solution. With limited resources (Figure 1 (b)), an upgrade of the new service's reward may result in an unfeasible set of tasks, which demands service degradation of some tasks. At each iteration, the configuration that minimises the decrease in the obtained reward for all services is selected.

From Figure 1, two important conclusions can be taken considering the desirable properties of an anytime algorithm [14]. First, the solution's quality measure is a non-decreasing function of time, since the current feasible configuration is only updated if, and only if, another feasible solution with a higher quality for the user's

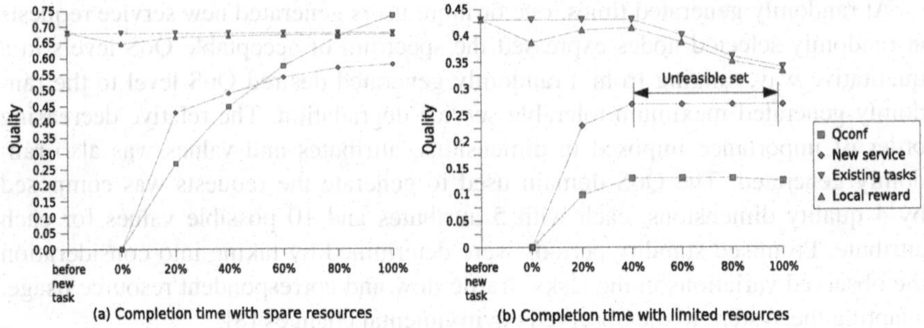

Fig. 1 Expected solution's quality in different scenarios

request under negotiation is found. Second, at an early stage of the computation the quality of the proposed solution is expected to be sufficiently close to its final value at completion time. With spare resources (Figure 1 (a)), at only 20% of the computation time, the solution's quality for the new service is near 74% of the achieved quality at completion time. When QoS degradation is needed (Figure 1 (b)), the configuration for the new service achieves near 85% of its final quality at 20% of the needed computation time.

A second study compared the computational cost required by the anytime approach to reach its optimal solution against the traditional version of the algorithm. The traditional local QoS optimisation proposed in [7] was extended to resolve any QoS dependencies present in its optimal solution and used in this comparison. It starts by selecting the user's preferred QoS level for the new service and stops when it finds a feasible solution that minimises the impact on the provided global level of service caused by the new service's arrival. The comparison's results were normalised with respect to the completion time of the longest solution.

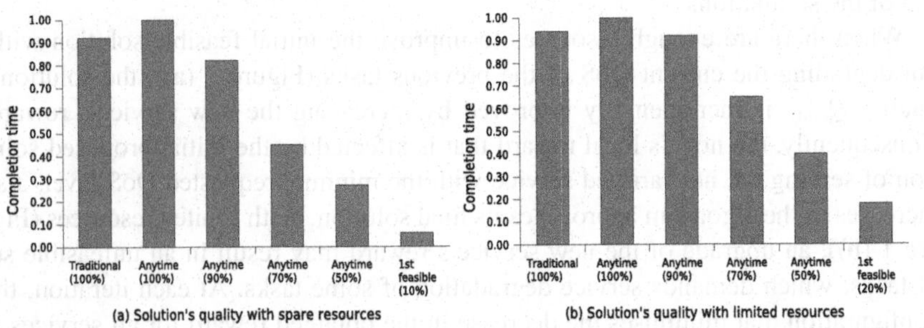

Fig. 2 Computational cost of both approaches

Figure 2 shows that the anytime version can take more time to achieve the same optimal solution in both scenarios. Two main reasons explain this difference. First, the anytime version resolves QoS inter-dependencies at each iteration. Recall that the goal is to be able to interrupt the algorithm at any time and still be able to return a valid solution. Without any restriction on the needed time to compute its optimal solution, the traditional version only has to resolve dependencies after finding the best configuration for the individual tasks in a second phase. Dependencies are resolved by relaxing the optimal values of some of the individual tasks to the maximum value constrained by the existing inter-dependency relations.

Second, the different approaches to achieve an optimal solution can have an impact on the number of needed iterations, particularly with spare resources. Since the anytime version tries to quickly find a feasible solution, it starts by considering the worst requested QoS values for the new service and iteratively improves that solution until the optimal one is found. On the other hand, the traditional version starts by trying to provide the best requested level of service for the new tasks and iteratively degrades all tasks, stopping when it finds a feasible, optimal solution.

Nevertheless, in both scenarios the anytime version is by far quicker to find a feasible solution. With spare resources, the first feasible solution with a quality near 10% of its optimal value is almost immediately found, and at near 20% of the running session the solution's quality is already around 50% of its optimal value. With limited resources, the anytime version takes about 20% of its computation time to reach a feasible solution with 20% of its optimal solution's quality, and at near 40% of the running session it achieves 50% of its optimal value. These results are in consonance with the performance profiles plotted in Figure 1, which further validate the ability of the proposed algorithm to quickly find a feasible solution and maximise the improvement in the expected solution's quality at each iteration.

5 Conclusions

It is not possible to predict in advance the characteristics of a dynamic open real-time system's computational load. Resource needs are usually data dependent and vary over time as tasks dynamically enter and leave the system. As such, nodes may need to cooperate with their neighbours in order to fulfil complex service requirements imposed by users. However, finding an optimal resource allocation that deals with both users' and nodes' constraints can be quite complex and may take a long time. The problem is even harder to solve within a useful time when tasks exhibit unrestricted inter-dependencies among them only known at admission time.

The proposed anytime approach is able to quickly find a sub-optimal solution at an early stage of the computation time. This service solution is then iteratively refined as the algorithm has more time to run. Such flexibility in the needed time to find a feasible service proposal allows a higher adaptation to the dynamically changing conditions of open real-time systems and, as the achieved results demonstrate, can be achieved with an overhead that can be considered negligible when compared against the introduced benefits.

Acknowledgements

This work was supported by FCT (CISTER Research Unit - FCT UI 608 and the CooperatES project - PTDC/EIA/71624/2006), and by the European Commission through the ARTIST2 NoE (IST-2001-34820).

References

1. Sourav Ghosh, Ragunathan (Raj) Rajkumar, Jeffery Hansen, and John Lehoczky. Integrated resource management and scheduling with multi-resource constraints. In *Proceedings of the 25th IEEE Real-Time Systems Symposium*, pages 12–22, Lisbon, Portugal, December 2004.
2. Xiaohui Gu, Alan Messer, Ira Greenberg, Dejan Milojicic, and Klara Nahrstedt. Adaptive offloading for pervasive computing. *IEEE Pervasive Computing Magazine*, 3(3):66–73, 2004.
3. Jingwen Jin and Klara Nahrstedt. Qos specification languages for distributed multimedia applications: A survey and taxonomy. *IEEE MultiMedia*, 11(3):74–87, 2004.
4. Ulrich Kermer, Jamey Hicks, and James Rehg. A compilation framework for power and energy management on mobile computers. In *14th International Workshop on Parallel Computing*, pages 115–131, 2001.
5. Averill M. Law and W. David Kelton. *Simulation modeling and analysis*. McGraw-Hill, 3rd edition, 2000.
6. Makoto Matsumoto and Takuji Nishimura. Mersenne twister: a 623-dimensionally equidistributed uniform pseudo-random number generator. *ACM Transactions on Modeling and Computer Simulation (TOMACS)*, 8(1):3–30, 1998.
7. Luís Nogueira and Luís Miguel Pinho. Dynamic qos-aware coalition formation. In *Proceedings of the 19th IEEE International Parallel and Distributed Processing Symposium*, page 135, Denver, Colorado, April 2005.
8. Luís Nogueira and Luís Miguel Pinho. Dynamic adaptation of stability periods for service level agreements. In *Proceedings of the 12th IEEE International Conference on Embedded and Real-Time Computing Systems and Applications*, pages 77–81, Sydney, Australia, August 2006.
9. Luís Nogueira and Luís Miguel Pinho. Iterative refinement approach for qos-aware service configuration. *IFIP From Model-Driven Design to Resource Management for Distributed Embedded Systems*, 225:155–164, 2006.
10. Luís Nogueira and Luís Miguel Pinho. Capacity sharing and stealing in dynamic server-based real-time systems. In *Proceedings of the 21th IEEE International Parallel and Distributed Processing Symposium*, page 153, Long Beach,CA,USA, March 2007.
11. Luís Nogueira and Luís Miguel Pinho. Shared resources and precedence constraints with capacity sharing and stealing. In *Proceedings of the 22th IEEE International Parallel and Distributed Processing Symposium (to appear)*, Miami,Florida,USA, April 2008.
12. Cheng Wang and Zhiyuan Li. Parametric analysis for adaptive computation offloading. In *Proceedings of the ACM SIGPLAN 2004 Conference on Programming Language Design and Implementation*, pages 119–130. ACM Press, 2004.
13. Shlomo Zilberstein. *Operational Rationality Through Compilation of Anytime Algorithms*. PhD thesis, Department of Computer Science, University of California at Berkeley, 1993.
14. Shlomo Zilberstein. Using anytime algorithms in intelligent systems. *Artificial Inteligence Magazine*, 17(3):73–83, 1996.

Topology-Aware Energy Efficient Task Assignment for Collaborative In-Network Processing in Distributed Sensor Systems

Baokang Zhao, Meng Wang, Zili Shao*, Jiannong Cao, Keith C.C. Chan, and Jinshu Su

Abstract In the emerging networked sensor systems, collaborative in-network processing provides a viable solution to overcome the limited energy and resource constraints of one single node. In this novel computing paradigm, it is very critical to perform task assignment. In this paper, we formally model TETA, an energy efficient topology-aware real time task assignment problem in wireless sensor networks, and prove its NP-completeness. We also propose an ant-based meta-heuristic algorithm to solve the TETA problem. We implement our algorithm and conduct experiments based on a simulation environment. The experimental results show that our approach can archive significant energy saving and improve the system lifetime effectively as well.

1 Introduction

With recent technological advances in sensing, computing, communication and wireless networking, distributed sensor systems are increasing deployed owing to their wide popularity of applications. In these systems, collaborative in-network data processing techniques have been proven to be an effective way to significantly reduce energy consumption. In this novel collaborative computing paradigm, applications are partitioned into tasks that are executed in a distributed manner. To meet the application requirements, these tasks should be assigned to different sensor nodes.

Baokang Zhao · Jinshu Su
School of Computer, National University of Defense Technology, Changsha, Hunan, P.R.of China
e-mail: bkzhao, sjs@nudt.edu.cn

Meng Wang · Zili Shao (the corresponding author) · Jiannong Cao · Keith C.C.Chan
Department of Computing, Hong Kong Polytechnic University, Hung Hom, Kowloon, Hong Kong, China
e-mail: csmewang, cszlshao, csjcao, cskcchan@comp.polyu.edu.hk

Please use the following format when citing this chapter:

Zhao, B., et al., 2008, in IFIP International Federation for Information Processing, Volume 271; *Distributed Embedded Systems: Design, Middleware and Resources*; Bernd Kleinjohann, Lisa Kleinjohann, Wayne Wolf; (Boston: Springer), pp. 201–211.

Hence, the task assignment problem is a fundamental issue and plays a critical role in the collaborative data processing.

Task assignment is a classical problem in the traditional computation paradigm. However, in distributed sensor systems, several distinct issues, such as energy efficiency,node location, network topology, should be particularly addressed. For instance, in high-performance computing and grid computing, there are many assignment techniques focused on interconnect or wired networks. In these models, processing units are either fully connected via interconnect or wired networks [3, 12], or some special topology such as chains[9], trees[2], 2D-mesh, 3D-Torus[10],etc.These topologies are different from those in wireless environments.

Recently,localized task assignment problem has been investigated in wireless sensor networks. In [4], Heemin et al. presented a simulated annealing framework for energy-efficient task assignment and migration in sensor networks. An Integer Linear Programming model is introduced by Yang and Viktor in [11], they also proposed a three-phase heuristic named EbTA. In [7], An algorithm named EcoMapS is proposed for jointly mapping and scheduling tasks in single-hop cluster. In [6], Yuan presented RT-Maps which can provide a real time guarantee. All the above techniques concentrate on task assignment in one hop. In practice, multi-hop collaboration is more popular in wireless sensor networks.

Latest studies have been conducted to multi-hop environments. In [5], Yuan et al. proposed a multi-hop collaborative in-network processing algorithm. However, network topology is not considered in their work. In wireless sensor networks, topology is a fundamental issue and should be taken into consideration.The approaches ignoring the location and topology of sensors may not work correctly.

In this paper, we focus on topology aware energy efficient task assignment problem in wireless sensor networks. To our best, this is a first attempt to deal with the task assignment problem in multi-hop sensor networks considering the underlying network topology. Our main contributions are summarized as follows:

- We study and address the topology-aware energy efficient task assignment problem for multi-hop sensor networks. We formally model TETA, an integrated model for both reducing the system-level energy consumption and providing real-time guarantee. We also prove its NP-completeness.
- We propose ANT-TETA, an ant based meta-heuristic algorithm to solve the TETA problem. Through multiple artificial ants travels the network and assign the tasks sequentially, this heuristic approach can exploit the underlying topology more better, and provides a good solution for TETA. Also, it can be easily extended to work in a decentralized and parallel way.
- We have implemented this work in a simulation environment, and compare it with the extension of existing approaches. The experimental results show that our approach can achieve significant energy saving and improve the system lifetime.

The rest of this paper is organized as follows.In section 2, we introduce the topology-aware energy efficient task assignment problem. Based on some system level assumptions, the formal definition of TETA is given. The proof of its NP-completeness is presented in section 3. We then propose the ANT-TETA algorithm in section 4. We provide the experiments results and analysis in section 5. Finally, the conclusion is given in section 6.

2 Problem Statement

In this section, we first introduce some realistic assumptions. Based on these assumptions, we formally define the application model, network model and energy model. Thereafter, the formal problem statement is given.

- System Assumptions

We assume the following system assumptions:

1. A sensor network consists of heterogeneous nodes. Each sensor node is equipped with a computing unit,sensors and a wireless module. Nearby nodes form a logical multi-hop computation environment called cluster. Applications are executed inside the cluster in a collaborative manner.
2. We adopt the collision free model[10]. The link collision can be avoided by link scheduling approaches.
3. The network topology information is available for sensor nodes inside the cluster.

- Application Model

In distributed and parallel computing, applications are modeled as DAG graphs. We assume the target application can be represented by $TG = (V_T, E_T, V_{ET}, vw, ew, TC)$. V_T denotes all the computational tasks,and vw represents tasks' computational overhead. E_T consists of communication edges between associated tasks,and ew is the function of communication throughput on the edges. In sensor applications, the entry tasks are always from special sensor nodes. The set of entry tasks is denoted as V_{ET}. The overall timing constraint is assumed to be TC.

- Network Model

The network topology is always modeled as a connected graph $NG = (V_G, E_G, cc, dw)$. V_G is the set of sensor nodes,E_G is the set of communication edges.To enhance the network lifetime,each sensor node can only perform limited computation,and this limitation is modeled as cc. The communication distance between two nodes is modeled as function dw.

- Energy Model

We adopt the same energy consumption model as [8].

$$P_{cpu} = \alpha C_L * V^2 * f + I_{leak} * f \tag{1}$$

$$P_{TX}(d) = E_{elec} + \varepsilon_{amp} d^{\partial} \tag{2}$$

$$P_{RX} = E_{elec} \tag{3}$$

In the CPU power model,α,C_L and I_{leak} are processor dependent parameters,V and f denote the working voltage and frequency,respectively.The transmitting and receiving power of the wireless module are shown in equation 2 and 3. E_{elec} and ε_{amp} are electronic parameters, d is the transmitting distance, and $2 \le \partial \le 4$. In our experiments, we adopt the parameters of μAMPS[8].

- Task Assignment

In general, the goal of task assignment is to assign tasks to sensor nodes. Assume m represents the assignment result.That is, task T_i is assigned to a sensor node $m(T_i)$.After the assignment is done, the communication edge is mapped to the shortest path between nodes. In a specified assignment m, we assume $E^{(m)}_{comp}(T_i)$ denotes the energy consumption of task T_i, $E^{(m)}_{comm}(e_{ij})$ denotes the energy consumption of communication edge e_{ij}, and $L(m)$ is the finish time of application.

- Problem Definition

Given task graph and network topology, the objective of task assignment is :

Minimize:

$$E^{(m)}_{total} = \sum_{t_i \in V_T} E^{(m)}_{comp}(t_i) + \sum_{e_{i,j} \in E_T} E^{(m)}_{comm}(e_{i,j}) \tag{4}$$

Subject to:

$$L(m) \le TC \tag{5}$$

3 Problem Complexity

In this section, we prove that the TETA problem is NP-complete by a reduction from the subgraph isomorphism problem.

Definition 1. the TATAS_DP problem:

Given a positive number K,TC, a task graph TG, a network topology NG, an assignment m, is the total energy consumption K, and the total execution time for the task graph $TG\ L(m) \le TC$?

Definition 2. Sub Graph Isomorphism problem:[1]

Given two graphs $G_1 = (V_1, E_1)$ and $G_2 = (V_2, E_2)$, G_1 is isomorphic to G_2 if there is a function f which maps the vertices of G_1 to vertices of G_2 such that for all pairs of vertices x,y in V_1, edge (x,y) is in E_1 if and only if the edge $(f(x), f(y))$ is in E_2.

Theorem 1. *the decision problem of the TATAS problem is NP-complete.*

Proof: Since we can check $E^{(m)}_{total}$ and $L(m)$ using equations (1-5), and this process can be finished in polynomial time, The TATAS_DP problem belongs to NP.

Assume $I =< G1, G2, f >$ is an instance of sub graph isomorphism, where $G_1 = (V_1, E_1)$ and $G_2 = (V_2, E_2)$, f is a mapping function from G_1 to G_2. We will construct a TATAS_DP problem instance from I.

Let a vertex d be any node in V_1, A task graph $TG = (V_1, E_1, \{d\}, vw, ew)$ is constructed from G_1 directly. The function vw and ew is configured to assign and for each node and edge G_1, respectively. A network topology $NG = (V_2, E_2, dw)$ from G_2.For each edge $e_{i,j}$ in E_2, $dw(e_{i,j}) = 1$.

We assume the total computation energy consumption as E_{comp}. We set TC to infinite and set K as

$$K = E_{comp} + e_{comm} * (2 * E_{elec} + \varepsilon_{amp}) * |E_1| \tag{6}$$

The mapping function f' from TG to NG can be constructed from f in polynomial time by:

$$\forall v \in V_1, f'(v) = f(v) \tag{7}$$

$$\forall e_{i,j} = (v_i, v_j) \in E_1, f'(e_{i,j}) = (f(v_i), f(v_j)) \tag{8}$$

We will prove that f' is a feasible solution to the TATAS_DP problem if and only if f is a solution to sub graph isomorphism decision problem I.

Suppose f is a solution to sub graph isomorphism decision problem I. In I', the total energy consumption of mapping f' will be

$$\begin{aligned} E_{total} &= E_{comp} + \sum_{e_{i,j} \in E_1} E(e_{i,j}) \\ &= E_{comp} + e_{comm} * (2 * E_{elec} + \varepsilon_{amp}) * |E_1| \leq K \end{aligned} \tag{9}$$

Thus, f' is a feasible solution to I'.

On the contrary, if a solution f' for I' is found, we can also prove f is a feasible solution by reduction to absurdity. If any edge in the task graph is mapped to a path with more than one edge, then the energy consumption in this communication will be larger than $e_{comm} * (2 * E_{elec} + \varepsilon_{amp})$. Therefore, the total energy consumption will be:

$$\begin{aligned} E_{total} &= E_{comp} + e_{comm} * (2 * E_{elec} + \varepsilon_{amp}) \sum_{e \in E_1} p(e) \\ &\geq E_{comp} + e_{comm} * (2 * E_{elec} + \varepsilon_{amp}) * |E_1| = K \end{aligned} \tag{10}$$

It violates the assumption that f' is a valid solution to I'. So the TETA problem is NP-complete.

4 The Proposed ANT-TETA Algorithm

Since the TETA problem is NP-complete, heuristic approaches can be proposed. Inspired by the efficiency of ant colony optimization in solving graph-related problems, we propose an ant based task assignment algorithm named ANT-TETA. In this section, we first introduce an overview of ANT-TETA, and then describe its key components in section 4.2.

4.1 Overview

The overview of the ANT-TETA algorithm is shown in Fig.1.

```
   Input: Task Graph TG, Network Topology Graph NG
   Output: assignment from TG to NG.
1  Initialize the pheromone matrix and other data structures.;
2  foreach ant k do
3  |   ant k build its task list L(k) via topological sorting using Depth-First Search;
4  end
5  while terminate condition is not meet do
6  |   foreach ant k do
7  |   |   L = L(k);
8  |   |   while L is not empty do
9  |   |   |   Pick out the next unassigned task i from L in sequential order;
10 |   |   |   Build the candidate node set CS(i);
11 |   |   |   For each node j in CS(i), calculate its probability through heuristics and
   |   |   |   pheromone;
12 |   |   |   Select node j stochastically according to its probability;
13 |   |   |   Assign task i to node j, update the assignment information and other
   |   |   |   information such as node capacity;
14 |   |   end
15 |   end
16 |   update the pheromone matrix;
17 |   update other statistics information;
18 end
19 Output the final solution;
```

Fig. 1 The ANTS-TETA algorithm

We assume the number of entry tasks is q. ANT-TETA tries to obtain a better assignment through the collaboration of q artificial ants. In step (2-4), each ant k will build a list $L(k)$ by topological sorting the task graph from its corresponding entry task nodes. $L(k)$ determines the task assignment order of ant i in step(8-12). From step (5), ANT-TETA performs task assignment in a standard ant system manner. In step (6-15), ant k assigns tasks to sensor nodes one by one following the sequential order of $L(k)$.Since the assignment of ants executes independently, this can be done in a distributed and parallel manner. After all the ants finish its assignment, the pheromone matrix and other information is updated as in step16-17. Since this process is based on the well known ant system, we will only focus on some critical steps in the next subsection.

4.2 Key Components

- Heuristic desirability

Heuristic desirability η_{ij} implies the fitness function of assign task i to node j. In ANT-TETA,let E_{ij} and $E_{ij}^{(total)}$ denotes increase and total energy consumption if task i is assigned to node j, and L_i denotes the application execution time after task i is assigned to node j,the heuristic desirability is defined as

$$\eta_{ij} = \begin{cases} \lambda \frac{E_{ij}}{E_{ij}^{(total)}} + \mu \frac{L_i}{TC} & \text{if } L_i \le TC \\ 0 & \text{otherwise} \end{cases} \quad (11)$$

where λ and μ is application specific parameters.

- Building candidate set

In step (10),let $rc(N_j)$ denotes the remain computation capacity in node N_j, ant k will construct a candidate node set $CS_{T_i}^{(k)}$ based on the computation requirements:

$$CS_{T_i}^{(k)} = \{N_j | rc(N_j) \ge cc(T_i)\} \quad (12)$$

- Probability of assignment

In step (11), it plays a critical role in calculating assignment probability. Let p_{ij}^k denotes the probability of ant k assigns task i on node j is given by

$$p_{ij}^k(t) = \frac{\sum_{l \in CS_{T_i}^{(k)}} [\tau_{ij}(t)]^\alpha \cdot [\eta_{ij}(t)]^\beta}{[\tau_{ij}(t)]^\alpha \cdot [\eta_{ij}(t)]^\beta} \quad (13)$$

Where t is the iteration number,and α, β determines the weight given to the heuristic information and pheromone, respectively.

- Update the pheromone information

In step(16), when all the ants find a solution, the pheromone matrix will be updated with

$$\tau_{ij}(t+1) = (1-\rho) \cdot \tau_{ij}(t) + \sum_{k=1}^{m} \Delta \tau_{ij}^k \quad (14)$$

, where ρ represents the pheromone evaporation,$\Delta\tau_{ij}^{k}$ is the amount of pheromone ant k deposits on the assignment (i,j):

$$\Delta\tau_{ij} = \begin{cases} Q/E_k^{total} & \text{if } i \text{ is assigned to } j \text{ by ant } k \\ 0 & \text{otherwise} \end{cases} \tag{15}$$

where E_k^{total} denotes the final energy consumption of assignment solution by ant k, and Q is a system parameter and it is application specific.

5 Simulation Results

We evaluate our ANT-TETA algorithm through simulations. In this section, we first introduce our simulation platform and parameters. Thereafter,we compare the results of our ANTS-TETA algorithm with the multi-hop extension of DCA[8]. Experimental results show that our algorithm can archive significant energy savings and improve the system lifetime.

5.1 Simulation Platform and Parameters

In order to evaluate the performance of the proposed algorithm, we build a simulation platform. As illustrated in Fig 2. This platform consists of three parts: DAG regulator, network topology generator(NTG),and assignment algorithms module.

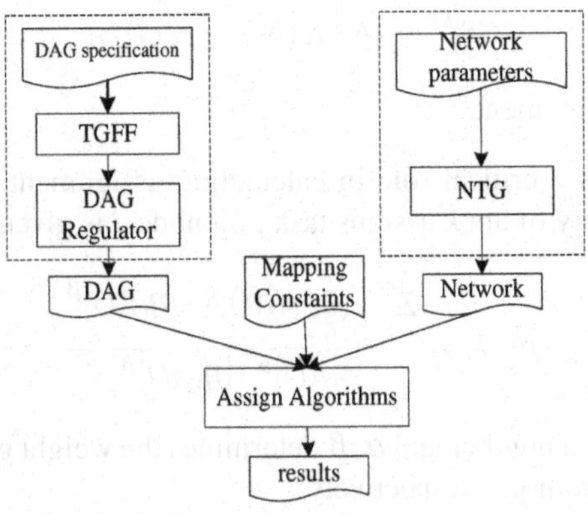

Fig. 2 The simulation platform

The DAG regulator is based on the **TGFF** tool. We use **TGFF** to generate DAG task graph,and regulate the results to meet the application requirements.In our experiments, we set the number of entry tasks to be 8, and set the maximum in degree and out degree to be 3 and 5,respectively. The computation workload and communication throughput are randomly chosen within the range of (100KCC, 600KCC) and (500bits, 1000bits). The raw sensing data is larger and is randomly chosen in the range of (4kbits, 8kbits).The computation workload and communication throughput are randomly chosen within the range of (100KCC, 600KCC) and (500bits, 1000bits),and its battery capacity is set to 1000Amh.

NTG is used to generate a random network topology. It assumes that the sink node is placed in the center of a 1km*1km area. It starts with placing specified number of randomly generated nodes within the area. Afterwards, it checks the connectivity. The nodes with a connectivity degree of zero is regarded as faulty nodes and will be replaced with new random nodes.This process continues until the node amount can meet the requirements.The computation capability of each node is selected within the range of (500KCC, 800KCC).

5.2 Results and Analysis

We compare our algorithm with the multi-hop extension of DCA. DCA represents the traditional and popular way of data processing. It executes the entry tasks on the corresponding sensing node, transmits raw data to the cluster head, and processes all the other tasks on the cluster head. We extend DCA with multi-hop support by constructing communication paths from entry sensors to the cluster head.

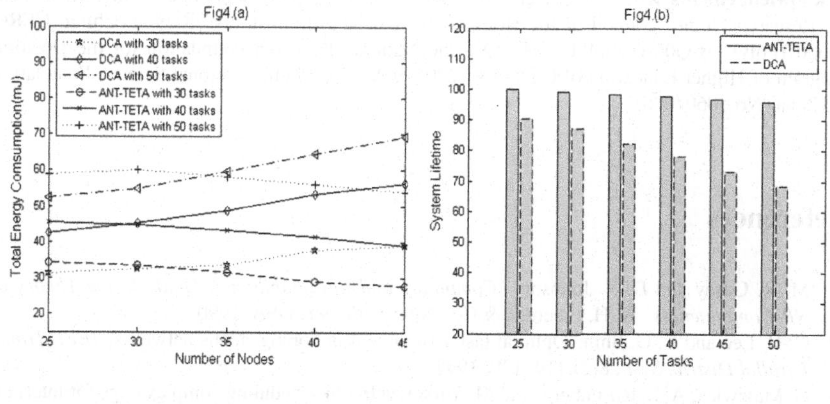

Fig. 3 The comparison between ANT_TETA and DCA

As shown in Fig 3, we compare ANT-TETA with DCA in terms of total energy consumption. With the number of nodes increases, the total energy consumption of DCA increases. Since DCA execute most tasks on the cluster head, its energy consumption depends on the communication activities. Thus, the change of network topology will influence it slightly. In contrast, the ANT-TETA is able to reduce its total energy consumption effectively for the underlying network topology.

The lifetime of sensor network is defined as the time after the first node runs out its battery.Compared with DCA, Our ANT-TETA can archive at most 28.9% improvements for the network lifetime. The reason is that DCA assigns too many tasks on the cluster head, which will exhaust the energy of the cluster head. What's more, this result comes from computation dominated applications. If the communication overhead is high, it will be more worse. Besides, in DCA, due to the huge size of raw sensed data, the other nodes in the transmitting path consume more energy. The result also indicates that the task assignment techniques of collaborative in-network processing are able to enhance the network lifetime dramatically.

6 Conclusion

In this paper, we formally define TETA, an energy efficient topology-aware real time task assignment problem in distributed sensor systems, and proved its NP-completeness. An ant-based meta-heuristic algorithm named ANT-TETA is proposed to solve the TETA problem. We also implement our algorithm in a simulation environment and conduct experiments. The experimental results show that our approach can archive significant energy saving and improve the system lifetime effectively as well.

Acknowledgements The work described in this paper is partially supported by the grants from the Research Grants Council of the Hong Kong Special Administrative Region, China (CERG 526007(PolyU B-Q06B), PolyU A-PA5X), the National Research Foundation for the Doctoral Program of Higher Education of China (No.20049998027), and the National Science Foundation of China (No.90604006).

References

1. M. R. Garey and D. S. Johnson. *Computers and Intractability; A Guide to the Theory of NP-Completeness.* W. H. Freeman & Co., New York, NY, USA, 1990.
2. C.-H. Lee and K. G. Shin. Optimal task assignment in homogeneous networks. *IEEE Trans. Parallel Distrib. Syst.*, 8(2):119–129, 1997.
3. G. Malewicz, A. L. Rosenberg, and M. Yurkewych. On scheduling complex dags for internet-based computing. In *IPDPS '05: Proceedings of the 19th IEEE International Parallel and Distributed Processing Symposium*, page 66, Washington, DC, USA, 2005.
4. H. Park and M. B. Srivastava. Energy-efficient task assignment framework for wireless sensor networks. Technical report, September 7 2003.
5. Y. Tian. Cross-layer collaborative in-network processing in multihop wireless sensor networks. *IEEE Transactions on Mobile Computing*, 6(3):297–310, 2007.
6. Y. Tian, J. Boangoat, E. Ekici, and F. Ozguner. Real-time task mapping and scheduling for collaborative in-network processing in dvs-enabled wireless sensor networks. *ipdps*, 2006.

7. Y. Tian, E. Ekici, and F. Ozguner. Energy-constrained task mapping and scheduling in wireless sensor networks. *IEEE International Conference on Mobile Adhoc and Sensor Systems Conference, 2005.*, pages 8 pp.– 12, 7-10 Nov. 2005.
8. A. Wang and A. Chandrakasan. Energy-efficient dsps for wireless sensor networks. *IEEE Signal Processing Magazine*, 43(5):68–78, 2002.
9. C.-C. Yeh. Power-aware allocation of chain-like real-time tasks on dvs processors. *IEICE - Trans. Inf. Syst.*, E89-D(12):2907–2918, 2006.
10. Y. Yu, B. Hong, and V. K. Prasanna. On communication models for algorithm design in networked sensor systems: a case study. *Pervasive Mob. Comput.*, 1(1):95–121, 2005.
11. Y. Yu and V. K. Prasanna. Energy-balanced task allocation for collaborative processing in wireless sensor networks. *Mob. Netw. Appl.*, 10(1-2):115–131, 2005.
12. M. Yurkewych. Toward a theory for scheduling dags in internet-based computing. *IEEE Trans. Comput.*, 55(6):757–768, 2006.

Data Partitioning Techniques for Partially Protected Caches to Reduce Soft Error Induced Failures

Kyoungwoo Lee, Aviral Shrivastava, Nikil Dutt, and Nalini Venkatasubramanian

Abstract Exponentially increasing with technology scaling, soft errors have become a serious design concern in the deep sub-micron embedded systems. Partially Protected Cache (PPC) is a promising microarchitectural feature to mitigate failures due to soft errors in embedded processors. A processor with PPC maintains two caches, one protected and the other unprotected, both at the same level of memory hierarchy. By finding out the data more prone to soft errors and mapping only that to the protected cache, the failure rate can be significantly improved at minimal power and performance penalty. While the effectiveness of PPCs has been demonstrated on multimedia applications – where the multimedia data is inherently resilient to soft errors – no such obvious data partitioning exists for applications in general. This paper proposes profile-based data partitioning schemes that are applicable to applications in general and effectively reduce failures due to soft errors at minimal power and performance overheads. Our experimental results demonstrate that our algorithm reduces the failure rate by 47× on benchmarks from MiBench while incurring only 0.5% performance and 15% power overheads.

1 Introduction

Reliability is becoming the paramount concern in system design in the deep sub-micron era [1]. With technology scaling, i.e., smaller feature size, lower voltage level, etc., microprocessors are becoming increasingly prone to transient faults [9]. A transient fault results in erroneous program states and eventually incorrect out-

Kyoungwoo Lee · Nikil Dutt · Nalini Venkatasubramanian
Department of Computer Science, School of Information and Computer Sciences, University of California, Irvine, CA 92697, USA, e-mail: {kyoungwl, dutt, nalini}@ics.uci.edu

Aviral Shrivastava
Department of Computer Science and Engineering, School of Computing and Informatics, Arizona State University, Tempe, AZ 85281, USA e-mail: Aviral.Shrivastava@asu.edu

Please use the following format when citing this chapter:

Lee, K., et al., 2008, in IFIP International Federation for Information Processing, Volume 271; *Distributed Embedded Systems: Design, Middleware and Resources*; Bernd Kleinjohann, Lisa Kleinjohann, Wayne Wolf; (Boston: Springer), pp. 213–225.

puts, but it is non-destructive, i.e., resetting the device, restores normal behavior. While transient faults occur due to several reasons, radiation is more responsible for transient faults than all the other causes combined [4]. Radiation-induced faults occur when a high energy radiation particle, e.g., an alpha particle, a neutron or a free proton, strikes the diffusion region of a CMOS transistor and produces charge, which results in toggling the logic value of the transistor. This phenomenon of change in the logic state of a transistor is called an *Upset*. An upset may result in a change in the architectural state of a processor. The changed architectural state of a processor is called an *Error*. An error can cause an observable difference in the behavior of the program, which is termed as a *Failure*.

Among all the microarchitectural features in a processor, on-chip caches are most susceptible to upsets. This is due to the fact that caches cover majority of chip area, and operate at much lower voltage than combinational circuits [7, 16]. In addition, while an upset in combinational circuits becomes an error only if it is latched at the right moment, the absence of latching-window masking in caches ensures that all upsets translate into errors. Indeed, more than 50% of errors occur in memories [17]. Consequently, it is very important to prevent errors in memory structures.

Several microarchitectural techniques have been proposed to reduce the impact of soft errors in memories, the most popular being the use of Error Correction Codes (ECC). While the ECC-based techniques are well suited for off-chip memories, they are inappropriate for caches, as they are highly sensitive to any power and performance overheads. In fact, implementing an ECC scheme in caches increases the cache access time by up to 95% [14] and power consumption by up to 22% [24]. Partially Protected Cache (PPC) was proposed by Lee et al. [13] to mitigate the impact of soft errors on caches. A PPC architecture has two caches, one *protected* against soft errors, and the other *unprotected*, at the same level of memory hierarchy. The intuition behind PPC is that when soft errors occur, some data is more likely to cause failures than others. By mapping only this data to the protected cache, the failure rate can be significantly reduced at minimal power and performance overheads. PPCs were demonstrated to be extremely effective for multimedia applications. In multimedia applications, the multimedia data itself is error-resilient. For example, in an image or video processing application, a soft error in the image or video only causes a slight loss in Quality of Service (QoS). In contrast, most other data, e.g, loop control variables, stack pointers, etc., are not error-resilient. Any soft error in these variables may lead to a failure. However, no obvious data partitioning exists for general applications. The absence of a data partitioning scheme for applications in general severely limits the applicability of PPC architectures.

In this paper, we propose schemes to partition the data of general applications into the two caches of PPC architecture and to achieve high reduction in failure rate, at minimal power and performance penalty. We develop and test several data partitioning algorithms. Monte Carlo exploration is unable to find interesting data partitions. While Genetic Algorithm efficiently searches the exploration space, it does not achieve high reduction in failure rate. Our approach, *DPExplore*, efficiently prunes the search space, and uncovers Pareto-optimal data partitions. Experimental results on the HP iPAQ h4600 [10]-like processor-memory subsystem running benchmarks from MiBench [8] demonstrate that the PPC architectures reduce the failure rate by 47× with 0.5% performance and 15% energy penalty on average.

2 Related Work

Radiation-induced soft errors have been under investigation since late 1970s. Due to incessant technology scaling, soft error rate (SER) has exponentially increased [9], and now it has reached a point, where it becomes a real threat to system reliability. Microarchitectural solutions attempt to reduce the number of upsets that translate into errors, and/or errors that result in failures. Solutions at the microarchitecture level can be categorized based on the components where they are applied: the combinational components, the sequential components, and the memory components.

Solutions for Combinational Logic Logic elements were considered more robust against soft errors than memory elements but many researchers predict that the logic soft errors will become one of main contributions to the system unreliability [4, 23, 28]. The simplest and most effective way to reduce failures due to soft errors in combinational logic is Triple Modular Redundancy (TMR) [25], which typically uses three functionally equivalent replicas of a logic circuit and a majority voter. But the overheads of hardware and power for conventional TMR exceed 200% [23]. Duplex redundancy [18, 23] is also available but it requires more than 100% area and power overheads without any optimization techniques. In order to reduce the high overheads in conventional redundancy techniques, Mohanram et al. in [18] presented a partial error masking by duplicating the most sensitive and critical nodes in a logic circuit based on the asymmetric susceptibility of nodes to soft errors. Recently, Nieuwland et al. in [23] proposed a structural approach analyzing the SER sensitivity of combinational logic to identify the critical components at circuits.

Solutions for Sequential Logic Temporal redundancy is another main approach that has been used to combat soft errors in circuits. In order to detect soft errors, Nicolaidis in [22] applied fine time-grain redundancy within the clock cycle greater than the duration of transient faults by using the temporal nature of soft errors. Similarly, Anghel et al. in [2] exploited the temporal nature to detect timing errors and soft errors by means of time redundancy. Krishnamohan et al. in [12] proposed the time redundancy methodology by using the timing slack available in the propagation path from the input to the output in CMOS circuits. A Razor flip-flop was presented in [6] to detect transient errors by sampling pipeline stage values with a fast clock and with a time-borrowing delayed clock.

Solutions for Memories By far, reducing soft errors in memories has been the most extensive research topic. Error detection and correction codes (EDC and ECC) have been widely investigated and implemented as the most effective schemes to detect and correct soft errors in memory systems. However, an ECC system consists of an encoding block as well as a decoding block responsible for detection and correction, and of extra bits storing parity values. Thus, ECC-based techniques consume extra energy and incur performance delay as well as additional area cost [14, 24, 25], and are therefore not suitable for caches. Thus, only a few processors such as the

Intel Itanium processor [26] protect L2 and L3 caches with ECC, but we are not aware of any processor employing ECC-based protection mechanism on L1-cache. This is mainly due to high overheads of ECC implementation [11, 19].

Mukherjee et al. in [20] proposed a cache scrubbing technique that can avoid potential double-bit errors by reading cache blocks periodically and fixing all single-bit errors. Li et al. in [15] evaluated the drowsy cache and the decay cache exploiting voltage scaling and shut-down schemes, respectively, in order to efficiently decrease the power leakage. They also proposed an adaptive error correcting scheme to different cache data blocks, which can save energy consumption by protecting clean data less than dirty data blocks. Kim in [11] proposed the combined approach of parity and ECC codes to generate the reliable cache system in an area-efficient way. However, they all exploit expensive error correcting codes in order to protect all the data unnecessarily. Recently, Sugihara et al. in [30] presented a task scheduling method to dynamically switch the operation modes between the performance and vulnerability in cache architectures of multiprocessor systems.

Partially Protected Cache Architecture Lee et al. in [13] proposed PPC architecture and demonstrated the effectiveness in reducing the failure rate with minimal power and performance overheads. However, the effectiveness of PPCs has been limited only on multimedia applications, and there is no known approach to use PPCs for general applications.

The contribution of this paper is in developing techniques to utilize PPC architectures for applications in general and establish PPC as an effective microarchitectural solution to mitigate failures due to soft errors.

3 Partially Protected Caches and Problem Definition

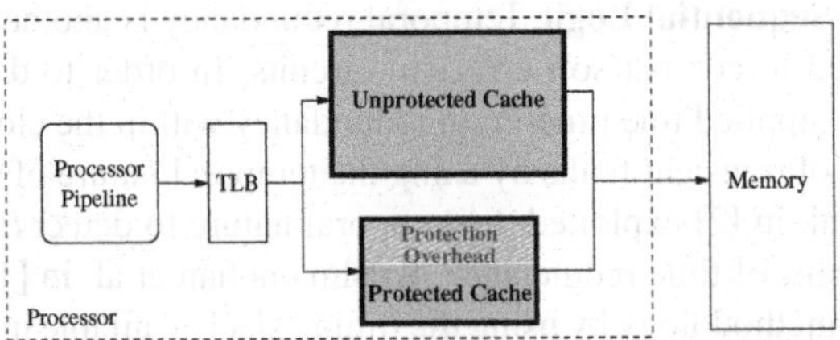

Fig. 1 Partially Protected Cache Architecture: one protected cache and the other unprotected cache at the same level of hierarchy

In a processor with *Partially Protected Cache* (PPC), the processor has two caches at the same level of memory hierarchy. As shown in Fig. 1, one of two caches is protected from soft errors, while the other is unprotected. Any protection mechanism can be implemented in the protected cache, e.g., increasing the thickness of oxide layer of the transistors, or adding redundancy logic like a Hamming Code [25]. The protected cache is typically smaller than the unprotected cache to keep the access latencies of both caches the same. Each page in the memory is mapped exclusively to one of the caches in a PPC architecture. The page mapping is set as a page attribute by the compiler. The mapping of the pages present in the cache resides in the Translation Lookaside Buffer (TLB). On a cache access, first a TLB lookup is performed to find out if the page is present in the cache, and if so, in which one? Thus, only one cache lookup is performed per cache access.

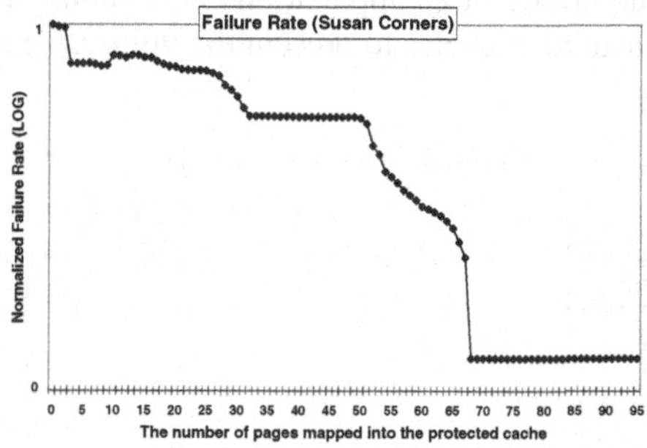

Fig. 2 Failure Rate Reduction by Moving Pages from the Unprotected Cache into the Protected Cache One by One in a PPC

While PPC architectures are very effective in reducing the failure rate with minimal performance and power overheads, the effectiveness hinges on the ability to partition the application data between the two caches in a PPC. To motivate for the need of page partitioning to reduce the failure rate, we perform a small experiment. First we map all the application pages to the unprotected cache, and then move the pages to the protected cache one by one. Fig. 2 plots the failure rate at each step of this exploration for *susan corners*, and shows that the failure rate drops rapidly as pages are moved from the unprotected cache to the protected cache. However, the pages have to be carefully moved to the protected cache, as it is small; mapping too many pages to the small cache increases the misses and results in significant penalties of performance and energy consumption due to frequent memory accesses. Therefore, the data partitioning is a multi-objective optimization problem in which we need to reduce the failure rate, at minimal overheads of performance and energy consumption. Since, even medium sized applications use a large number of pages; our benchmarks from [8] access 27 - 95 pages. Owing to its exponential complexity, enumerative techniques (e.g. trying all the possible page partitions) do not work.

We formulate our problem as: *Given an allowable performance degradation, determine the page partitioning to minimize the failure rate at minimal energy penalty.*

4 Our Approach

4.1 Vulnerability: A Metric for Failure Rate

To partition pages for a PPC architecture, we need a metric to quantitatively compare page partitions in terms of susceptibility to soft errors. We use the concept of vulnerability, proposed in [3, 21], to partition the data into the protected and unprotected caches in a PPC. If an error is injected in a variable that will not be used, the error does not matter. However, if the erroneous value is used in the future, then it will result in a failure. Thus a data is defined to be **vulnerable** for the time it is in the unprotected cache until it is eventually read by the processor or written back to the memory. The vulnerability of an application is the summation of the individual data vulnerability measured in cycles to present the vulnerable time of this data.

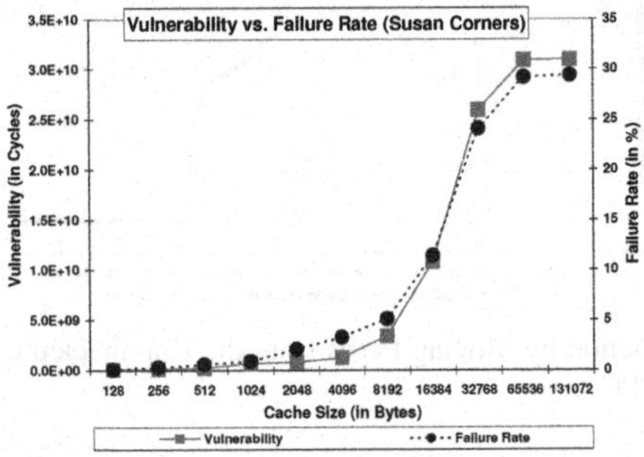

Fig. 3 Vulnerability and Failure Rate: vulnerability is a good metric for estimating failure rate

To validate our idea using vulnerability as a failure rate metric, we simulated the *susan corners* benchmark from [8] on a modified *sim-outorder* simulator from SimpleScalar [5] to model HP-iPAQ [10] like system for various L1 cache sizes. Our modified simulator calculated the vulnerability for each cache size as discussed above. To estimate the failure rate, we injected soft errors on data caches for each run of the benchmark, counted the number of failed runs out of a thousand runs, and calculated the failure rate in %. Each run is defined as a success if it ends and returns the correct output. Otherwise, it is a failure. Fig. 3 plots the *vulnerability* and the *failure rate* obtained by simulations and shows that the shape of the vulnerability closely matches the failure rate curve. Other applications also show similar trends. On average, the error in predicting the failure rate using vulnerability is less than 5%. In this paper, we use vulnerability as the metric to estimate the failure rate, and perform automated design space exploration to decide the page partitioning between the two caches of a PPC. Reducing vulnerability can be contrary to performance improvement. For example, to reduce the vulnerability of data, data should not remain in the cache for long. It is better to evict and reload the reused data to reduce the vulnerability, but this degrades performance. Therefore, there is a fundamental trade-off between performance improvement and vulnerability reduction.

4.2 Page Partitioning: DPExplore

Fig. 4 outlines our DPExplore partitioning algorithm, which starts from the case when no page is mapped to the protected cache. In each step, pages are moved from the unprotected to the protected cache, to minimize the vulnerability under the runtime penalty. Our page partitioning algorithm takes three inputs: (i) allowable runtime penalty (*rPenalty*), (ii) exploration width (*eWidth*), the number of partitions maintained as best configurations for the whole exploration, and (iii) *pCount*, the number of pages in a benchmark. DPExplore searches for page mappings that will suffer no more than the specified *rPenalty*, while trying to minimize the vulnerability. DPExplore maintains a set of best page mappings found so far (Line 05) in *bestConfigs*, sorted in an increasing order of vulnerability. After initialization, the algorithm goes into a forever loop in Line 07. It takes each existing best solution and tries to improve it by mapping a page to the protected cache (Lines 11-12). If the new page mapping is better than the worst solution in the *newBestConfigs*, then the new page mapping is saved in the list. The loop in Lines 09-21 is one step of exploration. After each step, the new set of page mappings is trimmed down to exploration width (Lines 22-24). The termination criterion of the exploration is when an exploration step cannot find any better page mapping. In other words, no page can be mapped to the protected cache to improve vulnerability (Lines 25, 27) under the runtime penalty. Otherwise, the global collection of the best page mappings are updated (Line 26).

```
DPExplore(rPenalty, eWidth, pCount)
01: pageMap0 = 0...0
02: runtime, power, vulnerability = simulate(pageMap0)
03: config0 = (pageMap0, runtime, power, vulnerability)
04: for (k = 0; k < eWidth; k++)
05:     bestConfigs.insert(config0)
06: endFor
07: for (;;)
08:     newBestConfigs = bestConfigs
09:     for (i = 0; i < eWidth; i++)
10:         for (j = 0; j < pCount; j++)
11:             testConfig = addPage(newBestConfigs[i], j)
12:             runtime, power, vulnerability = simulate(testConfig.pageMap)
13:             if (runtime < config0.runtime × (100+rPenalty)/100)
14:                 if (vulnerability < newBestConfigs[0].vulnerability)
16:                     newBestConfigs.insert(testConfig, runtime, power, vulnerability)
17:                     newBestConfigs.sort()
18:                 endIf
19:             endIf
20:         endFor
21:     endFor
22:     for (i = newBestConfigs.length(); i > eWidth; i--)
23:         newBestConfigs.delete[i - 1]
24:     endFor
25:     if (newBestConfigs[0].vulnerability < bestConfigs[0].vulnerability)
26:         bestConfigs = newBestConfigs
27:     else break;
28:     endIf
29: endFor
```

Fig. 4 DPExplore: an exploration algorithm for data partitioning

Note that our exploration technique is a profile-based approach, which works well if the page mapping of application codes and input data does not change. Our proposal, DPExplore, is very effective for such applications.

5 Experiments

5.1 Setup

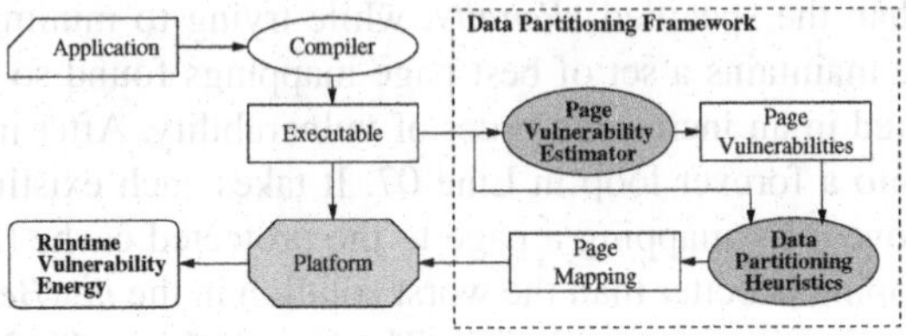

Fig. 5 DPExplore Page Partitioning Framework for PPC Architectures

To demonstrate the effectiveness of DPExplore in exploring and discovering the partition with minimal vulnerability at minimal power and runtime[1] penalty, we have built an extensive simulation framework. The application is first compiled to generate an executable. The application is then profiled, and the *Page Vulnerability Estimator* calculates the vulnerability of each page accessed by the application. The pages are then sorted according to their vulnerabilities, and then *Data Partitioning Heuristics* partitions and maps the pages to the two caches in the PPC architecture. Through the simulations, *Data Partitioning Heuristics* finds out the page mapping with minimal vulnerability under the runtime constraint. Finally, the executable and the page mapping are provided to the platform, which runs the application and generates outputs such as runtime, energy consumption, and vulnerability.

The platform is modeled using *sim-outorder* simulator from the SimpleScalar toolchain [5]. The simulation parameters have been setup so as to model an HP iPAQ h4600 [10] like processor memory system. We model a PPC architecture consisting of a 4 KB of unprotected cache and a 256 bytes of protected cache with line size of 32 bytes, 4 way set-associativity, and FIFO cache replacement policy. This model protects one small cache with an ECC-based technique such as a Hamming Code [25]. The overheads of power and delay for ECC protected caches are estimated and synthesized using the CACTI [27] and the Synopsys Design Compiler [31] as in [13]. And also SimpleScalar *sim-outorder* simulator has been modified to include the vulnerability computation. The memory subsystem includes the caches, external buses, and 2 off-chip SDRAMs. To estimate the memory subsystem energy consumption, we use the power models presented in [29].

The HP iPAQ is a wireless handheld device, and MiBench is the set of benchmarks that are representative of applications that run on wireless handheld devices [8]. MiBench suite is therefore the right set of benchmarks that are supposed to run on the iPAQ, and we choose them. However, we pick only those benchmarks in which the runtime difference between the cases when all data is mapped to the

[1] Here runtime and performance are used interchangeably and represent the number of cycles for execution of an application

4 KB unprotected cache, and when all data to the 256 bytes protected cache in the PPC is more than 5%. This is to avoid benchmarks for which only the small protected cache is enough. Note that although some of the benchmarks in MiBench are multimedia applications (for which an obvious data partitioning exists), we use DPExplore to partition the data of **all** applications in the selected benchmark suite.

We compare the effectiveness of our approach DPExplore with two traditional exploration techniques,

Monte Carlo (MC) In MC, several page partitions are randomly generated and tested by simulation for their effectiveness in power, runtime and vulnerability.

Genetic Algorithm (GA) For GA, initially, we form a randomly generated sequence, representing a page mapping. At each successive generation, the superior sequences in terms of vulnerability are selected as the evolutionary page mappings through the simulations. In order to generate the next sequence, we implemented two GA operations such as mutation and crossover. For the mutation operation, a pseudo-random number tells whether each page mapping in a sequence is modified or not. For the crossover operation, one point is selected in the current sequence and the bits are swapped on page mappings to generate the next sequence.

5.2 Results

5.2.1 Effectiveness of DPExplore

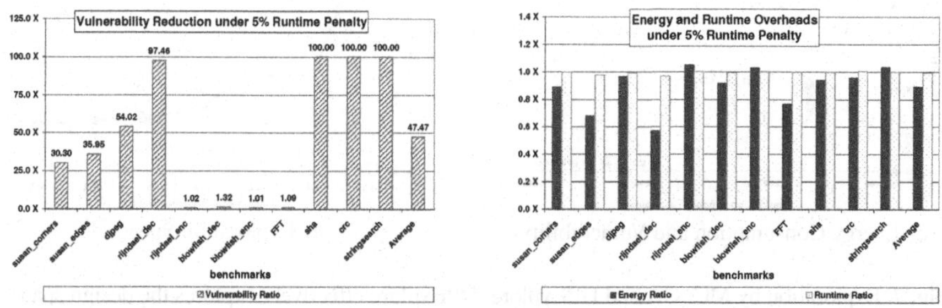

(a) Vulnerability Reduction (A bar greater than 1.0× indicates vulnerability reduction)

(b) Energy and Runtime Increase (A bar lower than 1.0× indicates the overhead)

Fig. 6 Evaluation under *5% Performance Penalty*: DPExplore significantly reduces the vulnerability at minimal runtime and power overheads

To demonstrate the effectiveness of DPExplore, we find the page partition with the least vulnerability under 5% performance penalty and exploration width 2. Fig. 6(a) plots the vulnerability ratio. *Vulnerability Ratio* indicates the ratio of the vulnerability of the *base case* to that discovered by DPExplore. Similarly, *Runtime Ratio* and *Energy Ratio* of the least vulnerability page partition obtained by DPExplore are presented in Fig. 6(b). Thus, each ratio greater than 1 implies the reduction of each metric. We observe 47× reduction in vulnerability on average, along with only 0.5% degradation in runtime, and 15% increase in the total energy consumption of the memory subsystem. Compared to the case when all data is mapped to the protected 4 KB cache, i.e., the completely protected cache, the runtime and the energy consumption of the page partition with DPExplore are improved by 36% and 9%, respectively. Thus, even very small runtime degradation allows DPExplore to find page mappings that can significantly reduce the vulnerability.

5.2.2 Comparison with Other Explorations

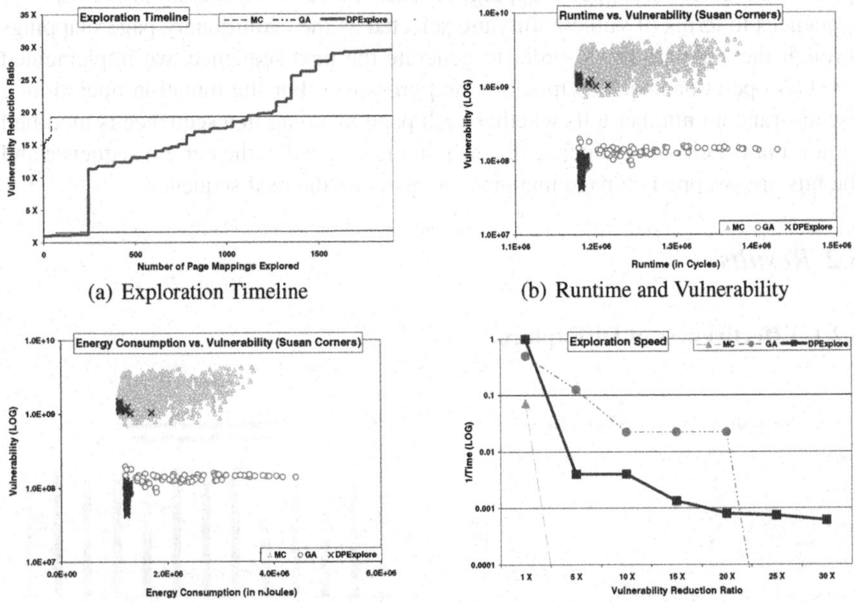

(a) Exploration Timeline (b) Runtime and Vulnerability

(c) Energy Consumption and Vulnerability (d) Exploration Speed

Fig. 7 Exploration by MC, GA and DPExplore: DPExplore effectively explores the design space

We detail the results of exploration using MC, GA, and DPExplore over the *susan corners* benchmark, when DPExplore is configured for 5% runtime penalty, and exploration width 2. Fig. 7(a) plots the vulnerability as the exploration progresses for MC, GA, and DPExplore. The plot shows that while MC is ineffective, GA improves vulnerability by about 20×, but DPExplore consistently finds better page mappings and is eventually able to reduce vulnerability by about 30×.

Fig. 7(b) and Fig. 7(c) plot the runtime, energy consumption, and vulnerability of the page partitions searched by MC, GA, and DPExplore. Note that the y-axis in these graphs – the vulnerability scale – is logarithmic. The most important observation that we make from these graphs is that DPExplore searches much more useful page mappings (low vulnerability with low runtime and energy overheads), as compared to MC and GA. We allow each exploration technique to evaluate 1,900 page mappings. Thus, in total there are 5,700 page mappings. Out of them only 83 are Pareto-optimal. A page mapping is Pareto-optimal, if it is no worse than any other configuration in all the three dimensions, i.e., runtime, vulnerability and energy. Out of these 83 Pareto-optimal page mappings, 68 were first drawn from DPExplore searches (82%), 12 came from GA (14%), and only 3 were discovered by MC (4%). This Pareto-optimal observation demonstrates the effectiveness of our algorithm as compared to MC and GA. The main reason for the effectiveness of DPExplore as compared to MC and GA explorations is that MC and GA ignore the effects of partitioning on the runtime and energy consumption.

Finally, we compare the speed of the various exploration algorithms. Fig. 7(d) plots the speed of exploration, i.e., inverse of the number of page partitions explored to achieve a required vulnerability reduction. The plot shows that MC is quite ineffective. Among GA and DPExplore, GA is a faster approach when low reduction in vulnerability is required, but it is unable to achieve high reductions in vulnerability. This is where, our approach is really effective.

6 Summary

Owing to the incessant technology scaling, soft errors, especially in caches, are becoming a critical design concern for system reliability. Partially Protected Cache (PPC) architecture has been proposed as an effective architectural means of improving system reliability without much power and performance penalty. However, the challenge is in partitioning pages among the two caches in a PPC. While page partitioning schemes have been proposed for multimedia applications, there is no page partitioning scheme for general applications. The page partitioning space is huge, and existing random techniques are unable to identify and explore the page partitions that lead to low vulnerability. In this paper, we develop DPExplore, a page partitioning algorithm at design time that effectively and efficiently finds page partitions resulting in 47 times reduction in vulnerability, i.e., in failure rate, at only 0.5% performance and 15% energy penalty on average. The main contribution of DPExplore is that it increases the applicability of PPC architectures and establishes PPC as the solution of choice to improve reliability of cache-based architectures.

Our future work includes intelligent schemes to improve the data partitioning in PPCs for the varying input data at runtime, and partitioning techniques for instruction PPC caches.

References

1. *International Technology Roadmap for Semiconductors 2005 Executive Summary.* http://www.itrs.net/Links/2005ITRS/ExecSum2005.pdf.
2. L. Anghel and M. Nicolaidis. Cost reduction and evaluation of a temporary faults detecting technique. In *IEEE/ACM Design, Automation and Test in Europe Conference (DATE)*, pages

591–597, 2000.
3. Ghazanfar-Hossein Asadi, Vilas Sridharan, Mehdi B. Tahoori, and David Kaeli. Balancing performance and reliability in the memory hierarchy. In *IEEE International Symposium on Performance Analysis of Systems and Software (ISPASS)*, pages 269–279, 2005.
4. Robert Baumann. Soft errors in advanced computer systems. *IEEE Design and Test of Computers*, pages 258–266, 2005.
5. Doug Burger and Todd M. Austin. The SimpleScalar Tool Set, version 2.0. *SIGARCH Computer Architecture News*, 25(3):13–25, 1997.
6. D. Ernst, N. S. Kim, S. Das, S. Pant, R. Rao, Toan Pham, C. Ziesler, D. Blaauw, T. Austin, K. Flautner, and T. Mudge. Razor: A low-power pipeline based on circuit-level timing speculation. In *IEEE/ACM International Symposium on Microarchitecture (MICRO)*, pages 7–13, 2003.
7. J. Gaisler. Evaluation of a 32-bit microprocessor with builtin concurrent error-detection. In *IEEE International Symposium on Fault-Tolerant Computing (FTCS)*, 1997.
8. M. Guthaus, J. Ringenberg, D. Ernst, T. Austin, T. Mudge, and R. Brown. MiBench: A free, commercially representative embedded benchmark suite. In *IEEE Workshop on Workload Characterization*, pages 3–14, 2001.
9. P. Hazucha and C. Svensson. Impact of CMOS technology scaling on the atmospheric neutron soft error rate. *IEEE Trans. on Nuclear Science*, 47(6):2586–2594, 2000.
10. Hewlett Packard, http://www.hp.com. *HP iPAQ h4000 Series - System Specifications.*
11. Soontae Kim. Area-efficient error protection for caches. In *IEEE/ACM Design, Automation and Test in Europe Conference (DATE)*, pages 1282–1287, Mar 2006.
12. S. Krishnamohan and N. R. Mahapatra. An efficient error-masking technique for improving the soft-error robustness of static CMOS circuits. In *IEEE International SOC Conference (SOCC)*, pages 227–230, Sep 2004.
13. Kyoungwoo Lee, Aviral Shrivastava, Ilya Issenin, Nikil Dutt, and Nalini Venkatasubramanian. Mitigating soft error failures for multimedia applications by selective data protection. In *International Conference on Compilers, Architecture, and Synthesis for Embedded Systems (CASES)*, pages 411–420, Oct 2006.
14. Jin-Fu Li and Yu-Jane Huang. An error detection and correction scheme for RAMs with partial-write function. In *IEEE International Workshop on Memory Technology, Design and Testing (MTDT)*, pages 115–120, 2005.
15. Lin Li, Vijay Degalahal, N. Vijaykrishnan, Mahmut Kandemir, and Mary Jane Irwin. Soft error and energy consumption interactions: A data cache perspective. In *International Symposium on Low Power Electronics and Design (ISLPED)*, pages 132–137, Aug 2004.
16. P. Liden, P. Dahlgren, R. Johansson, and J. Karlsson. On latching probability of particle induced transients in combinational networks. In *IEEE International Symposium on Fault-Tolerant Computing (FTCS)*, 1994.
17. Subhasish Mitra, Norbert Seifert, Ming Zhang, Quan Shi, and Kee Sup Kim. Robust system design with built-in soft-error resilience. *IEEE Computer*, 38(2):43–52, Feb 2005.
18. Kartik Mohanram and Nur A. Touba. Partial error masking to reduce soft error failure rate in logic circuits. In *IEEE International Symposium on Defect and Fault Tolerance in VLSI Systems (DFT)*, pages 433–440, 2003.
19. K. Mohr and L. Clark. Delay and area efficient first-level cache soft error detection and correction. In *IEEE International Conference on Computer Design (ICCD)*, 2006.
20. Shubhendu S. Mukherjee, Joel Emer, Tryggve Fossum, and Steven K. Reinhardt. Cache scrubbing in microprocessors: Myth or necessity? In *IEEE Pacific Rim International Symposium on Dependable Computing (PRDC)*, pages 37–42, 2004.
21. Shubhendu S. Mukherjee, Christopher Weaver, Joel Emer, Steven K. Reinhardt, and Todd Austin. A systematic methodology to compute the architectural vulnerability factors for a high-performance microprocessor. In *IEEE/ACM International Symposium on Microarchitecture (MICRO)*, pages 29–40, Dec 2003.
22. M. Nicolaidis. Time redundancy based soft-error tolerance to rescue nanometer technologies. In *IEEE VLSI Test Symposium (VTS)*, page 86, 1999.

23. A. K. Nieuwland, S. Jasarevic, and G. Jerin. Combinational logic soft error analysis and protection. In *IEEE International Symposium on On-Line Testing (IOLTS)*, pages 99–104, 2006.
24. Richard Phelan. Addressing soft errors in ARM core-based designs. Technical report, ARM, 2003.
25. D. K. Pradhan. *Fault-Tolerant Computer System Design.* Prentice Hall, 1996. ISBN 0-1305-7887-8.
26. Nhon Quach. High availability and reliability in the Itanium processor. *IEEE/ACM International Symposium on Microarchitecture (MICRO)*, pages 61–69, Sep–Oct 2000.
27. P. Shivakumar and N. Jouppi. CACTI 3.0: An Integrated Cache Timing, Power, and Area Model. In *WRL Technical Report 2001/2*, 2001.
28. P. Shivakumar, M. Kistler, S. Keckler, D. Burger, and L. Alvisi. Modeling the effect of technology trends on soft error rate of combinational logic. In *IEEE/IFIP International Conference on Dependable Systems and Networks (DSN)*, pages 389–398, 2002.
29. Aviral Shrivastava, Ilya Issenin, and Nikil Dutt. Compilation techniques for energy reduction in horizontally partitioned cache architectures. In *International Conference on Compilers, Architecture, and Synthesis for Embedded Systems (CASES)*, pages 90–96, 2005.
30. Makoto Sugihara, Tohru Ishihara, and Kazuaki Murakami. Task scheduling for reliable cache architectures of multiprocessor systems. In *IEEE/ACM Design, Automation and Test in Europe Conference (DATE)*, pages 1490–1495, 2007.
31. Synopsys Inc., Mountain View, CA, USA. *Design Compiler Reference Manual*, 2001.